Islam and the Plight of Modern Man

Seyyed Hossein Nasr

Islam and the Plight of Modern Man

Seyyed Hossein Nasr

LONGMAN
LONDON AND NEW YORK

LONGMAN GROUP LTD
London
Associated companies, branches and representatives throughout the world

First published 1975

ISBN 0 582 78053 5

Library of Congress Cataloging in Publication Data
Nasr, Seyyed Hossein.
Islam and the plight of modern man.

Includes bibliographical references.
1. Islam—20th century. I. Title.
BP163.N28 297'.09'04 75-29014
ISBN 0-582-78053-5

Published by the Longman Group Ltd
in association with
the World of Islam Festival Publishing Co Ltd.
Designer : Colin Larkin
General Editor : Daphne Buckmaster
Islamic Patterns : Issam El Said
Set in 11/12pt 'Monotype' Imprint

Printed in England by
W & J Mackay Limited, Chatham

for Vali and Laili

Other works by the author in European languages

An Introduction to Islamic Cosmological Doctrines, Cambridge (Mass.), Harvard University Press, 1964.

Three Muslim Sages, Cambridge, Harvard University Press, 1964.

Iran (French and English editions), Paris, UNESCO, 1966; Tehran, 1971 and 1973.

Ideals and Realities of Islam, London, George Allen and Unwin, 1966; French translation as *Islam: Perspectives et réalités*, Paris, Buchet–Chastel, 1974; Italian translation as *Ideali e realità dell'Islam*, Milano, Rusconi editore, 1974.

Islamic Studies—Essays on Law and Society, the Sciences, and Philosophy and Sufism, Beirut, Librairie du Liban, 1967.

Science and Civilization in Islam, Cambridge, Harvard University Press, 1968 and New York, Mentor Books, 1970.

The Encounter of Man and Nature, The Spiritual Crisis of Modern Man, London, Allen and Unwin, 1968.

Sufi Essays, London, Allen and Unwin, 1972; Albany, State University of New York Press, 1973; Italian translation as *Il Sufismo*, Milano, Rusconi editore, 1974.

Jalal ad-Din Rumi, Supreme Persian Poet and Sage, Tehran, High Council of Culture and Arts, 1974.

An Annotated Bibliography of Islamic Science, Vol. I, Tehran, Imperial Iranian Academy of Philosophy, 1975.

(with R. Beny) *Persia, Bridge of Turquoise*, McClelland and Stewart, Toronto, 1975.

Islamic Science, An Illustrated Study, World of Islam Festival Trust, London, 1976.

Collaboration with Henry Corbin and O. Yahya in the *Histoire de la philosophie islamique*, Paris, Gallimard, 1964.

اَللّٰهُ نُوْرُ السَّمٰوٰتِ وَالاَرْضِ مَثَلُ نُوْرِهٖ كَمِشْكٰوةٍ فِيْهَا مِصْبَاحٌ
اَلْمِصْبَاحُ فِيْ زُجَاجَةٍ اَلزُّجَاجَةُ كَاَنَّهَا كَوْكَبٌ دُرِّيٌّ يُوْقَدُ مِنْ شَجَرَةٍ مُبٰرَكَةٍ
زَيْتُوْنَةٍ لاَ شَرْقِيَّةٍ وَلاَ غَرْبِيَّةٍ

(سورة النور)

'Allah is the Light of the heavens and earth. The similitude of His light is as a niche wherein is a lamp. The lamp is in a glass. The glass is as it were a shining star. (This lamp is) kindled from a blessed tree, an olive neither of the East nor of the West . . .'

Quran (XXIV; 35). Pickthall translation

Contents

Transliteration

Arabic Letter	Transliteration
ء	ʼ
ب	b
ت	t
ث	th
ج	j
ح	ḥ
خ	kh
د	d
ذ	dh
ر	r
ز	z
س	s
ش	sh
ص	ṣ
ض	ḍ
ط	ṭ
ظ	ẓ
ع	ʻ
غ	gh
ف	f
ق	q
ك	k
ل	l
م	m
ن	n
و	w
ه	h
ة	t
ي	y

Short Vowels	
ـَـ	a
ـُـ	u
ـِـ	i

Long Vowels	
ـَا	ā
ـُو	ū
ـِي	ī

Diphthongs	
ـَوْ	aw
ـَيْ	ay
ـِيّ	iyy
ـُوّ	uww

Persian Letters	
پ	p
چ	ch
ژ	zh
گ	g

In the Name of God Most Merciful and Compassionate

بسم الله الرحمن الرحيم

Preface

Gradually the inner riches of Islam and its civilization are beginning to attract a greater number of men and women in the West at the very moment when the spread of Westernization is threatening the citadel of Islam itself. This paradoxical situation calls for a new affirmation of the principles of the Islamic revelation and a re-statement of the teachings contained in the branches of the tradition which issued forth from the Quranic revelation. This must be accomplished in order to present the teachings of Islam to the Western man in search of a way out of the morass within which modernism has confined him, and to the modernized Muslim in need of finding a means to combat the corrosive forces which threaten the very existence of Islamic civilization.

The present book is a humble step in this direction. We have sought to bring out the major issues which confront modern man in both East and West, to discuss means of studying the Islamic intellectual and spiritual heritage today and finally to present ways of applying the teachings of the Islamic tradition to solve the plight of modern man in both the Orient and the Western world. We are not of those who believe that the negative effects of modernism in the Occident are due merely to certain deficiencies existing in Western peoples alone, or that such effects might be avoided in the East. Nor is it our aim to contrast the Islamic world with the West simply geographically, or even culturally. Our concern is rather with the Truth, with Truth as contained in tradition (*al-dīn*) and as the criterion of all human activity in either East or West in all times past, present and future; it is with Islam as the last terrestrial expression of this Truth and as a living reality, a reality which can provide the necessary criteria to judge, according to permanent and immutable archetypes beyond the confines of time and space, the thoughts and actions of men living on earth today, whether they be non-Muslim Westerners or Muslims. We feel that it is especially important at this moment when so many people in the West are becoming more seriously interested in the achievements of Islamic civilization that they should also become aware of the living nature of the Islamic tradition and its pertinence to their present-day problems. Also we feel that it is high time for modernized elements within the Islamic world to become aware of the real nature of the forces under whose influence they have fallen and to become better prepared to defend the Islamic tradition against these forces which now threaten it from within the borders of the Islamic world itself.

We have incorporated into the text of this book a certain amount of material drawn from several of our essays written during the past few years relating to the subject matter in hand. We have also been forced to repeat certain arguments which appear in some of our other writings because of the nature of the subject matter with which we are dealing. In the exposition of traditional doctrines and their application to the present-day situation, a certain amount of repetition is in any case hardly avoidable and in fact at times necessary.

In conclusion, we wish to thank Mr William Chittick and Mr Peter Wilson for reviewing the text of the book and Mrs I. Hakemi for preparing the manuscript for publication.

Tehran
20 Shaʿbān 1394 (A.H. lunar)
17 Shahrīwar 1353 (A.H. solar)
8 September 1974

Part I

The Present-day Condition of Man

Chapter 1

Contemporary Western Man between the Rim and the Axis

Come you lost atoms to your Centre draw,
And *be* the Eternal Mirror that you saw:
Rays that have wander'd into Darkness wide
Return, and back into your Sun subside.

Farīd al-Dīn 'Aṭṭār, *Manṭiq al-ṭayr*
trans. E. Fitzgerald, Boston, 1899, p.187

My Guru spake to me but one precept. He said unto me, 'From without enter thou the inmost part!' That to me became a rule and a precept.

Lallā, the Female Saint of Kashmir, *Lallā Vakyāni*,
trans. by Grierson and Barrett, London, 1920, p. 107, para 94

Although the present work deals primarily with Islam and the Muslims, it is also concerned directly with the modern world—whose impact upon the Islamic world during the past century has brought havoc and confusion beyond comparison with anything that Islamic history has witnessed since its origin—and with the message of Islam and its significance for the contemporary West. Hence it is most appropriate to begin with the study of the situation of modern Western man, and by implication that of his imitators on other continents, a study which has become especially imperative and urgent as a result of the rapid deterioration of both modern society and the natural environment during the past few decades.

The confrontation of man's own inventions and manipulations, in the form of technology, with human culture, as well as the violent effect of the application of man's acquired knowledge of nature to the destruction of the natural environment, have in fact reached such proportions that many people in the modern world, especially in the West, are at last beginning to question the validity of the conception of man held in the Occident since the rise of modern civilization. But, despite this recent awareness, in order to discuss such a vast problem in a meaningful and constructive way, one must begin by clearing the ground of the obstacles which usually prevent the profoundest questions involved from being discussed. Modern man has burned his hands in the fire which he himself kindled when he allowed himself to forget who he is. Having sold his soul in the manner of Faust to gain dominion over the natural environment, he has created a situation in which the very control of the environment is turning into its strangulation, bringing in its wake not only ecocide but also, ultimately, suicide.

The danger is now evident enough not to need repetition. Whereas only two decades ago everyone spoke of man's unlimited possibility for development understood in a physical and materialistic sense, today one speaks of 'limits to growth'—a phrase well-known in the West today—or even of an imminent cataclasm. But the concepts and factors according to which the crisis is analyzed, the solutions sought after and even the colours with which the image of an impending doom are depicted are usually all in terms of the very elements that have brought the crisis of modern man into being. The world is still seen as devoid of a spiritual horizon, not because there is no such horizon present, but because he who views the contemporary landscape is most often the man who lives at the rim of the wheel of existence and therefore views all things from the periphery. He remains indifferent to the spokes and completely oblivious of the axis or the Centre, which nevertheless remains ever accessible to him through them.

The problem of the devastation brought upon the environment by technology, the ecological crisis and the like, all issue from the malady of *amnesis* or forgetfulness from which modern man suffers. Modern man has simply forgotten who he is. Living on the periphery of his own existence he has been able to gain a qualitatively superficial but quantitatively staggering knowledge of the world. He has projected the externalized and superficial image of himself upon the world.[1] And then, having come to know the world in such externalized terms, he has sought to reconstruct an image of himself based upon this external knowledge. There has been a series of 'falls' by means of which man has oscillated in a descending scale between an ever more externalized image of himself and of the world surrounding him, moving ever further from the Centre both of himself and of his cosmic environment. The inner history of the so-called development of modern Western man from his historic background as traditional man—who represents at once his ancestor in time and his centre in space—is a gradual alienation from the Centre and the axis through the spokes of the wheel of existence to the rim, where modern man resides. But just as the existence of the rim presupposes spokes which connect it to the axis of the wheel, so does the very fact of human existence imply the presence of the Centre and the axis and hence an inevitable connection of men of all ages with Man in his primordial and eternal reality as he has been, is, and will continue to be, above all outward changes and transformations.[2]

Nowhere is the tendency of modern man to seek the solution of many problems without considering the factors that have caused these problems in the first place more evident than in the field of the humanities in general and the sciences dealing specifically with man, which are supposed to provide an insight into human nature, in particular. Modern man, having rebelled against Heaven, has created a science based not on the light of the Intellect[3]—as we see in the traditional Islamic sciences—but on the powers of human reason to sift the data of the senses. But the success of this science was so great in its own domain that soon all the other sciences began to ape it, leading to the crass positivism of the past century which caused philosophy as perennially understood to become confused with logical analysis, mental acrobatics or even mere information theory, and the classical fields of the humanities to become converted to quantified social sciences which make even the intuitions of literature about the nature of man inaccessible to many students and seekers today. A number of scientists are in fact among those most critical of the pseudo-humanities being taught in many Western universities in an atmosphere of a psychological and mental sense of inferiority *vis-à-vis* the sciences of nature and mathematics, a 'humanities' which tries desperately to become 'scientific', only to degenerate into a state of superficiality, not to say triviality.[4] The decadence of the humanities in modern times is caused by man's loss of the direct knowledge of himself and also of the Self that he has always had, and by reliance upon an externalized, indirect knowledge of himself which he seeks to gain from the outside, a literally 'superficial' knowledge that is drawn from the rim and is devoid of an awareness of interiority, of the axis of the wheel and of the spokes which stand always before man and connect him like a ray of light to the supernal sun.

It is with a consideration of this background that certain questions created by the confrontation between the traditional concept of man and the 'scientific' one must be analyzed and answered. The first of these questions that often arise in people's minds is 'What is the relation of piecemeal scientific evidence about human behaviour to what has been called traditionally "human nature"?' In order to answer this question it is essential to remember that the reality of the human state cannot be exhausted by any of its outward projections. A particular human action or behaviour always reflects a state of being, and its study can lead to a certain kind of knowledge of the state of being of the agent provided there is already an awareness of the whole to which the fragment can be related. Fragmented knowledge of human behaviour is related to human nature in the same way that waves are related to the sea. There is certainly a relationship between them that is both causal and substantial. But unless one has had a vision of the sea in its vastness and illimitable horizons—the sea which reflects the Infinite and its inimitable peace and calm—one cannot gain an essential knowledge of it through the study of its waves. Fragmented knowledge can be related to the whole only when there is already an intellectual vision of the whole.

The careful 'scientific' study of fragmented human behaviour is incapable of revealing the profounder aspect of human nature precisely because of an *a priori* limitation that so many branches of the modern behaviouristic sciences of man—veritable pseudo-sciences if there ever were any[5]—have placed on the meaning of the human state itself. There has never been as little knowledge of man, of the *anthropos*, in different human cultures as one finds among most modern anthropologists today. Even the medicine men of Africa (not to speak of the Muslim sages) have had a deeper insight into human nature than the modern behaviourists and their flock, because the former have been concerned with the essential and the latter with the accidental. Now, accidents do possess a reality, but they have a meaning only in relation to the substance which supports them ontologically. Otherwise one could collect accidents and external facts indefinitely without ever reaching the substance, or what is essential. The classical error of modern civilization, to mistake the quantitative accumulation of information for qualitative penetration into the inner meaning of things, applies here as elsewhere. The study of fragmented behaviour without a vision of the human nature which is the cause of this behaviour cannot itself lead to a knowledge of human nature. It can go around the rim of the wheel indefinitely without ever entering upon the spoke to approach the proximity of the axis and the Centre. But if the vision is already present, the gaining of knowledge of external human behaviour can always be an occasion for recollection and a return to the cause by means of the external effect.

In Islamic metaphysics, four basic qualities are attributed to Ultimate Reality, based directly on the Quranic verse, 'He is the First and the Last, the Outward and the Inward' (LVII; 3). This attribution, besides other levels of meaning, also has a meaning that is directly pertinent to the present argument. God, the Ultimate Reality, is both the Inward (*al-Bāṭin*) and the Outward (*al-Ẓāhir*), the Centre and the Circumference. The religious man sees God as the Inward; the profane man who has become completely oblivious to the world of the Spirit sees only the Outward, but precisely because of his ignorance of the Centre does not realize that even the outward is a manifestation of the Centre or of the Divine. Hence his fragmented knowledge remains incapable of encompassing the whole of the rim or circumference and therefore, by anticipation, the Centre. A segment of the rim remains nothing more than a figure without a point of reference or Centre, but the whole rim cannot but reflect the Centre. Finally the sage sees God as both the Inward and the Outward. He is able to relate the fragmented external knowledge to the Centre and see in the rim a reflection of the Centre. But this he is able to do only because of his *a priori* awareness of the Centre. Before being able to see the external world—be it the physical world about us or the outer crust of the human psyche—as a manifestation of the Inward, one must already have become attached to the Inward through faith and knowledge.[6] Applying this principle, the sage could thus relate fragmented knowledge to the deeper layers of human nature; but for one who has yet to become aware of the Inward dimension within himself and the Universe about him, fragmented knowledge cannot but remain fragmentary, especially if it is based upon observation of the behaviour of a human collectivity most of whose members themselves live only on the outermost layers of human existence and rarely reflect in their behaviour the deeper dimension of their own being.

This last point leads to an observation that complements the discussion of principles already stated. Western man lives for the most part in a world in which he encounters few people who live on the higher planes of consciousness or in the deeper layers of their being. He is therefore, for the most part, aware of only certain types of human behaviour, as can be readily seen in the writings of most Western social scientists, especially when they make studies of such traditions as Islam. Fragmented knowledge of human behaviour, even if based solely on external observation, could aid modern man to become at least indirectly aware of other dimensions of human nature, provided a study is made of the behaviour of traditional man—of the man who lives in a world with a Centre. The behaviour of traditional men of different societies, especially at the highest level of the saints and sages—be they from the Chinese, the Islamic, the North American Indian or any other traditional background—in the face of great trials, before death, in presence of the beauty of virgin nature and sacred art, or in the throes of love both human and divine, can certainly provide indications of aspects of human nature for the modern observer. Such behaviour can reveal a constancy and permanence within human nature that is truly astonishing and can also be instrumental in depicting the grandeur of man, which has been largely forgotten in a world where he has become a prisoner to the pettiness of his own trivial creations and inventions. Seen in this light, a fragmented knowledge of human behaviour can aid in gaining a knowledge of certain aspects of human nature. But in any case a total knowledge of this nature cannot be achieved except through a knowledge of the Centre or axis, which also 'contains' the spokes and the rim. A famous saying of the Prophet of Islam states, 'He who knows himself knows his Lord'. But precisely because 'himself' implies the Self which resides at the Centre of man's being, from another point of view this statement can also be reversed. Man can know himself completely only in the light of God, for the relative cannot be known save with respect to the Absolute.

The second query which is often posed today and to which we must address ourselves concerns the relationship of scientific 'objectivity' and its findings to the criteria of the universal and unchanging implied by the phrase 'human nature' as used traditionally. To answer this query, it is necessary before all else to define once again what is meant by scientific objectivity, especially when it concerns the study of man. It has become commonplace, at least for non-specialists in the philosophy of science, to attribute objectivity to modern science almost as if the one implied the other. No doubt modern science possesses a limited form of objectivity in its study of the physical world, but even in this domain its objectivity is encompassed by the collective subjectivity of a particular humanity at a certain moment of its historical existence when the symbolist spirit has become atrophied and the gift of seeing the world of the Spirit through and beyond the physical world has been almost completely lost. Certainly what the traditional Muslim sees 'objectively' is not the same as the vision of the world seen by modern men today 'objectively' but without the dimension of Transcendence. Even in the physical world, all that cannot be caught in the net of modern science (to quote the well-known image of Sir Arthur Eddington) is collectively neglected, and its non-existence 'objectively' avowed. It is as if an audience of deaf people at a concert testified together that they did not hear any music and considered the unanimity of their opinion as a proof of its objectivity.

Now if, in the domain of the physical world itself, the concept of the so-called 'objectivity' of modern science must be employed with great prudence and the qualitative and symbolic aspects of nature not neglected because they lie outside the 'objectively' defined world view of modern science, so much more does this 'objectivity' need to be reconsidered in the field of the study of man. The aping of the methods of the physical sciences in the study of man has enabled Western scientists to gather a great deal of information about men of all ages and climes, but little about man himself, for the simple reason that the philosophical background of modern science, ultimately Cartesian, is incapable of providing the necessary background for the study of man. Already in the seventeenth century the body-mind dualism of Descartes perverted in the European mind the image of the much more profound tripartite division of the being of man—*corpus*, *anima* and *spiritus*—expounded so fully in the Hermetic tradition and repeated so often in works of Islamic philosophy. To this error a worse illusion was added in the nineteenth century which prevented even the collecting of facts about men of different ages from becoming a way of reaching at least some form of knowledge of man himself.

This illusion is that of evolution as it is usually understood today. Evolution is no more than a scientific hypothesis that has been parading itself for the past century as a scientific fact; despite the lack of the least proof of its having taken place in the biological plane, it is usually taught in schools as proven. The present discussion does not allow our entering into debate about biological evolution, although writings by biologists and geologists against it, especially works written in recent years, are far from few in number.[7] But as far as the study of man is concerned, it is precisely the intrusion of the idea of evolution into anthropology that has made the potentially positive relation of scientifically accumulated facts to an understanding of the universal and unchanging aspect of human nature well-nigh impossible. Western scientists and scholars in the fields of anthropology, the social sciences, and even the humanities are trained almost completely to study only change. Any alteration, no matter how trivial, is more often than not considered as a significant change, while the immutable is almost unconsciously identified with the unimportant or the dead. It is as if man were trained to study only the movement of clouds and to remain completely oblivious of the sky, with its immutable and infinite expanses, which provides the framework for the observations of the cloud movements. No wonder that so much of the study of man provided by modern disciplines is really no more than a study of triviality, producing most often petty results and failing at almost every step to predict anything of significance in the social order. Many a simple traditional folk tale reveals more about man than thick tomes with pages of statistics on what are usually described as 'vital changes'. In fact the only vital change that is occuring today is the ever greater alienation of man from his own permanent nature and a forgetfulness of this nature, a forgetfulness which cannot but be transitory but is bound at the same time to have catastrophic effects upon that type of man who has chosen it. But this is precisely the one change which 'objective' scientific methods are incapable of studying.

Yet, in principle, there is no necessary contradiction between scientific facts accumulated objectively and the concept of human nature with its permanent and universal implications. Were the impediments of that mental deformation called evolutionary thinking, which is neither objective nor scientific, to be removed, the accumulation of facts about man would display in a blindingly evident fashion the extra-spatial and extra-temporal character of man, if not beyond history—for this would lie beyond the reach of facts—at least in periods of history and in various regions of the world. Such an exercise would depict human nature as something constant and permanent (that nature to which the Holy Quran refers as *al-fiṭrah*), from which at certain moments of history and among certain peoples there have been deviations and departures that have soon been corrected by tragedies or catastrophes leading to a re-establishment of the norm. Sacred books such as the Quran contain, besides other levels of meaning, a history of the human soul which emphasizes in a majestic fashion this conception of human nature.[8] That is why the goal that is placed before man in all sacred books is to know and to return to the norm, to man's permanent and original nature, to the *fiṭrah*. As the *Tao-Te Ching* (XIX) states, 'Realize thy Simple Self. Embrace thy Original Nature'. For the goal of man cannot but be the knowledge of himself, of who he is.

> He who knows others is wise;
> He who knows himself is enlightened.
>
> *Tao-Te Ching*, XXXIII

Or, to quote a mediaeval Western contemplative,

> If the mind would fain ascend to the height of Science,
> let its first and principal study be to know itself.
>
> Richard of St Victor

In the light of the understanding which both revelation and intellectual vision have provided over the ages concerning the nature of man, the answer to the often posed question 'Can scientific knowledge capture something essential about man?' can only be the following: We cannot gain an *essential* knowledge of man through any method that is based on an externalization of man's inner being and the placing of this externalized man, of the man who stands at the rim of the wheel of existence, as the subject that knows. If 'essential' has any meaning at all it must be related to the *essence*, to the Centre or axis which generates at once the spokes and the rim. Only the higher can comprehend the lower, for 'to comprehend' means literally 'to encompass', and only that which stands on a higher level of existence can encompass that which lies below it. Man is composed of body, psyche and intellect, the last being at once above man and at the centre of his being. The essence of man, that which is essential to human nature, can be understood only by the intellect, through the 'eye of the heart' (*'ayn al-qalb* in Arabic or *chishm-i dil* in Persian) as traditionally understood, the intellect which is at once at the centre of man's being and encompasses all the other levels of his existence. Once the eye of the heart becomes closed and the faculty of intellection, in its original sense, atrophied, it is not possible to gain an essential knowledge of man. That reflection of the intellect upon the plane of the psyche and the mind which is called reason can never reach the essence of man, nor for that matter the essence of anything else, no matter how much it concerns itself with experiment and observation or how far it carries out its proper function of division and analysis, the legitimate and rightful function of *ratio*. It can gain peripheral knowledge of accidents, of effects, of external behaviour, but not of the essence. Reason, once divorced from the guiding light of the intellect, can at best confirm the existence of the *noumena*, of the reality of the essences of things, as we see in the philosophy of Kant, who, having limited intellect to reason, accepted the reality of *noumena* but denied the possibility of ever knowing them in themselves. But reason alone cannot *know* the essence itself. The knowledge that is essential is one that is ultimately based on the identity of the knower and the known, on the known being consumed by the fire of knowledge itself.

Man is at a particular vantage point to know one thing in essence, and that is himself, were he only to overcome the illusion of taking (to use Vedantic terms) the externalized and objectivized image of himself for his real Self, the Self which cannot be externalized because of its very nature. Scientific knowledge, like any other form of knowledge which is based by definition on the distinction between a subject that knows and an object that is known, must of necessity remain content with a knowledge that is peripheral and not essential.

One is naturally led to ask what is the relationship of particular scientific research in the modern sense to the quest for other kinds of knowledge about mankind in general. A relation of a legitimate and meaningful kind can exist—as seen in the Islamic sciences—provided the correct proportion and relation between ways of knowing is kept in mind. And that is possible only if a knowledge that transcends science, as currently understood, is accepted. The rim can serve as a point of access to the axis and the Centre only if it is taken for what it really is, namely the rim. Once the fact that the rim is the periphery is forgotten, the Centre also ceases to possess meaning and becomes inaccessible. Were a true metaphysics, a *scientia sacra*, to become once again a living reality in the West, knowledge gained of man through scientific research could be integrated into a pattern which would also embrace other forms of knowledge ranging from the purely metaphysical to those derived from traditional schools of psychology and cosmology.

But in the field of the sciences of man, as in that of the sciences of nature, the great impediment is precisely the monolithic and monopolistic character which modern Western science has displayed since the seventeenth century. Putting aside the great deal of pseudo-science and simply erroneous theories prevalent in the modern sciences of man such as anthropology and psychology, the elements that are based on careful observation of human behaviour or the human psyche under different circumstances could be related, without any logical contradictions, to what traditional schools of psychology, such as those found in Sufism, or Yoga, or Zen, have also discovered about the human psyche, and especially about certain aspects of it totally unknown to most of our contemporaries.[9] But to relate these elements to traditional schools is possible only if the doctrine of man in his totality, as expounded in traditional metaphysics—the 'Universal Man' (*al-insān al-kāmil*) of Islamic esotericism— is accepted, for as already stated only the greater can embrace the lesser. To claim to know the human psyche without the aid of the Spirit (or the Intellect) and to claim a finality for this knowledge as 'truly scientific', independent of any other form of knowledge, cannot but result in the very impasse which in fact the modern world faces today. It can only end in a truncated and incomplete, not to say outright erroneous, 'science of man', which is asked to play a role for which it has no competence. Such a science is most often more dangerous than ignorance pure and simple, for there is nothing more dangerous than simple ignorance except an ignorance which has pretensions to being knowledge and wisdom.

Scientific research into the nature of man can possess a constructive relationship to the universal and perennial ways of knowing man only if it realizes its own limitations and does not seek to transgress them. It can be legitimate only if it is able to overcome the 'totalitarian rationalism' inherent in modern science[10]—even though not accepted by many scientists—and to assent to become what it really is, namely a limited and particular way of knowing things through the observation of their external aspects, their *phenomena*, and of ratiocination based upon this empirical contact with things; a way that would be acceptable if taken for what it is, because things do also possess a face turned toward the external and the exteriorized.

The answer to the question concerning the worth of scientific research as a source of universal or essential knowledge about man—research which is being aped everywhere in the world today—must then be that it is worthless if considered as a source. How can a knowledge which negates the universal order in the metaphysical sense and denies the possibility of essential knowledge serve as the source of a knowledge that is essential and universal? Scientific research can become a source of essential knowledge only under the condition that 'scientific' is understood in the traditional sense as *al-ʿilm,* as a knowledge that issues from and leads to the principial order.

There is, however, one way in which scientific research can aid in gaining an awareness of something essential about the present predicament of modern man, if not of man's eternal nature. This is to make use of the experimental method employed by science to study modern scientific and industrial civilization itself. In science, whenever an experiment does not succeed, it is discontinued, no matter how much effort has been put into it, and an attempt is made to learn from the errors which were responsible for its lack of success.

Modern civilization as it has developed in the West since the Renaissance is an experiment that has failed[11]—failed in such an abysmal fashion as to cast doubt upon the very possibility of any future for man to seek other ways. It would be most unscientific today to consider this civilization, with all the presumptions about the nature of man and the Universe which lie at its basis, as anything other than a failed experiment. And in fact scientific research, if not atrophied by that totalitarian reign of rationalism and empiricism alluded to above, should be the easiest way of enabling contemporary man to realize that modern civilization has failed precisely because the premises upon which it has been based were false, because this civilization has been based on a concept of man which excludes what is most essential to the human state.

Paradoxically enough, the awareness of the shortcomings of modern civilization has dawned upon the general Western public—and not upon a small intellectual élite of the kind that warned of the crisis facing the modern world as far back as half a century ago[12]—not because of a sudden realization of man's forgotten nature but because of the rapid decay of the natural environment. It is a symptom of the mentality of modern man that the deep spiritual crisis which has been causing the very roots of his soul gradually to wither away had to come to his attention through a crisis within the physical environment.

During the past few years, so much has been written about the environmental and ecological crisis that there is no need here to emphasize the dimensions of the problems involved. The famous study that has emanated from M.I.T., *Limits to Growth*, has sought to apply the very methods of modern science to a study of the effects of the application of this science in the future. The authors of that work, as well as many others seriously concerned with the ecological crisis, have proposed a change in man's concept of growth, a return to non-material pursuits, a satisfaction with fewer material objects and many other well-meaning suggestions for change. But very few have realized that the pollution of the environment is no more than the after-effect of a pollution of the human soul which came into being the moment Western man decided to play the role of the Divinity upon the surface of the earth and chose to exclude the transcendent dimension from his life.[13]

In this late hour of human history, we observe two tragedies, one in the West and the other in the East. In the Occident, where the crisis of modern civilization—a crisis which is after all the product of the West—is most fully felt, since it is related usually to the environmental crisis, solutions are proposed which contain the very factors that led to the crisis in the first place. Men are asked to discipline their passions, to be rational humanists, to be considerate to their neighbours, both human and non-human. But few realize that these injunctions are impossible to carry out as long as there is no spiritual power to curb the infernal and passionate tendencies of the human soul. It is the very humanist conception of man that has dragged him to the infra-human. It is as a result of an ignorance of what man is, of the possibilities of the depths of darkness as well as the heights of illumination that he carries within himself, that such facile solutions are proposed. For millennia religions have taught men to avoid evil and to cultivate virtue. Modern man sought to destroy first the power of religion over his soul and then to question even the meaning of evil and sin. Now many propose as a solution to the environmental crisis a return to traditional virtues, although usually they do not describe the virtues in such terms because for the most part such people remain secular and propose that the life of men should continue to be divorced from the sacred.

It might be said that the environmental crisis, as well as the psychological unbalance of so many men and women in the West, the ugliness of the urban environment and the like are the results of the attempt of man to live by bread alone, to 'kill all the gods' and announce his independence of Heaven. But man cannot escape the effect of his actions, which are themselves the fruit of his present state of being. His only hope is to cease to be the rebellious creature he has become, to make peace with both Heaven and earth and to submit himself to the Divine. This itself would be tantamount to ceasing to be modern as this term is usually understood, to a death and a rebirth. That is why this dimension of the problem is rarely considered in general discussions of the environmental crisis. The missing dimension of the ecological debate is the role and nature of man himself and the spiritual transformation he must undergo if he is to solve the crisis he himself has precipitated.

The second tragedy, occurring in the East in general and the Islamic world in particular, is that this world is for the most part repeating the very errors which have led to the failure in the West of urban-industrial society and the modern civilization that has produced it. The attitude of the East towards the West should be to view it as a case study to learn from rather than as a model to emulate blindly. Of course the politico-economic and military pressures from the industrialized world upon the non-Western world are so great as to make many decisions impossible and many choices well-nigh excluded. But there is no excuse for committing certain acts whose negative results are obvious, or for having no better reason for undertaking this or that project than the fact that it has been carried out in the West. The earth cannot support additional mistakes of the kind committed by Western civilization. It is therefore most unfortunate that no present-day power on earth has a perspective wide enough to keep the well-being of the whole earth and its inhabitants in mind.

Of these two tragedies, certainly the first overshadows the second, for it is action carried out in the modernized, industrialized world that affects more directly the rest of the globe. For example, were the ecological crisis really to be taken seriously by any of the major industrial powers in their economic and technological policies rather than just in verbal statements, it would have an immeasurable influence upon those who of necessity emulate these powers in such fields. How different would the future of man be if the West were to remember again who man is, before the East forgets the knowledge it has preserved over the ages about man's real nature!

What contemporary man needs, amidst this morass of confusion and disorder of the mental and physical world which surrounds him, is first and foremost a message that comes from the Centre and defines the rim *vis-à-vis* the Centre. This message is still available in a living form in the Eastern traditions such as Islam and can be resuscitated within the Western world. But wherever this message be found, whether in the East or the West, if it issues from the Centre which is neither of the East nor of the West it is always a call for man who lives on the periphery and the rim of the wheel of existence to follow the spokes to the axis or Centre which is the Origin at once of himself and of all things. It is a call for man to realize who he is and to become aware of that spark of eternity which he contains within himself.

> There is in every man an incorruptible star, a substance called upon to become crystallized in Immortality; it is eternally prefigured in the luminous proximity of the Self. Man disengages this star from its temporal entanglements in truth, in prayer and in virtue, and in them alone.[14]

He who has crystallized this star within himself is at peace with both himself and the world. Only in seeking to transcend the world and to become a star in the spiritual firmament is man able to live in harmony with the world and to solve the problems that terrestrial existence by its very nature imposes upon him during this fleeting journey in the temporal which comprises his life on earth.

Notes to Chapter 1

1. It must be remembered that, in the West, man first rebelled against Heaven with the humanism of the Renaissance; only later did the modern sciences come into being. The humanistic anthropology of the Renaissance was a necessary background for the scientific revolution of the seventeenth century and the creation of a science which, although in one sense non-human, is in another sense the most anthropomorphic form of knowledge possible, for it makes human reason and the empirical data based upon the human senses the sole criteria for the validity of all knowledge.

Concerning the gradual disfiguration of the image of man in the West, see G. Durand, 'Défiguration philosophique et figure traditionnelle de l'homme en Occident', *Eranos-Jahrbuch*, XXXVIII, 1971, pp. 45–93.

2. If such a relation did not exist, it would not even be possible for man to identify

himself with other periods of human history, much less for the permanent aspects of human nature to manifest themselves even in the modern world as they have in the past and continue to do today.

3. Throughout this book the word 'intellect' is used in its original Latin sense as *intellectus* or the Greek *nous*, which stands above reason and is able to gain knowledge directly and immediately. Reason is only the reflection of the intellect upon the mirror of the human mind.

4. There is little more pathetic in this type of pseudo-humanities than the attempt now being made in some Islamic countries to introduce this decadence into the very bosom of Islamic culture in the name of progress.

Certain American scholars such as William Arrowsmith and William Thompson have already criticized what could be called the 'pollution of the humanities', but the tendency in this field as in the question of the pollution of the environment is mostly to try to remove the ill effects without curing the underlying causes.

5. In modern times, the occult sciences, whose metaphysical principles have been forgotten, have become known as the 'pseudo-sciences', while in reality they contain a profound doctrine concerning the nature of man and the cosmos, provided their symbolism is understood. Much of the social and human sciences today on the contrary veil and hide a total ignorance of human nature with a scientific garb and are, in a sense, the reverse of the occult sciences. Hence they deserve much more than the occult sciences the title of 'pseudo-science'.

6. This theme is thoroughly analyzed by F. Schuon in his *Dimensions of Islam*, trans. by P. Townsend, London, 1970, Chapter 2. Concerning the sage or the Sufi, he writes: 'The Sufi lives under the gaze of *al-Awwal* (the First), *al-Ākhir* (the Last), *al-Ẓāhir* (the Outward) and *al-Bāṭin* (the Inward). He lives concretely in these metaphysical dimensions as ordinary creatures move in space and time, and as he himself moves in so far as he is a mortal creature. He is consciously the point of intersection where the Divine dimensions meet; unequivocally engaged in the universal drama, he suffers no illusions about impossible avenues of escape, and he never situates himself in the fallacious "extra-territoriality" of the profane, who imagine that they can live outside spiritual Reality, the only reality there is.' pp. 36–37.

7. See, for example, L. Bounoure, *Déterminisme et finalité, double loi de la vie*, Paris, 1957; his *Recherche d'une doctrine de la vie*, Paris, 1964; G. Berthault, *L'évolution, fruit d'une illusion scientifique*, Paris, 1972; and D. Dewar, *The Transformist Illusion*, Murfreesboro, 1957. See also S. H. Nasr, *The Encounter of Man and Nature, The Spiritual Crisis of Modern Man*, London, 1968, pp. 124 ff., where works and views opposed to evolution are discussed.

8. For the episodes of the Quran considered as events of the human soul and its inner 'history', see F. Schuon, *Understanding Islam*, trans. by D. M. Matheson, London, 1963 and Baltimore (Penguin Metaphysical Series), 1972, Chap. 2.

9. Unfortunately very few serious studies based on the traditional point of view, which alone matters, have as yet been made of the traditional psychological sciences of the various Oriental traditions, sciences which can be understood only in the light of metaphysical principles and can be practised only with the aid of the spiritual grace present in a living tradition. See A. K. Coomaraswamy, 'On the Indian and Traditional Psychology, or rather Pneumatology', in *Selected Writings of Ananda K. Coomaraswamy*, ed. by R. Lipsey, Princeton, (in press).

10. F. Schuon, *Light on the Ancient Worlds*, trans. by Lord Northbourne, London, 1965, p. 117.

11. 'But, properly, urban industrialism must be regarded as an *experiment*. And if the scientific spirit has taught us anything of value, it is that honest experiments may well fail. When they do, there must be a radical reconsideration, one which does not flinch even at the prospect of abandoning the project. Surely, as of the mid-twentieth century, urban-industrialism is proving to be such a failed experiment, bringing in its wake every evil that progress was meant to vanquish.' T. Roszak, *Where the Wasteland Ends, Politics and Transcendence in Postindustrial Society*, Garden City, New York, 1973, p. xxiv of introduction.

12. Such men as R. Guénon in his *Crisis of the Modern World*, trans. by M. Pallis and R. Nicholson, London, 1962, whose original French edition first appeared in 1927, followed by other traditional authors, especially F. Schuon and A. K. Coomaraswamy, have written extensively during the past few decades on the crisis of the West on the basis of the application of perennial metaphysical criteria to the contemporary situation. But their writings were ignored in academic circles for a long time and continue to be so to a large extent even today. The crisis had to appear on the physical level in order to bring the dangerous tendencies of modern civilization before the eyes of modern men.

13. We have dealt with this theme extensively in our *The Encounter of Man and Nature, the Spiritual Crisis of Modern Man*. 'What, after all, is the ecological crisis that now captures so much belated attention but the inevitable extroversion of a blighted psyche? Like inside, like outside. In the eleventh hour, the very physical environment suddenly looms up before us as the outward mirror of our inner condition, for many the first discernible symptom of advanced disease within.' T. Roszak, *op. cit.*, p. xvii of introduction.

14. F. Schuon, *Light on the Ancient Worlds*, p. 117.

Chapter 2

The Dilemma of the Present-day Muslim

> And it (the resurrection) will not take place until you see affairs which will cause you to ask one another whether your Prophet has mentioned anything concerning them, and until the mountains will be displaced from their stations.
>
> (Prophetic *ḥadīth*)

When we turn to the contemporary Muslim as he finds himself in today's world, we discover that although his problems are not identical with those of Western man, he too lives in a situation which presents him with numerous difficulties, one which puts his faith (*īmān*) to the most arduous test possible. One can find in the Islamic world today a full spectrum of people ranging from purely traditional elements, through those who are caught between traditional values and modernism, to the blatant modernists who nevertheless still move within the Islamic orbit, and finally to the few who no longer consider themselves to belong to the Islamic universe at all.[1] With this latter group we are not concerned, for they can no longer be considered as the representative of *homo islamicus* who is the subject of our present discussion, although they, too, often return finally to the Islamic pattern of things. It is the *īmān* of the other groups, who already possess faith in one degree or another, that is put to the test in a world which makes the real appear illusory and the illusory real, a world which seduces men into believing that spiritual reality—the only reality there is—is out-moded in comparison with a supposedly 'real' world which is dissolving before the bewildered eyes of modern man like sand running through his fingers.

The major difference between the contemporary Muslim and his Western counterpart is that the former, in contrast to the latter, lives in a society where the Centre is still visible and therefore the rim can also be seen for what it really is.[2] He lives in a world where the transcendent dimension is still present, where the majority of men still perform their religious rites and duties, where the Divine Law or *Sharīʿah* is still considered to be the ultimate law, even if not fully practised by everyone, and where the figure of the saint and sage is still a living one, although now perhaps less easy to find than before. There is also the basic difference that the contemporary Muslim knows less about the modern world than does Western man, that his intelligence has been tested in fewer ways and that he has not in general developed the kind of discernment found among those in the West who have re-discovered tradition and by the same token come to know the real nature of the modern world. The situation of contemporary Muslims, like that of other Orientals in general, is also in one aspect more difficult than that of Western man in that changes now taking place in the East are more rapid and often more devastating. In a sense, the West has little more to lose to the onslaught of modernism, whereas there are still many things of spiritual value in the East which are being threatened every day, whether by means of books, the radio or the bulldozer. The contemporary Muslim must and cannot but wage a continuous holy war (*jihād*), not only within himself to keep his mind and soul healthy and intact, but also outwardly to protect what he can of the marvellous spiritual and artistic heritage his forefathers have bequeathed him in the expectation that he too will preserve and transmit it to the next generation. In this sense then, that he is being pulled by the forces of the Islamic tradition on the one hand and of secularism and modernism on the other, the contemporary Muslim, especially of the class thoroughly influenced by the modern world, may also be said to be situated between the rim and the axis, although his 'existential' situation differs from that of Western man in secularized post-industrial society because of the different elements which have conditioned his mind and soul.

The contemporary Muslim who lives in the far corners of the Islamic world and has remained isolated and secluded from the influence of modernism may be said to live still within a homogeneous world in which the tensions of life are those of normal human existence. But the Muslim who lives in the centres of the Islamic world touched in one degree or another by modernism lives within a polarized field of tension created by two contending world views and systems of values. This tension is often reflected within his mind and soul, and he usually becomes a house divided against itself, in profound need of re-integration. If he is of an intellectual bent, he sees on one side the rich intellectual heritage of Islam as a still-living reality, a heritage which is precisely a message from the Centre and a guide for man in his journey from the rim to the Centre. It is a world view based on the supremacy of the blinding reality of God before whom all creatures are literally nothing, and then on the hierarchic Universe issuing from His Command (*Amr*) and comprising the multiple levels of being from the archangelic world to the level of material existence.[3] It is a *Weltanschauung* based on viewing man as the 'image of God' (*khalaqa'llāhu Ādama ʿalā ṣūratihi*)[4], as God's vicegerent (*khalīfah*) on earth but also as His perfect servant (*ʿabd*) obeying His every command. It is based on the idea that all phenomena in the world of nature are symbols reflecting divine realities and that all things move according to His Will and their spiritual nature (*malakūt*), which is in His Hands.[5] It is based on the conception that only the law of God, the *Sharīʿah*, has ultimate claim upon the allegiance and respect of men and that it alone can provide for their felicity in its true sense.

On the other side and in contrast to this world view, the contemporary Muslim sees the basic assumptions of modern Western civilization, nearly all of which are the very antithesis of the Islamic principles he cherishes. He sees philosophies based either on man considered as a creature in rebellion against Heaven or on the human collectivity seen as an ant-heap in which man has no dignity worthy of his real nature. He sees the Universe reduced to a single level of reality—the spatio-temporal complex of matter and energy—and all the higher levels of reality relegated to the category of old wives' tales or—at best—images drawn from the collective unconscious. He sees the power of man as ruler upon the earth emphasized at the expense of his servanthood so that he is considered to be not the *khalīfatallāh*, the vicegerent of God, but the *khalīfah* of his own ego[6] or of some worldly power or collectivity. He sees the theomorphic nature of man either mutilated or openly negated. He reads the arguments of Western philosophers and scientists against the symbolic concept of nature, a concept which is usually debased by being called 'totemistic' or 'animistic' or some other term of that *genre*, usually loaded with pejorative connotations. He is, in fact, made to believe that the transformation from seeing the phenomena of nature as the portents or signs (*āyāt*) of God to viewing these phenomena as brute facts is a major act of progress which, however, only prepares nature for that ferocious rape and plunder for which modern man is now beginning to pay so dearly. Finally, the contemporary Muslim is taught to believe that the law is nothing but a convenient agreement within a human collectivity and therefore relative and ever-changing, with the implication that there is no such thing as a Divine Law which serves as the immutable norm of human action and which provides the measures against which man can judge his own ethical standards objectively.

These and many other intellectual and philosophical questions beset constantly the mind of that contemporary Muslim who is touched in one degree or another by the influence of modernism. Not all the questions present themselves with the same force to everyone, nor is every modernized Muslim modernized to the same degree. For this reason the dilemma of every contemporary Muslim is not the same. But, nevertheless, the tension between two world views of a contradictory nature is to be observed widely, the kind and degree of tension differing, of course, from one *milieu* and even one individual to another.

The same confrontation of world views and the same dilemma is also to be observed in other domains. In education—in its universal sense as the most important means of transmitting the tradition from one generation to another—again two contending systems vie with each other, with the contemporary

Muslim caught in between. On the one hand, there are the classical channels of education ranging from the laps of grandparents and parents to Quranic schools (*maktabs*) to traditional universities (*madrasahs*) to Sufi centres (*khānaqāhs* or *zāwiyahs*), not to speak of ateliers and guild centres where the arts and crafts are taught. On the other hand, there are radio and television programmes mostly dubbed from European languages, and on the formal level the modern educational systems of various Muslim countries, nearly all of which consist of poor imitations of various Western models at a time when the Western educational system itself is undergoing a crisis of unparalleled dimensions.[7] The difference between the relation of parent to child or teacher to student in the two systems, as well as the content of the subject matter taught, is as great as can be imagined. In the more modernized circles of the Islamic world, even small children face this tension, as on the one hand they still learn the various traditional stories which contain the profoundest wisdom in simple language from the mouth of a grandparent or a nanny and, on the other hand, they watch murder stories and the like on television screens. Among the adults, the opposition and the tension are even more evident, with two contending educational systems providing a natural battlefield upon which the contemporary Muslim, both as an individual who wishes to receive education and as a parent wanting to select a school for his or her child, stands bewildered.[8] The transition from the traditional educational system to the modern ones has in most cases been abrupt and disruptive and one of the major causes of the confusing state which the contemporary Muslim now faces.[9]

It might be thought that the dilemma of the contemporary Muslim under the influence and pressure of modernism is limited to the intellectual and educational realm, but this is far from true. Actually, a crisis of the same intensity, and perhaps of an even more direct effect, exists in the world of forms with which art is concerned. In this domain, the remarkably homogeneous yet diversified world of Islamic art, which has succeeded in creating an Islamic ambience for the Muslim within which he has lived and died, is threatened from every direction. Traditional Islamic architecture has been at a peak during nearly all of its long history and can be cited as a supreme example of that architecture which Goethe referred to as 'music grown silent'.[10] Today, in many Islamic cities, architecture is no longer music grown silent but sheer noise and cacophony petrified. An art which was a direct call from the Centre and which reflected the Centre and the Transcendent in nearly everyone of its forms[11] is now threatened by an 'art' of the most debased and opaque nature whose source of inspiration is revealed by the veil of ugliness with which it shrouds the environment.

The same conflict is to be seen in the auditory arts. Classical Arabic, Persian and North Indian music, all of which are among the highest expressions of Islamic art, have to compete with music of a much lower order of inspiration, to put it mildly, not only on a particular programme but sometimes even within the same composition. Classical poetry likewise has to contend with an army of young poets often cut off from their own traditional roots but bent on imitating at all costs not only the content but even the form of modern European and American poetry. Even the chanting of the Holy Quran, that supreme form of Islamic sacred art, is sometimes mutilated beyond recognition in many city centres where indiscriminate use is made of loudspeakers as if people wished to compete with the traffic noise through sheer volume.[12] Altogether, in the realm of forms as in the realm of ideas, there remains an acute tension and confrontation between two contending worlds within which the contemporary Muslim has to live and to make daily decisions.

As far as political, social and economic life are concerned, the conflicts and tensions are so many and at the same time so evident that there is no need to delve into them here. Numerous studies have already been devoted to them in the East and the West. The general trend in these domains as elsewhere is towards the secularization of the economic and political life of the Muslim peoples in total contrast to the Islamic conception, which has sacralized man's daily life including, of course, his political and economic activities and institutions.

As an example of the contrasts created within these fields and the dilemmas brought into being for the present-day Muslim who is aware of the world about him may be mentioned the concept of freedom.[13] In the traditional Islamic view, absolute freedom belongs to God alone and man can gain freedom only to the extent that he becomes God-like. All the restrictions imposed upon his life by the *Sharīʿah* or upon his art by the traditional canons are seen not as restrictions upon his freedom but as the indispensable aids which alone make the attainment of real freedom possible. The concept of *ḥurriyyah* (the word into which 'freedom' is usually translated today in modern Arabic) is taken from the post-Renaissance idea of individual freedom, which means ultimately imprisonment within the narrow confines of one's own individual nature. This totally Western idea is so alien to traditional Islam that this word cannot be found in any traditional text with the same meaning it has now gained in modern Arabic. In the Islamic world-view, freedom to do evil or to become severed from the source of all existence is only an illusory freedom. The only real freedom is that which enables man to attain that perfection which allows him to approach and ultimately become unified with the One Who is at once absolute necessity and absolute freedom. How far removed is this concept from the current Western notion of freedom, and what confusions are created within the mind of a man who is attracted by the pull of both ideas! These confusions affect nearly all of his daily decisions and his relations with nearly all the institutions of society from the family to the state. And they reflect upon art as well as morality, influencing individual patterns of behaviour in matters as far apart as sex and literary style.

These are only some of the dilemmas the contemporary Muslim in contact with the modern world faces. Many more could be added in nearly every domain of life. Together these contending factors have succeeded in converting the life and thought of most modernized Muslims into a patchwork of conflicting thoughts and actions whose contradictory nature remains often hidden from themselves. It might, of course, be asked why this dilemma must exist at all. Why cannot Muslims simply evaluate modern civilization according to the principles of their own tradition and simply reject what is opposed to these principles? The answer lies in the state of mind of most modernized Muslims, who, having been witness to the superior power of the modern West in the economic and military fields, fall under the spell of everything else that comes from the West, from philosophy to ethics, from social theories to canons of beauty. Moreover, many of them display a sense of inferiority *vis-à-vis* the West which is truly amazing. They take much too seriously the various currents that issue forth from the West and usually last but a short time, and they make every effort possible either to conform to them or to distort the teachings of Islam to appear in harmony with these currents. The source of the tension that exists within the soul of the modernized Muslim is precisely the strong pull of the modern world upon a segment of the Islamic *ummah* (Islamic community) whose hold upon its tradition and whose roots within the tradition have been weakened during, and as a result of, that very historical process which has enabled modernism to spread throughout the Islamic world.

It must, however, be added that there is also a vast segment of the Islamic world which, although touched by the storm of modernism, has its roots firmly grounded in the Islamic tradition and, in fact, sees in the events that pass over the surface of the earth today a confirmation rather than a denial of Islam, for these very events concerning the latter days were predicted long ago in traditional Islamic sources. The Holy Prophet (upon whom be peace) spoke more than once of conditions arising at the end of time about which men would question whether the Prophet had mentioned anything concerning them, that is, events which would break the mould of traditional Islamic life completely. He spoke of mountains being moved from their station, alluding to the devastation brought upon the natural environment. He spoke through his God-given knowledge of these and many other events to which the modern world is now becoming witness.

These confirmations cannot but strengthen the faith of those contemporary Muslims who are firmly rooted in their own tradition, while those whose faith has become shaken as a result of the corroding influence of modernism are suspended within a field of tension, between the rim and the axis, between secularism and modernism on the one hand and the sacred and the traditional on the other. Such people are therefore also in profound need of a message from the Centre, a message that would be authentic and at the same time re-interpreted in a fresh manner to save them from their particular condition of animated suspension and intellectual paralysis. Although their condition differs from that of Western man both psychologically and mentally, their need for a return to the Centre is as urgent, for they, like Western man who in an earlier period of his history became cut off from his spiritual traditions, are faced with the uncertainties of life and death, with a vacuum which cannot be filled save by the sacred. However, in contrast to modern Westerners, contemporary Muslims belong to a tradition which is still fully alive and needs only to be re-lived and to have its immutable principles applied again to existing conditions for them to be saved from the whirlpool of doubt and uncertainty into which they have cast themselves almost with the innocence of children imitating a 'sophisticated' adult, but without being truly innocent. For as the Quran has asserted so often, man is responsible for his actions before God, and the modernized Muslim is certainly no exception to this divinely ordained principle.

Notes to Chapter 2

1. This last group is small indeed, but nevertheless it is beginning to make its presence felt in some modernized cities of the Islamic world. There are also a few Muslims who are trying to rediscover tradition and have a deep nostalgia for it but who are lost in the maze of pseudo-traditional movements that have swept over the West recently. There is, of course, also a small élite which, having absorbed Western culture to its very roots, has rediscovered and returned to the Islamic tradition, but its number at the moment is very limited indeed.

2. In certain schools of Islamic esotericism, the *Sharī'ah* itself has been compared to the rim or the circumference, the *Ṭarīqah* to the spokes and the *Ḥaqīqah* to the centre of the wheel. See S. H. Nasr, *Ideals and Realities of Islam*, London, 1966, and Boston, 1972, p. 122. But here we have used the symbolism of the rim and the axis in the sense given to it in the first chapter rather than in the sense used by these schools.

3. Concerning Islamic cosmology, see S. H. Nasr, *An Introduction to Islamic Cosmological Doctrines*, Cambridge (USA), 1964.

4. This well-known *ḥadīth* of the Holy Prophet, which means 'God created man according to His form', must not, however, be understood in an anthropomorphic sense. See F. Schuon, *Understanding Islam*, Chap. 1; and S. H. Nasr, *Ideals and Realities of Islam*, p. 18.

5. The Holy Quran says,

قُلْ مَنْ بِيَدِهِ مَلَكُوتُ كُلِّ شَيْءٍ

Say: In whose hand is the dominion (*malakūt*: meaning also essence or spiritual root) over all things? (XXIII, 88; Pickthall translation).

6. In fact if man cannot remain *khalīfatallāh*, he is dragged ultimately to the state of becoming *khalīfat al-shaiṭān*, the vicegerent of Satan. A humanism cut off from God cannot but lead to the infra-human. One would think that the experiment carried out by Western man since the Renaissance should be sufficient 'experimental' proof of this metaphysical assertion. But for certain types of mentalities hypnotized by the glitter of the modern world even such 'experimental' evidence does not seem to be sufficient, although usually such people are the loudest defenders of the 'scientific' and the 'experimental' approach without usually understanding what it really means. We have dealt more extensively with this and other basic principles of Islam and their parodies in the modern world in our other writings.

7. See I. Illich, *Deschooling Society*, New York, 1970. It is curious that despite this crisis in many Muslim countries, not only do the national educational systems seek to imitate ever more closely Western models, but also the foreign schools which were once run by missionaries continue to expand under the veil of 'neutrality', which means in reality substituting for Christian missionary activity missionary zeal in the name of the spread of Western culture or, ultimately, secularism. If there are some exceptions to be observed, they are only exceptions which prove the rule.

8. See H. A. R. Gibb, *Modern Trends in Islam*, Chicago, 1945, Chap. 3, for a profound analysis of this situation in the contemporary Islamic world. See also W. C. Smith, *Islam in Modern History*, New York, 1957; S. H. Nasr, *Islamic Studies*, Beirut, 1966, Chap. 2.

9. For the transition from traditional education to modern as far as the Arab world is concerned, see A. L. Tibawi, *Islamic Education: Its Traditions and Modernization into the Arab National Systems*, London, 1972.

10. 'A noble philosopher has spoken of architecture as frozen music and has thereby caused much raising of eyebrows. We know of no better way to re-introduce this beautiful thought than by calling architecture "music grown silent".' *Maximen und Reflexionen*, 1207, cited in S. Levarie and E. Levy, 'The Pythagorean Table', *Main Currents in Modern Thought*, New York, Vol. 30, no. 4, March–April 1974, p. 124.

11. For the metaphysical foundations of Islamic art, see T. Burckhardt, 'Perennial Values in Islamic Art', in J. Needleman (ed.), *The Sword of Gnosis*, Baltimore, 1974, pp. 304–316; also N. Ardalan and L. Bakhtiyar, *The Sense of Unity—The Sufi Tradition in Persian Architecture*, Chicago, 1973.

12. The indiscriminate use of loudspeakers, which accompany some people in the Islamic world from the cradle to the grave, is a sign of the loss of discernment and artistic taste among many contemporary Muslims affected by the influence of modernism.

13. See. F. Rosenthal, *The Muslim Concept of Freedom Prior to the Nineteenth Century*, Leiden, 1960, where the meaning of this concept during the various periods of Islamic history is analyzed.

Part II

The Comparative Method and the Study of the Islamic Intellectual Heritage in the West

Chapter 3

Metaphysics and Philosophy East and West: Necessary Conditions for Meaningful Comparative Study

There is an Arabic proverb according to which a fish always begins to decay from its head. This echoes the well-known Latin proverb *corruptio optimi pessima*: 'the corruption of the best is the worst'. What occurred in the West during the Renaissance and is now happening in so many parts of the Islamic world is precisely the corruption of the best, the decay of the head of the fish whose body is still intact. To oppose this process and to cater to the real needs of man in both East and West, therefore, it is likewise necessary to begin from the 'head', from the teachings related to the most sublime aspect of tradition contained in its spiritual and intellectual dimensions which are the first to become inaccessible and 'veiled', rather than the social and practical dimensions of the tradition which usually remain more accessible. It is the decay of the best or most intellectually gifted and hence influential in the long run that must be combated with the help of sapiential doctrines, the message from the Centre the forgetting of which is at the root of the pathetic plight of modern man now observable on such a vast scale. It is, therefore, to the metaphysical dimension of tradition contained at the heart of religion that we must turn before all else.

A great deal has been written during the past decades on the methodology of comparative religion, on various approaches taken by Western scholars, ranging from historians to phenomenologists, in studying Eastern religions. With this already extensively debated subject we will not concern ourselves here.[1] Rather, we shall limit ourselves to the question of Oriental and particularly Islamic metaphysics and traditional philosophy, of which the understanding in the West is sought by so many but is attained by so few, remembering that, in this domain, what holds true for the Islamic tradition applies to other Oriental traditions as well.

In contrast to the extravagant claims made for world-wide communication between peoples of various cultures and races, the Tower of Babel in which modern man resides makes communication of serious matters most difficult at a time when outward contact between men seems to have become easier than at any other period of human history. The common language of wisdom having been lost, there exists for modernized men no common ground to make any meaningful communication possible, especially between the modern world and the traditions of the East. Men talk of a single humanity at a time when there has never been so little inner communication between components of the human race. Today, outwardly cut off from the umbilical cord that has always connected them to the common Divine Ground, men are reduced to islands set apart by an insuperable chasm which no amount of humanism can bridge. In no field is this as true as in metaphysical doctrines and traditional 'philosophy', or in that corpus of knowledge which determines the ultimate framework of all man's other modes of knowledge as well as the values of his actions.

Because of the lack of discernment which characterizes the modern world and which is to be seen even more among Westernized Orientals, Muslim and otherwise, than among Westerners themselves, all kinds of fantastic excesses on both sides have for the most part prevented a meaningful intellectual communication and a comparative study of philosophy and metaphysics worthy of the name. The greatest gnostics and saints have often been compared with sceptics, and different levels of inspiration have been totally confused. A Tolstoy has been called a Mahatma; Hume's denial of causality has been related to Ashʿarite theology on the one hand and to Buddhism on the other; Śaṇkara has been compared with the German idealists, and Nietzsche with Rūmī. Western students of Oriental doctrines have usually tried to reduce these doctrines to 'profane' philosophy, and modernized Orientals, often burdened by the half-hidden sense of inferiority already alluded to, have tried to give respectability to the same doctrines and to 'elevate' them by giving them the honour of being in harmony with the thought of this or that Western philosopher, who in fact is usually out of vogue by the time such comparisons are made. On both sides, usually, the relation of the 'philosophy' in question to the experience or direct knowledge of the Truth which is the source of this 'philosophy' is forgotten, and levels of reality are confused.

A first step toward a solution of this problem is to clear the ground of existing confusions in order to clarify exactly what is being compared with what. One must first of all ask what we mean by 'philosophy'. To this extremely complicated question one can provide a clear answer provided that the light of metaphysical certainty is present. But precisely because this light is lacking in most discussions, the worst kind of confusion reigns over the very attempt at a definition of the subject matter in hand. Moreover, the traditions of the East and the West have given different meanings to this term, although at the highest level of the *philosophia perennis*, the *sanatana dharma* of Hinduism or the *ḥikmah laduniyyah* of Islam, there has always been the profoundest agreement concerning the nature of the *sophia* which all true philosophers 'love' and seek and in whose bosom alone can the East and West meet.[2]

To begin with it can be said that, if we accept the meaning of the term 'philosophy' current in the West in most European languages, then it is nearly synonymous with logic[3]—leaving aside the recent anti-rationalist movements based upon such sentiments as anxiety and fear. In the West, philosophy as usually understood has sometimes allied itself with revelation and theology or true intellectual intuition ('intellect' being understood in its original sense) as in St Bonaventure or St Thomas;[4] at other times it has become wedded to mathematics or to the physical sciences, as in certain schools of the seventeenth century and again of the twentieth century; and at yet other times it has sought to analyze and dissect the data of the senses alone, as in British empiricism, and to serve solely the function of praxis.

Also in the West, at least in its main intellectual current, metaphysics in its real sense, which is a sapiential knowledge based upon the direct and immediate experience of the Truth, has become reduced—thanks to the Occidental interpretation of Aristotle—to a branch of philosophy. As a result, men like Plotinus, Proclus, Dionysius, Erigena and Nicolas of Cusa have been treated as ordinary philosophers, whereas if we accept the meaning of philosophy given above, they cannot by any means be classified in the same category as men like Descartes and Kant, nor even with the Aristotelian and Thomist philosophers, who occupy an intermediary position between these two groups, namely the post-mediaeval European philosophers on the one hand and the gnostics and metaphysicians on the other. As a result of the forgetting of the fundamental distinction between the intellect, which knows through immediate experience or vision, and reason, *ratio*, which can only know through analysis and division, the fundamental distinction between metaphysics as a *scientia sacra* or Divine Knowledge and philosophy as a purely human form of mental activity has been blurred or forgotten.[5] Things have reached such a point that in the modern world all the different philosophical schools ranging from the purely metaphysical to the feeblest efforts of atrophied minds have been put into a single category and their content has been reduced to a lowest common denominator.

To make the problem more difficult, despite the currently accepted definition of philosophy in the West, the echo of philosophy as the doctrinal aspect of an integral spiritual way, or as metaphysics and theosophy in its original sense, still lingers on in the meaning of the word and continues to possess a marginal existence. One can in fact distinguish, at least in popular language in the West, two meanings of the term philosophy:[6] one in the technical sense alluded to above and the other in the sense of 'wisdom'. Against this latter meaning, in fact, most professional modern European and American philosophy has rebelled more than ever before, so that these modes of thought could hardly be called *philo-sophia*, for they do not love but hate wisdom. Logically they should be called *miso-sophia*.

As far as the Oriental traditions such as Buddhism, Taoism, Hinduism and

Islam are concerned, the situation is just the reverse. Except for certain schools such as the *mashshāʾī* or Peripatetic school of Islam, which corresponds in many ways but not completely to Aristotelianism and Thomism in the West,[7] certain individual Islamic figures such as Muḥammad ibn Zakariyyāʾ al-Rāzī, and some of the peripheral schools in India, there is nothing in the Oriental traditions which could be considered 'philosophy' in the current Western sense of the term, precisely because the major intellectual traditions of the Orient are always wedded to a direct experience of the spiritual world and intellectual intuition in the strictest sense of the term. What is usually called Oriental philosophy is the doctrinal part of a total spiritual way, tied to a method of realization and inseparable from the revelation or tradition which has given birth to the way in question. That is why to speak of rationalistic philosophy and of Chinese or Hindu philosophy in the same breath is a contradiction in terms, unless we use the word 'philosophy' in two different senses: of thought processes being wedded to spiritual experience, and of thought being completely cut off from this experience. It is a lack of awareness of this basic distinction that has made a sham of so many studies of comparative philosophy and has helped to blind to the real significance of Oriental metaphysics those in the West whose sources of knowledge are the usual academic works on the subject. Far from being the object of mental play, this metaphysics has the function of enabling man to transcend the mental plane itself.

When one has taken into consideration the above differences as well as the essential role of religion and methods of spiritual realization in the creation and the sustaining of what is usually called 'Oriental philosophy'—in contrast to what is found in modern Western philosophy—the first necessary condition for a meaningful comparative study will be complete awareness of the structure and the levels of meaning of the religious and metaphysical traditions of East and West. One can compare religions themselves; that belongs to the field of comparative religion. One can also compare the mystical and esoteric teachings of the East and the West in the field which has recently come to be called 'comparative mysticism'[8] and which is in reality an aspect of comparative religion. These are disciplines apart from what is now becoming known as comparative philosophy, a discipline which seeks to study the intellectual heritage of various Oriental traditions and that of the Occident through the comparative method.

Now comparative philosophy *per se* is either a shallow comparison of apparently similar but essentially different teachings, or, if it is to be serious, it is a comparative study of different ways of thinking and various matrices determining different sciences and forms of knowledge in reference to the total vision of the Universe and of the nature of things, a vision which is inseparable from the religious and spiritual background that has produced the 'philosophy' in question. The outward comparison of an Emerson and a Ḥāfiẓ or a Saʿdī will never have any meaning unless what each has said is considered in the light of Protestant Christianity and Islam respectively.

Comparative philosophy without reference to the religious background, whether the religion in question has had a positive influence or has even been treated negatively, is as absurd as comparing single notes of music without reference to the melody of which they are a part.

Nor is comparative philosophy between East and West possible without considering the hierarchic nature of man's faculties and the modes of knowledge accessible to him. One of the most unfortunate and in fact tragic elements that has prevented most modern Western men from understanding Oriental teachings and in fact much of their own tradition is that they wish to study traditional man in the light of the model of two-dimensional modern man deprived of the transcendent dimension, the type of man with whom they are usually closely associated. The very concept of man's identity prevalent in the modern world is the greatest obstacle to an understanding of traditional man, who has been and continues to be aware of the Centre and also of the multiple levels of existence and the grades of knowledge accessible to him.[9] If a blind man were to develop a philosophy based upon his experience of the world derived from his four other senses, surely it would differ from one based upon those four senses as well as upon sight. How much more would a 'philosophy' based upon man's rational analysis of sense data differ from one that is the result of the experience of a world which transcends both reason and the sensible world? The functioning of the eye of the heart (*'ayn al-qalb* or *chishm-i dil* of the Sufis, which corresponds to the 'third eye' of the Hindus) makes accessible a vision or an experience of reality which affects man's 'philosophy' about the nature of reality as completely as perception by the eye colours our view of the nature of material existence.

Without a full awareness of the hierarchy of knowledge—which can be reduced to at least the four basic levels of the intellectual, the imaginative (in its positive sense of *imaginatio* or *khayāl* in Arabic),[10] the rational and the sensible—again no meaningful comparative study is possible. When people say that Śaṇkara said so and so, which was confirmed by Berkeley or some other eighteenth century philosopher, it must be asked whether the same means of gaining knowledge was accessible to both. Or when it is said that this or that existential philosopher has had an 'experience of being' like a Mullā Ṣadrā or some other Muslim sage,[11] it must first be asked whether it is possible for a philosopher who negates Being to have an experience of It, for in reality we can have an experience of Being only through the grace provided by Being Itself and by means of the paths provided by It through those objective manifestations of the Universal Intellect called religion or revelation. Whenever comparisons are to be made, it must be asked what the source of the 'philosophy' in question is, whether it comes from ratiocination, from empirical analysis or from spiritual vision, or in other words upon which aspect of the being of the knower it depends. One must always remember the *dictum* of Aristotle that knowledge depends upon the mode of the knower.

In certain limited fields such as logic or the 'philosophy of nature', comparisons can be made for the most part legitimately without recourse to the total background alluded to above, although even here elements cannot be divorced totally from their background. But to a certain degree it is possible to compare Indian or Islamic logic with the various logical schools in the West, or atomism as it developed in India or among the Muslim Ashʿarites with atomism in the West, at least before the modern period. But once this limit is passed, the total background and the question of the 'source' of the knowledge in question become factors of paramount importance which one can neglect only at the expense of forsaking the possibility of true comprehension.

For example, it is possible to make serious comparative studies between Indian or Persian and Greek doctrines, or between Islamic philosophy and Western scholastic philosophy before the modern period. These studies can be meaningful because of both morphological resemblances and historical relations. But once we come to the modern period, the situation changes completely.[12] From the point of view of Oriental metaphysics, the whole movement of thought in the West from the period after Nicolas of Cusa to Hegel, not to speak of twentieth century philosophy, is a movement toward 'anti-metaphysics' and an ever greater alienation from all that constitutes the very basis of all true 'philosophy', namely the twin sources of truth, which for traditional or perennial philosophy are none other than revelation and intellectual intuition or spiritual vision. Comparative studies made of this period should be concerned either with showing dissimilarities, conflicts and contradictions, or with the schools that have stood at the margin away from the mainstream of the history of European thought. A comparative study showing similarities between Oriental doctrines and modern Western 'thought' could have meaning only in the case of such Western figures as those known by the collective name of the Cambridge Platonists, or Jacob Boehme, Claude St Martin, Franz van Baader and the like, who are not even generally well known in the West, to say nothing of the East. Otherwise, to say that this or that statement of Hegel resembles the Upanishads or that Hume presents ideas similar to Nagarjuna is to fall into the worst form of error, one which prevents any type of profound understanding from being achieved, either for Westerners wanting to understand the East or *vice-versa.*

In this order of indiscriminate comparisons without regard for the real nature of the ideas involved and for their meaning within the total context of things, Orientals have been even more at fault than the Western scholars who concern themselves with Oriental studies. In many instances found over and over again in the writings of modernized Orientals, the nature of the experience upon which the 'philosophy' in question is based and the total world view in which alone it possesses meaning are completely overlooked. And often the sentimental desire to bring about harmony between completely contradictory and incompatible premisses—such as those upon which the traditional societies and the anti-traditional modern civilization are based—causes such writers to speak of apparent resemblances where there are in fact only the deepest contrasts and contradictions. This attitude reduces the role of comparative philosophy to that of a sentimental charity, whereas its function should be to serve the truth and to reveal contrasts and differences wherever they exist.

In speaking of differences we must also turn our glance for a moment to the question of the comparative study of doctrines, not between East and West but between the Eastern traditions themselves. One of the results of Western colonization of Asia during the last century has been that even today the different civilizations of Asia see each other, even if they be neighbours, in the mirror of the Occident. 'Comparative philosophy' is taken for granted to mean the comparison of ideas between East and West. Moreover, Oriental authors who undertake comparative studies usually take their own tradition and the West into consideration and nothing else. A Muslim considers only Islam and the West, and a Hindu Hinduism and Western thought, whereas the situation should be otherwise. For example, as far as relations between Hinduism and Islam are concerned, contemporary Hindu and Muslim scholars should strive to their utmost to attain today, through comparison, a degree of understanding of their respective traditions similar to what was achieved by Dārā Shukūh and Mīr Abu'l-Qāsim Findiriskī three centuries ago. Only recently, in fact, have a handful of Oriental scholars begun to take seriously comparative studies within the Oriental traditions themselves, and a few outstanding works have been composed in this domain,[13] but a great deal more needs to be done in this fertile but almost unexplored field.

In the domain of comparing various Oriental doctrines, one finds, of course, a much firmer ground for comparison than when dealing with the modern West, seeing that Oriental civilizations are all of a traditional character, rooted in the Divine Principle which presides over and dominates them. But even here it is necessary to proceed with a spirit of discernment, avoiding shallow and sentimental comparisons and equations, and situating each school and doctrine in its appropriate place within the total matrix of its tradition. Although in a profound sense there is an East or Orient which stands *vis-à-vis* the Occident, a more detailed panorama of the intellectual landscape, which would give the appropriate depth to comparative studies, would reveal several Orients juxtaposed against a modern Occident whose historical tradition has, however, possessed elements and periods akin to the Orient, a term which, more than a geographical location, symbolizes most of all a spiritual reality, the world of light and illumination.[14]

It might be asked, 'What use is the comparative study of philosophy and metaphysics?' To the West, its primary function can be to provide the criteria necessary to criticize in depth Western philosophy itself, which although outwardly critical of earlier schools of philosophy rarely turns the sharp edge of criticism against itself and is hardly ever exposed to criticism of its totality and of its basic premisses. Moreover, Oriental doctrines can fulfil that most fundamental and urgent task of reminding the West of truths that have existed within its own tradition but which have become so completely forgotten that it appears to many as if they had never existed. Today, it is in fact nearly impossible for Western man to rediscover the whole of his own tradition without the aid of Oriental metaphysics.[15] This is particularly so because the sapiential doctrines and the appropriate spiritual techniques necessary for their realization are hardly accessible in the West, and 'philosophy' has become totally divorced from experience of a spiritual nature. In the traditional East the very opposite holds true. 'Philosophy' as a mental play or discipline which does not transform one's being is considered meaningless and in fact dangerous. The whole of the teachings of such Islamic philosophers as Suhrawardī and Mullā Ṣadrā and all of Sufism are based on this point, as are all the schools of Hinduism and Buddhism, especially Vedanta and Zen. The very separation of knowledge from being which lies at the heart of the crisis of modern man is avoided in the Oriental traditions, which consider legitimate only that form of knowledge that can transform the being of the knower. The West could learn no greater lesson from the East than the realization of the central role of spiritual discipline in the attainment of any knowledge of permanent value.

As far as modern Easterners are concerned, one observes among most of those who are at once interested in the intellectual life and affected by the modernist spirit the most abominable lack of discernment and the dangerous tendency to mix the sacred and the profane, thus creating an eclectic conglomeration of sacred doctrines and profane and transient 'thoughts' which becomes a most deadly instrument for the destruction of all that still survives of true intellectuality and spirituality in the East. The errors committed by Easterners in this domain are perhaps even graver than those of Western scholars, because, here as in instances already cited, there is more possibility of spiritual damage in the East, where traditions have been better preserved. Some of the most destructive of those forces that have played havoc in Eastern societies during the past century are the result of shallow and facile 'syntheses' of Eastern and Western thought and superficial attempts at their unification. A more serious comparative study would therefore also serve Eastern scholars by enabling them to know better the very complex and complicated thought patterns of the modern world and the real nature of the modern world itself, so that they may be able to defend more carefully the authenticity of their own traditions while seeking at the same time to express their timeless truths in a contemporary manner without betraying their essence. In this supreme task that today stands before every genuine Oriental intellectual in general and Muslim intellectual in particular, the fruits of comparative study carried out on a serious basis can be of much value.

Finally, a comparative study in depth of Eastern doctrines and Western schools can help to achieve an understanding between East and West based not on the shifting sands of human nature nor on some form of humanism but on immutable truths, of which the attainment is made possible by the spiritual experience that is accessible to qualified men, whether of East or of West. It is intellectual intuition, and the spiritual experience of which a metaphysical doctrine is in a sense the fruit, that alone can make possible the attainment of that Unity which in its transcendence comprehends both the East and the West. Today, many men who have been exposed to the modern world in a sense carry the Orient and the Occident as two poles and tendencies within themselves. A comparative study in depth can make possible, through the removal of that complex of current errors which constitutes the modern world, the vision of that 'tree that is neither of the East nor of the West',[16] wherein alone can the East and the West be united. To seek this noble end, which would mean also the discovery of the immutable nature of man and which is the only way possible to correct the optical illusions to which the modern world is victim, must be the purpose of all serious studies of Eastern and Western doctrines and philosophies. It is a goal to the achievement of which the truly contemplative and intellectual élite of both East and West are urgently summoned by the very situation of man in the contemporary world, a situation which demands such a study, whatever be the differences in the problems faced by men living in the East and in the West.

Notes to Chapter 3

1. Numerous contemporary historians of religion such as M. Eliade, W. C. Smith, C. Adams and R. H. L. Slater have dealt with this subject, which now occupies much attention among scholars of comparative religion. On the incomparable method of studying various religions employed by F. Schuon, who more than any other living authority has provided Western man with the key to the understanding of Oriental traditions, see H. Smith, 'The Relation between Religions', in *Main Currents in Modern Thought*, Vol. 30, no. 2, Nov–Dec, 1973, pp. 52–57, Rochester, N.Y.

2. 'We recognize that the only possible ground upon which an effective entente of East and West can be accomplished is that of the purely intellectual wisdom that is one and the same at all times and for all men, and is independent of all environmental idiosyncrasy.' A. K. Coomaraswamy, 'On the Pertinence of Philosophy', *Contemporary Indian Philosophy*, London, 1952, p. 160.

3. 'Philosophy, in the sense in which we understand the term (which is also its current meaning) primarily consists of logic; this definition of Guénon's puts philosophic thought in its right place and clearly distinguishes it from "intellectual intuition", which is the direct apprehension of a truth.' F. Schuon, *Language of the Self*, trans. by M. Pallis and M. Matheson, Madras, 1959, p. 7.

4. 'Logic can either operate as part of an intellection, or else, on the contrary, put itself at the service of an error; moreover, unintelligence can diminish or even nullify logic, so that philosophy can in fact become the vehicle of almost anything; it can be an Aristotelianism carrying ontological insights, just as it can degenerate into an "existentialism" in which logic has become a mere shadow of itself, a blind and unreal operation; indeed, what can be said of a "metaphysic" which idiotically posits man at the centre of the Real, like a sack of coal, and which operates with such blatantly subjective and conjectural concepts as "worry" and "anguish"?' *ibid*, p. 7.

5. 'A metaphysical doctrine is the incarnation in the mind of a universal truth. A philosophical system is a rational attempt to resolve certain questions which we put to ourselves. A concept is a "problem" only in relation to a particular ignorance.'

F. Schuon, *Spiritual Perspectives and Human Facts*, trans. by D. M. Matheson, London, 1953, p. 11. This distinction has also been thoroughly discussed by R. Guénon in his many works.

6. Coomaraswamy also distinguished between two kinds of philosophy whose unity is embraced by wisdom alone: 'Philosophy, accordingly, is a wisdom about knowledge, a *correction du savoir-penser* . . . Beyond this, however, philosophy has been held to mean a wisdom not so much about particular kinds of thought, as a wisdom about thinking, and an analysis of what it means to think, and an enquiry as to what may be the nature of the ultimate reference of thought.' *op. cit.*, pp. 151–152.

7. See S. H. Nasr, *Three Muslim Sages*, Cambridge (USA), 1964, Chap. 1.

8. This field has attracted the attention of several well-known scholars during the past few decades, men such as R. Otto, L. Gardet, D. T. Suzuki and A. Graham. It has received its profoundest treatment, however, in the writings of F. Schuon, who has followed the path, trodden before him by R. Guénon and A. K. Coomaraswamy, to its sublimest peak.

9. See S. H. Nasr, 'Who is Man? The Perennial Answer of Islam', *Studies in Comparative Religion*, Vol. 2, 1968, pp. 45–56; also in J. Needleman (ed.), *The Sword of Gnosis*, pp. 203–217.

10. See H. Corbin, *Terre céleste et corps de résurrection*, Paris, 1961.

11. See H. Corbin (ed.), *Le livre des pénétrations métaphysiques* (*Kitāb al-mashā'ir* of Mullā Ṣadrā), Tehran–Paris, 1964, Introduction.

12. In the case of certain seventeenth century philosophers such as Descartes and Spinoza it is also, of course, possible and legitimate to trace the influence of Islamic and Greek as well as Scholastic philosophy upon them, as has been done so ably by such scholars as E. Gilson and H. A. Wolfson.

13. We have in mind especially the two-volume work of T. Izutsu, *A Comparative Study of the Key Philosophical Concepts in Sufism and Taoism: Ibn 'Arabī and Lao-Tsŭ, Chuang-Tzŭ*, Tokyo, 1966–67, which contains a profound study of these men and a comparison of their doctrines.

14. This symbolism is the basis of Suhrawardī's 'Theosophy of the Orient of Light' (*ḥikmat al-ishrāq*), which is at once Oriental and illuminative. See Nasr, *Three Muslim Sages*, pp. 64 ff. and the two prolegomena of H. Corbin, to Suhrawardī, *Opera metaphysica et mystica*, Vol. 1, Istanbul, 1945; Vol. 11, Tehran–Paris, 1952.

15. Concerning the teachings of Guénon on this subject, Coomaraswamy writes, 'It is only because this metaphysics still survives as a living power in Eastern societies, in so far as they have not been corrupted by the withering touch of Western, or rather, *modern* civilization . . . , and not to Orientalize the West, but to bring back the West to a consciousness of the roots of her own life and . . . values . . . , that Guénon asks us to turn to the East'. 'Eastern Wisdom and Western Knowledge', *The Bugbear of Literacy*, London, 1949, pp. 69–70.

16. This is in reference to the verse from 'The Light' (*āyat al-nūr*) in the Quran (XXIV, 35), quoted at the beginning of this work.

Chapter 4

The Significance of the Comparative Method for the Study of the Islamic Intellectual and Spiritual Heritage

Having dealt with the problems and the significance of 'the comparative method', we must now apply this method to the Islamic universe, with which we are particularly concerned. It can be said with certainty that the comparative method, in the sense given to it in the previous chapter, is the most suitable means to explain and elucidate the Islamic intellectual and spiritual heritage for Western man. And although obviously not necessary for Muslims who wish to study their own tradition, even in their case it can be helpful to those who have received some form of modern education and whose matrix of thought and attitudes is often determined to some degree by elements drawn from the context of Western history and culture.

In applying the comparative method to the Islamic intellectual and spiritual heritage, we must emphasize once again that the term 'philosophy' (*al-falsafah* or *al-ḥikmah*) used in a traditional Islamic context must not be confused or equated with the modern use of the term,[1] and also that the basic distinction between Oriental metaphysics and profane philosophy must be kept in mind.[2] Moreover, the traditional Islamic 'philosophy' which is usually the subject of comparative studies fills, in fact, an intermediate position in the spectrum of Islamic intellectual life between the pure metaphysics contained in various forms of Islamic esotericism, especially Sufism but also the inner aspect of Shiʿism, and rationalistic philosophy, which through its gradual decadence in the West led to the completely profane philosophy of today. For it must be remembered that the post-mediaeval development of Western philosophy—after the Scholastic school, which is closely related to the Islamic philosophy in question—is based on the gradual decomposition of the concept of Being, which was so central to mediaeval European philosophy, and the gradual estrangement of reason, the tool *par excellence* of modern European philosophy, from the light of the Intellect.[3]

With these distinctions in view, we can proceed to apply the comparative method to Islamic intellectuality and spirituality, both the 'philosophy' mentioned above, which is usually the subject of comparative and also pure metaphysics, and gnosis (*maʿrifah*) in both its theoretical and its practical aspects, keeping in mind the hierarchy of knowledge that forms the basis of traditional Islamic intellectual life. In this domain, we must also be aware of the full breadth of the rich Islamic intellectual heritage which includes the several forms of gnostic doctrines contained in Sufism and various forms of Shiʿism, the school of illumination (*ishrāq*) of Suhrawardī, the 'transcendent theosophy' (*al-ḥikmat al-mutaʿāliyah*) of Mullā Ṣadrā, Ismāʿīlī philosophy and theology, Peripatetic philosophy, later *Kalām*, the principles of jurisprudence (*uṣūl al-fiqh*), both Sunni and Shiʿite, and many other schools, not all of which can be enumerated here. The teachings of all of these schools can be brought back to life by comparing them with metaphysical and philosophical schools of a corresponding order in other traditions and, as far as Western man is concerned, of course by comparing them with the major traditions that have dominated the West, namely the Graeco-Alexandrian and the Judeo-Christian. Moreover, the profound intellectual crisis of modern man can be brought into focus especially for Muslims through a comparison which would show the contrast between the sapiential teachings of these Islamic schools and what passes for philosophy or 'thought' in the West today.[4] Finally, the operative and practical aspects of attaining gnosis or *maʿrifah* which are contained in the teachings of Sufism can be studied in the light of the current needs of contemporary man, to which we shall turn in the next chapter, as well as with respect to the present-day condition of Muslims themselves.

The application of the comparative method to the Islamic intellectual heritage can be particularly fecund for the study of metaphysics and philosophy in both the East and the West because of the special function and role of Islam in human history. Because of the integrating power of Islam and the fact that it was destined to cover the 'middle-belt' of the world, it came historically into contact with many modes of thought, including the Graeco-Alexandrian, Persian, Indian and even, to a certain extent, Far Eastern. The basis of Islamic intellectual life was therefore cosmopolitan and international in conformity with the world-wide perspective of Islam itself and the universal nature of the fundamental Islamic doctrine of Unity (*al-tawḥīd*).[5] Moreover, because it was the last revelation and therefore the synthesis of the messages of the traditions before it, Islam developed an extremely rich intellectual life into which was integrated much of the heritage of mankind that had preceded it, a heritage that became transformed by the light of Unity and converted into a building block in the new edifice of the Islamic arts, sciences and philosophy. Islamic philosophy, if considered in its totality and not only in terms of the Peripatetic school known in the West, is extremely rich and possesses schools that can be compared with most of the intellectual perspectives and traditional philosophies of the East, of the ancient Mediterranean world and of mediaeval Europe. Comparative studies would be fruitful as an adjunct to historical methods of research and would be basic in bringing out the morphological structure of the different Islamic schools by comparing and contrasting them with similar schools elsewhere. Sometimes even these two approaches, namely the historical and the comparative, can be combined, as for example a study of atomism in *Kalām* and a comparison of it with Buddhist schools of atomism, which could clarify the historical roots of the idea[6] and bring out the similarities and differences between the atomism of *Kalām* and that of the Buddhist schools. There are many pages and passages in the history of Islamic philosophy which could be clarified in this way.

Comparative philosophy can also play an important function for Muslims themselves, not only by making the Western intellectual tradition as well as its modern deviations better known to them, but also by drawing their attention to non-Western traditions and re-establishing the balance destroyed by the unilateral domination of Western civilization over the East during the past century. As mentioned above, today for most people in the East, not only Muslims but also Indians, Japanese and others, comparative philosophy means comparing the 'philosophy' of their own civilization with that of the West and, in fact, only the modern West. Outside the small circle of traditional writers whose works are in any case still not well known in the Islamic world, it is rarely that one finds serious comparative studies made between Islamic metaphysics and philosophy and those of India and the Far East.[7] The cultivation of the comparative approach in the field of Islamic metaphysics and philosophy could make Muslims aware of the vast riches of the traditional doctrines of India and the Far East, and through them could put Western philosophy in a more just perspective. Moreover, because of the nature of Oriental doctrines, the very awareness of these doctrines could help Muslim scholars discover other aspects of the Western intellectual tradition greatly neglected in the Islamic world until now precisely because of the paralyzing influence of modern European thought upon 'educated' classes in the Islamic world. The sapiential nature of Oriental doctrines and the very depth of their metaphysical teachings could be instrumental in a direct fashion in making the awareness of the Western intellectual tradition among Muslims more profound. It could thereby provide for Muslim scholars a key to the better understanding of the West and the sapiential teachings contained in the writings of such groups as the early Church Fathers, the apophatic theology of the Eastern Church, the school of Chartres, intellectual currents of mediaeval and renaissance Christian mysticism—especially of the school of Eckhardt and Angelus Silesius—and Western alchemy and Hermeticism.[8] In any case, to introduce comparative philosophy in the serious sense into the domain of Islamic philosophy would influence the very concept of the relation of Islamic philosophy to Western thought and that of the nature of Western thought itself held by most educated Muslims today.

As far as the effect of the comparative approach upon a better understanding of Islamic philosophy itself is concerned, the extent of its possibilities is evident to anyone acquainted with the structure of Islamic thought. A few illustrations will bring out the role comparative philosophy can play in different areas. To start with the Graeco-Alexandrian tradition, we must recall that there are, of course, outstanding problems of an historical nature which deal on the one hand with the Greek roots of many facets of Islamic philosophy and on the other with the survival of important elements of the Graeco-Alexandrian heritage, particularly of the late period, in Arabic. This is a subject for historical research, and many scholars in both East and West have devoted themselves to both of its dimensions.[9]

But, in addition, morphological comparisons could play an important role in bringing out the differences as well as the similarities between the Greek and the Islamic traditions and reveal how the elements of Greek thought that were accepted by the Muslims were transformed by them into elements of a new intellectual structure possessing a significance beyond what the purely historical method of tracing influences can reveal. A comparative study of Hermetic philosophy in Alexandria and alchemical philosophy in Islam, of Greek sapiential and gnostic teachings of the Middle and Neo-platonists—especially of Plotinus himself—and the masters of Islamic gnosis like Ibn ʿArabī, of the Greek Pythagorean teachings of Nichomachus and the Muslim Pythagoreans like the Ikhwān al-Ṣafā' and many other instances would reveal the structural similarities and also the differences between doctrines of a similar or corresponding order in traditions possessing differing characteristics.

In the Graeco-Alexandrian case, comparative studies should complement the historical ones. The historical method would reveal the roots of many ideas adopted by Islamic philosophy from the Greek heritage, and the comparative method would cast light—because of the living nature of the Islamic tradition and its esoteric and gnostic teachings—upon certain forgotten features of the Graeco-Alexandrian tradition itself. It could be especially helpful in enabling Western scholars to re-evaluate their own judgment of Greek philosophy, in which they usually make no distinction between purely human philosophy and a wisdom of a supra-human inspiration. The Muslim intellectuals, thanks to the grace (*barakah*) of the Islamic revelation and the particular light of the 'Muḥammadan' message which enabled them to penetrate into the very heart of non-Islamic traditions when necessary, discerned almost automatically the basic distinction between the sapiential doctrines of such schools as the Pythagorean, Platonic, Aristotelian and Neoplatonic on the one hand and the Sophist, the Epicurean and the like on the other. This distinction between a teaching of an ultimately divine inspiration and a purely profane philosophy was so natural for them that they separated the two immediately and did not even consider the latter type of thought to be philosophy at all. It must be recalled that Suhrawardī asserted that Aristotle was the last of the Greek philosophers and not the first, as the post-Renaissance philosophy of the West has claimed in its interpretation of the Greek heritage. The understanding of this basic distinction between a metaphysics of a purely traditional order couched in philosophical language and alone considered as philosophy, and a purely profane philosophy which the Muslims did not consider worthy of being called philosophy at all is essential for any serious re-interpretation of the Graeco-Alexandrian heritage by contemporary Western man in search of the roots of his own metaphysical heritage. If the West were to understand today the true nature of Ibn ʿArabī's doctrines, which belong to a still living spiritual and intellectual tradition, these doctrines in turn could serve as a key for an understanding of a Plotinus or a Proclus, metaphysicians and gnostics who belong to a tradition the living sources of which are no longer accessible, and who are moreover usually innocently classified with modern academic philosophers. As for Muslims, the comparative method could reveal much more to them of the true structure and nature of the Graeco-Alexandrian antiquity than could facile translations of standard Western histories of Greek philosophy, works which are usually coloured by current and passing modes and fashions of thought and yet are beginning to influence the contemporary Muslim's view of the heritage of antiquity which he had viewed until now through the eyes of his own sages and metaphysicians.

A somewhat similar situation exists *vis-à-vis* the intellectual tradition of pre-Islamic Persia. Here also there are certain historical influences the understanding of which is important for a full grasp of the genesis of Islamic philosophy. But the comparative method can reveal another dimension which in this case is also a key for an understanding of the spiritual and intellectual destiny of the Persian peoples.[10] To compare the angelology of Suhrawardī with that of Zoroastrianism or the story of Kay Khusraw with the visionary narratives of Suhrawardī is more than anything to penetrate into the way in which the universe of the pre-Islamic Persians was transformed into the Islamic one. Many of the profounder reasons for the continuation of the life of Islamic philosophy in Persia after its cessation in the Western lands of Islam can also be understood through the comparative method. Moreover, many of the deepest characteristics of the tradition of Islamic philosophy in Persia can be discovered with the help of a comparative study of Islamic philosophy and the *Weltanschauung* of the pre-Islamic Persians.[11]

The situation of the mediaeval West in relation to Islamic philosophy is somewhat similar to that of Islamic philosophy *vis-à-vis* the Greek heritage. There are, naturally, extensive historical relations, and the work that has been carried out during the past few decades in making better known the Latin corpus of the writings of Ibn Sīnā and Ibn Rushd, as well as of other Muslim authors, and in tracing their influence in the West is, of course, precious. Without it, one would not be able to understand the genesis of Scholasticism. But there are studies of a profounder nature based upon the comparative method which could enable Westerners to better understand Islam and *vice versa*. As already stated, a comparative and morphological study of such figures as Eckhardt with Ibn ʿArabī or Rūmī, Erigena or other Western Illuminationists with Suhrawardī, or St Augustine with al-Ghazzālī, would give a greater insight into the structure of the Islamic and Christian traditions than an attempt merely to discover lines of influence.

As for the Asian world, it presents an arena of almost unlimited possibility for the application of the comparative method. As far as the Indian world is concerned, besides such historical influences as that of Buddhist and Hindu moral philosophy and possibly of atomism upon early Islam, and Sufism upon certain mediaeval *bhaktic* schools in India, there is the whole world opened by the translation of Sanskrit works into Persian, and Persian and Arabic works into Sanskrit and other Indian languages during the Moghul period. The *Majmaʿ al-baḥrayn* of Dārā Shukūh and the Persian commentary of Mīr Findiriskī upon that memorable expression of pure *jñāna*, the Yoga Vaśiṣṭha, are already based upon morphological and structural comparisons. Many other works of this kind also exist which need to be studied and explored. Moreover, the rich intellectual structures of Hinduism and Buddhism naturally present many resemblances to Islamic intellectuality, since all of them possess a traditional character. These resemblances can be best brought to light through the comparative method. The *Advaita Vedānta* school of Śaṇkara can obviously be best understood by a Muslim by comparing it with the doctrine of *waḥdat al-wujūd* (unity of being) of Ibn ʿArabī and his followers; for a Muslim who cannot understand the doctrine of *waḥdat al-wujūd* is unlikely to comprehend the Advaita doctrine, which is like the reflection of the former doctrine in another spiritual universe. There are variations and subtle modifications of the doctrine of *waḥdat al-wujūd* and *waḥdat al-shuhūd* (unity of consciousness) developed by Indian Sufis and unknown in other Muslim lands precisely because of the challenging presence of certain Hindu metaphysical doctrines, especially Śaṇkara's non-dualism. The correlation and the correspondence that exist on the purely metaphysical level can, moreover, be detected on the level of the cosmological sciences and of natural philosophy, and comparative studies can be made with great profit between the other *darśanas* such as the *Sāṇkhya* and the corresponding Islamic schools.[12]

As for the Far East, it represents a domain that in relation to Islamic philosophy should be studied almost entirely from the vantage point of comparative philosophy, for here, except for certain early alchemical ideas that reached eastern Islam from China and certain exchanges of ideas during the Mongol period, the whole relation is morphological rather than historical. For a Muslim to understand Lao-Tzŭ or Chuang-Tzŭ there is no better way than to make a comparative study between Taoism and Sufism or particular doctrines of the two traditions, such as that of the Universal Man, which present striking resemblances. This is a nearly unresearched field, which could be explored extensively to make the Far Eastern tradition better known to Muslims, and the Islamic intellectual and spiritual tradition more comprehensible for the people of the Far East and especially for those of Japan, where there now seems to be a genuine interest in Islamic metaphysics and philosophy.

In conclusion then, it can be said that for Muslims themselves the comparative method can play a basic role in making them aware of the great civilizations of the East and also in making the Western intellectual tradition more readily understandable in its true nature, as well as revealing to them the remarkable shortcomings and weaknesses of modern philosophy, a philosophy which many have taken much too seriously until now. It can be an instrument in combating the sense of inferiority towards the West which has developed among so many modernized Muslims, and a necessary shock to awaken them from their hypnotic trance before the modern West. For non-Muslims interested in an understanding of Islamic metaphysics and philosophy, the comparative method can be instrumental in removing the erroneous conception of Islamic philosophy as merely a phase in the transmission of ideas to the West. This method can also help to reveal the immense treasures contained in the Islamic intellectual tradition and to make manifest the true structure of this tradition as it stands between the traditions of the Orient and those of the Mediterranean world and the West. Finally, when applied to the operative and practical aspects of Islamic spirituality, it can uncover before the eyes of modern man treasures which can provide for his profound spiritual needs. For these and many other reasons the comparative approach deserves to be applied to many aspects of the Islamic intellectual and spiritual heritage. It cannot but enrich present-day knowledge of a tradition of which many elements are still unexplored. And it cannot but provide some of the keys with which modern man can open the doors of the prison within which he has confined himself through his own ignorance and forgetfulness.

Notes to Chapter 4

1. On the meaning of *al-ḥikmah* and *al-falsafah* in Islam see S. H. Nasr, 'The Meaning and Role of "Philosophy" in Islam', *Studia Islamica*, Vol. 37, 1973, pp. 57–80.

2. On the basic distinction between Oriental metaphysics, which as already mentioned is wedded to a spiritual discipline, and profane philosophy, see R. Guénon, *La Métaphysique orientale*, Paris, 1939; translated by J. C. Cooper, 'Oriental Metaphysics', *Tomorrow* (London), Vol. 12, 1964, pp. 6–16; also in *The Sword of Gnosis*, pp. 40–56. It need hardly be mentioned, at least for those acquainted with the contemporary traditional writers in the West such as Guénon, Coomaraswamy, T. Burckhardt and especially F. Schuon, that the approach of these writers represents the application of the 'comparative method' at its highest and most sublime level, an achievement that is made possible by the presence of a remarkable power of intellectual penetration which, at the level displayed in these writings, can come solely from attachment to a tradition and the realization of its metaphysical teachings.

3. See E. Gilson, *The Unity of Philosophical Experience*, New York, 1937.

4. Comparison through bringing out contrasts is the very opposite of what so many modernized Muslims seek to do by belittling the contrasts and exaggerating insignificant similarities between the teachings of various Islamic schools and profane philosophy in order to show that Islam is 'modern' after all.

5. See S. H. Nasr, *Science and Civilization in Islam*, Cambridge (USA), 1968, and New York, 1970, Introduction.

6. This has been already attempted by S. Pines in his well-known *Beiträge zur islamischen Atomenlehre*, Berlin, 1936.

7. As far as the Far East is concerned, the already cited (Chap. 3, note 13) study of T. Izutsu, *A Comparative Study of the Key Philosophical Concepts in Sufism and Taoism*, is unique. For India there are a few studies made mostly by Indian scholars and one or two by Persians, but most of them deal with historical influences rather than morphological comparisons.

8. The paralyzing effect of modern Western thought upon the East in general and the Muslim world in particular is proved by the fact that in the hundreds of comparative studies made by Orientals themselves between various Eastern sages and Western figures practically no attention has been paid to the authentic representatives of the Western metaphysical and spiritual tradition. For every hundred studies which compare a Śaṇkara or an Ibn 'Arabī with some 'Idealistic' follower of Hegel, hardly one seeks to compare them with a St Denis the Areopagite, an Erigena, an Eckhart or an Angelus Silesius.

9. The writings of Bergsträsser, Walzer, Badawī, Goerr and many others have brought into the open the significance of Islamic philosophical sources for material lost in the original Greek, including especially the writings of the Alexandrian commentators and Galen.

10. See, for example, H. Corbin, *Terre céleste et corps de résurrection;* also S. H. Nasr 'The Life of Mysticism and Philosophy in Iran: Pre-Islamic and Islamic', *Studies in Comparative Religion*, Autumn, 1971, pp. 235–240.

11. A notable example of this kind of study is H. Corbin, *En Islam iranien*, 4 Vols., Paris, 1971–72, where comparative studies have also been made between Islamic schools and Taoism on the one hand and the Grail tradition in the West on the other.

12. See, for example, D. Shayegan, *Les relations de l'hindouisme et du soufisme d'après le 'Majma' al-Baḥrayn'* (Thèse de 3e cycle, Sorbonne, 1968).

Part III

The Islamic Tradition and the Current Problems of Modern Man

Chapter 5

The Spiritual Needs of Western Man and the Message of Sufism

The need to recover a vision of the Centre becomes ever more urgent for Western man as the illusory world he has created around himself in order to forget the loss of the transcendent dimension in his life begins to reveal ever more fully its true character. In such a situation, the response cannot, of course, come from anywhere but sacred tradition in all its authentic forms. But inasmuch as we are concerned here with Islam, the last of these traditions to manifest itself on the scene of human history, it is to this tradition that we shall confine ourselves, although much of what we have to say would apply to other traditions as well. Moreover, since in viewing a mountain from far away it is first of all the peak that is seen and then sought after, it is Sufism, the peak as well as the spiritual essence and esoteric dimension of Islam, which attracts most of those who feel the need to recover the Centre by submitting themselves to the message from the Centre in its Islamic form. The amazing increase of interest in the West in recent years in the study of Sufism, much of which is unfortunately diverted by counterfeit presentations of Sufi teachings, is a result of both the growing spiritual need felt by many men today and the particular characteristics which Sufism possesses as the esoteric dimension of the Islamic tradition. A perspicacious application of the comparative method, taking into account the structure of the Islamic and the Occidental traditions, would reveal that nearly every aspect of the Islamic tradition, from the procedures of law at Shariʿite courts to the description of Divine Beauty in poetry, can be of immense benefit in solving the problems of modern man. But it would also show that it is most of all the purely metaphysical and gnostic teachings of Islam, contained primarily in Sufism,[1] which can provide the answers to the most pressing intellectual needs of men today, and that it is the spiritual presence contained within Sufism which can quench more readily the thirst of aspirants in search of God.

Today the need to benefit from the teachings of sacred tradition leads naturally, because of the anomalous situation of the modern world where the usual channels of transmission no longer exist, to the heart or to the most universal aspect of various sacred traditions, to the *Bhagavad-Gītā* and the *Tao-Tē Ching*, rather than to their more outward expressions. Islam is no exception to this general tendency, and as more Westerners seek outside the confines of their own civilization for ways of escaping from the labyrinth within which they have become imprisoned, and turn in the direction of Islam, the interest in Sufism and in its amazingly rich message grows, a message which on the doctrinal level contains so wide a range, from the simple aphorisms of Abū Madyan to the vast metaphysical compendia of Ibn ʿArabī, from the gnostic prayers of Abu'l-Ḥasan al-Shādhilī to the ocean of mystical poetry of Rūmī.

Before turning specifically to Sufism, it is necessary to make a few general remarks about the meaning of sacred tradition and its relation to the present spiritual and intellectual needs of Western man. In order to understand sacred tradition and to discuss the truth in its metaphysical sense, there must be (besides interest and the sense of need) the aid of Heaven and the presence of a discerning intelligence. It is, therefore, necessary first of all to turn an eye to the meaning of 'sacred tradition', of which Islam is an eminent example, and also to the real nature of man's present-day spiritual needs. So much confusion has been cast upon these subjects as a result of the recent 'pseudo-spiritual' explosion in the West that there is no way of understanding what kind of contribution Sufism can make to the task of saving man from his current plight without clearing the ground of prevalent errors and misconceptions.

Today many people speak of tradition in ways very different from the usage we employ here and throughout our writings. It is therefore necessary to clarify the meaning of this key term once again. Those who are acquainted with the majestic works of the traditional authors in the West such as F. Schuon, R. Guénon and A. K. Coomaraswamy already have an understanding of the meaning of this term. It is the definition of tradition contained in the writings of these authors to which we adhere fully in all of our works. Therefore, by 'tradition' we do not mean habit or custom or the automatic transmission of ideas and motifs from one generation to another, but rather a set of principles which have descended from Heaven and which are identified at their origin with a particular manifestation of the Divine, along with the application and deployment of these principles at different moments of time and in different conditions for a particular humanity. Tradition is therefore already sacred in itself and the term 'sacred tradition' is, in a sense, a pleonasm which we have used only for the sake of emphasis. Moreover, tradition is both immutable and a living continuity, containing within itself the science of Ultimate Reality and the means for the actualization and realization of this knowledge at different moments of time and space. To quote Schuon, 'Tradition is not a childish and outmoded mythology but a science that is terribly real.'[2] Tradition is ultimately a sacred science, a *scientia sacra*, rooted in the nature of Reality, and itself the only integral means of access to this Reality, which at once surrounds man and shines at the innermost centre of his being. It is the call from the Centre which alone can allow man to return from the rim to the Centre.

As far as Sufism is concerned, strictly speaking it should not be classified along with other integral traditions such as Hinduism and Buddhism, because Sufism is itself a part of Islam and not an independent tradition. Islam can be spoken of as a tradition in the same way as one speaks of Christianity or Buddhism, whereas Sufism must be understood as a dimension of the Islamic tradition. This rather obvious point needs to be laboured because often today in certain circles Sufism is taken out of its Islamic context with particular motives in mind and then discussed along with other Oriental or Occidental traditions.

Sufism is actually like the flower of the tree of Islam, or in another sense the sap of that tree. Or it can be called the jewel in the crown of the Islamic tradition. But whatever image is used, there remains the undeniable fact that, taken out of the context of Islam, Sufism cannot be fully understood, and its methods, of course, can never be practised efficaciously, to say the least. Nor can one do justice to the wholeness of the Islamic tradition and its immensely rich spiritual possibilities by putting aside its inner dimension.[3] In speaking about Sufism, therefore, in reality we shall be speaking about the Islamic tradition itself in its most inward and universal aspect.

As for the question of the present needs of Western man which the message of sacred tradition in general and Sufism in particular can fulfil, it is essential to analyze fully its content and meaning, considering the cloud of illusion which surrounds modern man and makes the clear discernment of his environment and 'living space', both external and internal, well-nigh impossible. As already mentioned in the first chapter, there has been so much talk during the past century about change, becoming and evolution that the permanent and abiding inner nature of man has been nearly forgotten, along with the most profound needs of this inner man. In fact the pseudo-dogma of evolution, as generally understood, which continues to dominate the horizon of much of modern anthropology and philosophy in the teeth of rapidly accumulating evidence concerning the essentially unchanged nature of man during the many millennia that have passed since his entering upon the stage of terrestrial history, has made it impossible for those who adhere to it to understand who man is.[4] Moreover, the permanent nature of man having been forgotten, the needs of man are reduced to the sphere of accidental changes which affect only the outer crust of man's being. When people speak of human needs today, most often they mean the man who is confined to the rim and cut off from the Centre, the man who is only accidentally human and essentially animal, the man who no longer fulfils his primordial mandate as God's vicegerent (*khalīfah*) upon the earth.

In reality, the needs of man, as far as the total nature of man is concerned, remain forever the same, precisely because of man's unchanging nature. 'Man is what he is, or he is nothing.'[5] The situation of man in the universal hierarchy of being, his standing between the two unknowns which comprise his state before terrestrial life and his state after death, his need for a 'shelter' in the vast stretches of cosmic existence and his deep need for certainty (*yaqīn* in the vocabulary of Sufism) remain unchanged. This latter element, the need to gain certainty, is in fact so fundamental that the Sufis have described the stages of gaining spiritual perfection as so many steps in the attainment of certainty.[6]

The very fact that in the West there is so much interest today in Oriental metaphysics and spirituality, the fact that so many people in Europe and even more in America search avidly for books of instruction or poetry and music associated with Sufism, is itself indirect proof of the fact that there is a profounder nature in man which does not 'evolve', a nature whose needs remain unchanged. This more permanent nature may be temporarily eclipsed but it cannot be permanently obliterated. The rationalistic philosophers of the eighteenth and nineteenth centuries never dreamt that a century or two after them so many people in the Western world would again become interested in religion, in metaphysics and cosmology, and even in the occult sciences, which in their unadulterated form are applications of the traditional cosmological sciences. These men would be surprised to discover that, a century or two after them, the works of Taoist sages or the Rishis of India or Sufi masters would be read more avidly than their own writings. The rationalistic philosophers of the past two centuries along with their anti-rationalist but still profane opponents regarded only the outer crust or rim of man's being, and they saw in its condensation and consolidation, its gradual separation from the world of the Spirit or the Centre, a progress and an evolution which they thought would be a continuous process. They did not realize that the crust would break of its own accord as a result of the advancement of the very process of its solidification, and that the needs of the inner man would manifest themselves once again on the scale we see before us today.

It was once asked of the Prophet of Islam what existed before Adam. He answered, 'Adam'. The question was repeated. He again answered, 'Adam', and added that if he were to answer this question to the end of time he would repeat, 'Adam'. The profound meaning of this *ḥadīth* is that man in his essential reality has not undergone evolution and that there is no 'before man' in the sense of a temporal predecessor or a state from which man developed 'in time'. A million years ago men already buried their dead and believed in the Invisible World.[7] Over ten thousand years ago, man not only produced masterpieces of art but even described the motion of the heavens in a most remarkable manner in myths and stories which reveal a power of abstraction that could match any of the feats of men of later periods of history.[8]

It is this man—obliterated temporarily by the progressive and evolutionary theories of the past few centuries in the West—to whom tradition addresses itself and it is this inner man whom tradition seeks to liberate from the imprisonment of the ego and the suffocating influence of the purely externalized and forgetful aspect of man. Moreover, it is tradition alone which possesses the means for his liberation, and not the pseudo-religions so prevalent today, which, seeing the resurgence of the needs of the inner man, try to entice those with a less discerning eye by means of parodies of the teachings of the sacred traditions, to which they almost invariably add something of the evolutionary pseudo-philosophy to make sure that men do not discover who they really are. But that inner man continues to abide within all men and to make its demands upon man no matter how far he seeks to escape from his own Centre and no matter what means he uses to obliterate the traces of the inner man upon what he calls 'himself'.

Of course when all is said concerning the permanent needs of man—needs which in fact must be emphasized in the strongest terms possible because they have been so forgotten in the modern world—it must be remembered that these needs concern only one pole of man's being, namely the essential pole. As far as the other pole is concerned, the pole which involves man's temporality and the historico-cultural conditions that colour the outer crust of his being, it can be said that man's needs *have* changed. They have changed not in their essence but in their mode and external form. Even in traditional societies, all of which have been based on immutable transcendent principles, the form in which the spiritual needs of a Japanese have been fulfilled has not been the same as that of an Arab. So much more is this true in the modern world, where men live in a desacralized *milieu* divorced from principles, where the psyche is separated from the Spirit which is its own source of life, where the experience of time and space, not to speak of all kinds of human relations, have altered completely and where the sense of authority has gradually disappeared. In such conditions there naturally appear new modes through which even the deepest human needs must be fulfilled.

The very fact of the advancement of the process of the consolidation of the world has introduced cracks in the closed world of materialism which permit not only the dark forces from below to enter into this world[9] but also light from above. This process implies at the same time a reawakening of man to his real needs, which leads naturally to a desperate attempt to find means of fulfilling these needs. But precisely because of the changed external circumstances, many modern men do not understand the conditions or are not willing to undergo the necessary sacrifices to become worthy of receiving the message of Heaven, which in its unadulterated form is contained only within the living orthodox and sacred traditions of the world. Also, many authorities from these traditions—not to speak of the pretenders who have recently flooded the Western scene—have become habituated to the traditional world from which they have issued and therefore are not aware of the differences existing between the psyche of Western man and that of men of traditional societies, nor of the different forms that Western man's spiritual needs take because of the particular world in which he has been nurtured.

In speaking of present needs, it is essential to keep in mind both these poles, namely the permanent nature of man's needs, which makes all the traditional teachings about man and his final end pertinent and in fact vital, and the changed form of man's needs due to the particular experiences of modern man, which necessitates the application of these teachings to existing conditions. It must be remembered that traditional authority and authenticity must be preserved, that Truth cannot evolve, that it is man who must make himself worthy of becoming the recipient of the message of Heaven, not *vice versa*, that Truth cannot be distorted to suit the passing whims and fashions of a particular period and that there is an objective Reality that determines the value of man and his thoughts and actions and finally judges them and determines the mode of his existence in the world to come. At the same time, it has to be recalled that this sacred tradition must be applied to the particular problems of modern man with a consideration of the anomalous conditions in which he lives, without this process distorting or destroying the authenticity of the tradition. The modern world is witness to an array of men and organizations which attempt to cater to the spiritual needs of modern man, ranging from authentic masters and organizations from the East unaware of the particular nature of the audience they are addressing,[10] to the rare few who have succeeded in applying traditional teachings to the particular conditions of modern man,[11] to the vast number of pseudo-masters and dubious organizations, ranging from the innocuous to the veritably satanic, which remind one of the saying of Christ about false prophets arising at the end of time. To draw from the resources of sacred tradition to fulfil present needs is to remain totally within the matrix of sacred tradition and at the same time to apply its methods and teachings to a world in which men have needs that are at once perennial and yet conditioned by the particular experiences of modern man.

An important condition which has coloured deeply the mental processes of modern man and today lies at the heart of the new religious movement in the West, albeit usually unconsciously, is Cartesian dualism and the reaction which has set in against materialism in the West within the context of this dualism. Cartesian dualism divided reality into the material and the mental, positing a non-material substance which somehow engulfs all the levels of non-material existence and reduces them to a single reality. The excessive materialism of the past centuries has now led many people to reject this materialism itself. But just as in physics a reaction is opposed to an existing action, so also has this philosophical and religious reaction set in within the already existing framework of the classical Cartesian dualism. For a large number of people, the reaction against materialism means, almost unconsciously, attraction towards the other pole of Cartesian dualism, namely the non-material, without there being any discrimination within the non-material domain between the Spirit and the psyche, the *rūḥ* and the *nafs* of Sufism. Hence, for many people who are unaware of this fundamental distinction, psychic phenomena have come to replace the spiritual and the religious.

Islam teaches that the rebellion against God takes place on the level of the psyche, not on that of the body. The flesh is only an instrument for the tendencies originating within the psyche. It is the psyche that must be trained and disciplined so as to become prepared for its wedding to the Spirit. Both the angelic and the demonic forces manifest themselves in this intermediate psychic plane, which is neither purely material nor purely spiritual. The paradisial and the infernal states refer to the macrocosmic counterparts of the various levels of this intermediate substance as it becomes moulded by angelic or demonic influences. This substance, moreover, within the microcosm, or man, stretches from the corporeal to the Divine Centre within the heart of man. Therefore, to identify all that is non-material with the religious or spiritual is sheer folly and a most dangerous error, which has come into being as a result of the optical illusion lingering from the delimitation of Reality into two domains by Cartesian dualism. But it is an error that is very prevalent in the new religious movements in the West and especially in America today, an error which in certain cases can open the soul of man to the most infernal and dissipating influences, throwing the personality of those who fall prey to them into disequilibrium. To simply identify the non-material with the spiritual is to misunderstand the nature of Reality, the complexity of the human soul, the source and reality of evil and the spiritual work necessary to reach the Fountain of Life which alone can satisfy in a permanent and not an illusory and transient manner the spiritual needs of man.

This mistaking the psychic for the spiritual, so characteristic of our times, is reinforced by another powerful tendency issuing from man's need to break the boundaries of his limited world of experience. The Sufis have always taught that man is in quest of the Infinite and that even his endless effort toward the gaining of material possessions and his dissatisfaction with what he has is an echo of this thirst, which cannot be quenched by the finite. That is why the Sufis consider the station of satisfaction (*riḍā'*)[12] to be an exalted spiritual condition attainable only by those who have reached the 'proximity' of the Infinite and have shed the bonds of finite existence. This need to seek the Infinite and overcome the limits of whatever is finite is clearly discernible in the new religious ferment in the West today. Many modern men are tired of the finite psychic experiences of everyday life no matter how materially comfortable that life may be. Having no access to the authentic spiritual experience which in traditional societies provides the natural means of breaking the limits of finite existence, they turn to psychic experiences of all kinds which open for them new worlds and horizons, even if they be infernal. The great concern with psychic phenomena, 'trips', extraordinary 'experiences', and the like, is deeply related to this inner urge to break the suffocating and limited world of everyday life in a civilization which has no purpose beyond moving with accelerated speed toward an illusory ideal state of material well-being that is always just round the corner.

This tendency, added to the one which unconsciously identifies the non-corporeal with the spiritual, has succeeded in bringing about a most dangerous confusion in the religious life of modern man in the West and particularly in America, where the need for a rediscovery of the world of the spirit is most keenly felt. From the Sufi point of view, which has always distinguished clearly between the psychic and the spiritual, so many of those who claim to speak in the name of the Spirit today are really speaking in the name of the psyche, and are taking advantage of the thirst of modern man for something beyond the range of experiences that modern industrial civilization has made possible for him. It is precisely this confusion which lies at the heart of the profound disorder one observes in the religious field in the West today, and which enables elements that are as far removed as possible from the sacred to absorb the energies of men of good intention and to dissipate rather than to integrate their psychic forces.

The sacred, as already stated, is related to the world of the Spirit and not of the psyche. It is whole and holy; it illuminates and integrates rather than causing men to wander aimlessly through the labyrinth that characterizes the psychic and mental worlds whenever these worlds are deprived of the light of the Spirit. The sacred, precisely because it comes from God, asks of us all that we are. To sacralize life and to reach the sacred we must become ourselves sacred, like a sacred work of art. We must chisel the substance of our soul into an icon which will reveal us as we really *are* in the Divine Presence, as we were when we were created, the *imago Dei*; for as the Prophet of Islam has said, 'God created man upon His Own image.' In order for man to become this work of art, to become him-*self* again, he must surrender and dedicate himself fully to the commands of the Spirit, to the sacred. It is only the sacred that *can* enable man to remove the veil which hides his true nature from himself and makes him forget his own primordial, theomorphic nature (the *fiṭrah* mentioned in the Quran). And it is only the sacred, which comes from the Spirit and not the psyche, that can be the source of ethics, of aesthetics in its traditional sense, of metaphysical doctrine and of methods of realization. The psyche may appear fascinating or absorbing. But in itself it is always no more than amorphous, full of impressions that are transitory and partial. It is only the spiritual or the sacred which is permanent and total and which precisely because of its totality embraces the psychic and even the corporeal aspects of man and transforms and illuminates them.

The application of sacred tradition—whether it be Sufism or some other Way—to the actual needs of man cannot begin at a more critical point than this present juncture of human history, where it can provide the means of discerning between the spiritual and the psychic and, by extension, between those whose teachings are of a truly spiritual nature and those whose message is rooted only in the psychic and supported solely by psychic phenomena, related to experiences which without the protective matrix of sacred tradition can lead to the most infernal depths of cosmic existence and to states that are much more dangerous to the soul of man than various forms of crass materialism.

Turning to the Sufi tradition itself, it must be said that the understanding of it, as of many other traditions, is made difficult in the modern West because of the presence of another optical illusion which mistakes the mental understanding of metaphysics for the full realization of its truths. This illusion, which is the result of the separation between the mental activity of certain men and the rest of their being, and which is directly related to a lack of spiritual virtues, is a major hindrance in the application of the sacred teachings of various traditions to the present needs of Western men. There are those who possess intellectual intuition, itself a gift of Heaven, and who can understand the doctrines of Sufism or other forms of Oriental metaphysics, but who are not willing to live their lives in accordance with the teachings of the sacred tradition whose flower they are able to scent from far away.[13] Such people mistake their vision of the mountain peak, *theoria* in its original sense, for actually being on top of the mountain. They therefore tend to belittle all the practical, moral and operative teachings of tradition as being below their level of concern. Most of all they mistake the emphasis upon the attainment of spiritual virtues (*faḍā'il* in Sufism) for sentimentality, and faith (*īmān*) for 'common religion' belonging only to the exoteric level,[14] forgetting the fact that the greatest saints and sages have spoken most of all of spiritual virtues and that one of the most widely used names for Sufism is 'Muḥammadan poverty' (*al-faqr al-muḥammadī*).[15] Without this poverty or *faqr*, the cup of man's existence has no empty space into which the nectar of Divine Wisdom can be poured. Without it no spiritual attainment is possible, no matter how keen the intelligence may be.

This prevalent error of identifying the theoretical understanding of metaphysics with spiritual realization is related to the anomalous situation of our times in which the purest metaphysical teachings of various traditions are easily available in translation for just a few shillings at every bookshop, works ranging from the *Song of Solomon* to the *Tao-Tē Ching*. Obviously, such has never been the case in a normal situation. In a traditional society, most of those drawn to the metaphysical and gnostic aspects of their tradition are attracted through gradual instruction which prepares them for the reception of gnostic doctrines only after long training. Moreover, their knowledge of tradition is through personal contact. They live the exoteric form of the tradition—which is absolutely necessary and indispensable—in their everyday lives, and they contact esotericism most often by encountering a master or his disciples, or by visiting the tomb of a saint, or by having a dream which incites them to seek a particular master or go to a particular place. Even when their contact with esotericism is through reading, it is most often through literature and parables which gradually arouse their interest in the Way. For every thousand people in the Islamic world who read the poetry of Ḥāfiẓ or Rūmī, only one or two read the purely doctrinal treatises of Sufism.

Today in the West there is a truly anomalous situation in which the contact of most men with tradition must of necessity begin from the top and through the channel of the written word or books, which play a special role in an age when the usual channels of oral transmission have become blocked in so many parts of the world. As a matter of fact, the very availability of the highest metaphysical teachings of not one but most of the sacred traditions today—not to speak of the remarkable expositions of the authentic traditional writers in the West—is a result of the Divine Mercy, which has made possible this compensation during an age of spiritual eclipse, inasmuch as one irregularity deserves another. But the danger present in this situation is precisely the mistaking of the mental understanding of some sacred text for the living of a tradition, which involves not only the mind but the whole of man's being.

With this reserve in mind, it must nevertheless be added that even on the plane of the mind the presence of expositions of traditional doctrines, whether they be of a metaphysical or a cosmological order, can fulfil one of the deepest needs of modern man, who can be characterized as a being who thinks too much and often wrongly, and who is over-cerebral. Even a mental understanding of traditional doctrines can therefore be like a blanket of snow which brings with it peace and calm and quiets the agitation of the sceptical and questioning mind. It can bestow upon man an intellectual certitude which corresponds to what in traditional Sufi terminology is called 'the science of certainty' (*ʿilm al-yaqīn*)[16] and therefore make the person who has attained such a degree of knowledge aware of the fact that the ultimate aim of knowledge is not to collect an ever-increasing number of facts and to chart areas *beyond* the present 'frontiers' of knowledge, but to reach the Centre within and to gain a vision of or even *become* the knowledge which has always been and will always be. This calming of the agitated mind by providing answers to questions posed by reason, answers which are the fruit of revelation, illumination or intellection, then provides the necessary background for the actual illumination of the mind and, in fact, of the whole being of him whose reason has been nourished by traditional knowledge rather than left to its own machinations.[17]

Considering the importance of doctrinal works in this process of calming the mind and preparing the person of a contemplative bent for true intellection, it is unfortunate that, as far as Islamic metaphysics is concerned, few of its riches in this domain have been translated into English in comparison with what one finds from Hindu, Buddhist and Taoist sources. A few of the greatest masterpieces of Islamic metaphysics, such as the *Fuṣūṣ al-ḥikam* of Ibn ʿArabī and *al-Insān al-kāmil* of al-Jīlī are now known and partially translated,[18] but a vast treasury of works by both Sufis and Islamic theosophers such as Suhrawardī, Ibn Turkah al-Iṣfahānī, Mīr Dāmād and Mullā Ṣadrā, who have composed major doctrinal and metaphysical treatises, remain almost completely inaccessible to a Westerner without a mastery of Arabic or Persian.[19] In this way, the application of the teachings of Islam in its esoteric and metaphysical aspects to the present-day needs of Western man is handicapped by a lack of well-translated material which would make the vast treasures of this tradition accessible to those capable of reaping their fruit. Also, the true appreciation of all that the Islamic tradition can offer to contemporary man has become difficult, since in the case of other traditions their most universal teachings are relatively well-known, but in the case of Islam most studies in Western languages have been devoted to its legalistic and formal aspects, while its most universal aspects have not received the attention they deserve.

Some who wish to follow a tradition today are in fact deceived by this situation into thinking that Islam is concerned only with law, Divine justice and punishment, rigour, etc., while it is possible to follow other traditions by simply reading their gnostic treatises or even by taking some particular initiatic practice out of context and practising it, without having to be burdened with moral considerations or questions of Divine justice and punishment. Actually, this is a most unfortunate modern delusion arising from the fact that, as a result of a reaction against an unintelligible moralism within certain forms of modern Christianity, many people today belittle the importance of morality, and as a result of the rebellion of modern man against Heaven and of the loss of the meaning of authority, the importance of the fear of God in religious life has been well-nigh forgotten by most Western men today. The prophetic utterance, 'Fear of God is the beginning of Wisdom' (*ra's al-ḥikmah makhāfat Allāh*), which echoes the well-known Pauline dictum, holds true not only for Islam or Christianity but for all traditions. In Islam there is a Divine Law (*Sharīʿah*) which concerns man's actions and which all Muslims, Sufis or non-Sufis, must follow.[20] There is also emphasis upon the fear of God, and an eschatology which is related to God's judgment of human action on earth. But then these elements are also present, in other forms, in Hinduism and other Oriental traditions. Hinduism has not only produced the *Gītā* and the *Vedānta* but also elaborate treatises on *pralaya*, the Last Judgment, and on *karma* and the serious consequences of human action on earth for man's posthumous states. It would be the worst illusion to imagine that one can practice, let us say, Yoga and forget all about morality or the consequences of human acts in the eyes of God simply because one has moved from one tradition to another. In every integral tradition one can find the fear, the love and the knowledge of God in one form or another. As Al-Ghazzālī has said, he who fears the Creator runs towards Him and loves Him, and he who loves Him knows Him.

The historic manifestations of Sufism reveal the phases of fear (*makhāfah*), love (*maḥabbah*) and knowledge (*maʿrifah*), and the cycle repeats itself within the soul of every man who is able to attain spiritual realization. If one can complain from one point of view that the gnostic and metaphysical works of Islam have not been translated widely enough, one can be thankful from another point of view that the integral teachings of Islam, including the *Sharīʿah*, are there to test the seriousness of those who would aspire to reach its inner chamber, by requiring them to become first of all aware of the justice and majesty of God. Such an awareness creates in man an awe and fear that is absolutely positive and that melts away from the substance of the soul all that is alien to its primordial nature.

In fact, it is in order to evade this test and this protecting criterion that recently pretenders have appeared in the West who wish to divorce Sufism from Islam and present it as if it had nothing to do with the teachings of Islam and its *Sharīʿah*, which provides the Divine matrix for human action and protects the man who follows it from the wrath of God. This effort is no more than sheer delusion. In all authentic manifestations of Sufism, the fear of God, described so majestically in the Quran and incorporated in the attitudes promulgated by the *Sharīʿah*, prepares the ground for the love of God, and the love of God in turn leads to gnosis, the knowledge of God, which cannot sink its roots into the being of man unless the soil of this being has been prepared for such a Divine plant by the fear of God and His love, a love which in Islamic spirituality always accompanies knowledge.

So far, most of what has been said concerns all traditions, but it is now appropriate to ask what is unique about Sufism itself as it concerns the present needs of man. There is an Arabic saying which states that 'the doctrine of Unity is unique' (*al-tawḥīd wāḥid*). This means that at the highest level there is only one truth, in which all traditions are unified. But as the Divine Truth descends from the one peak downwards towards men, it takes on the characteristics which distinguish one tradition from another.

Sufism, being the inner dimension of Islam, shares, in its formal aspect, in the particular features of this tradition. Since Islam is based on Unity (*al-tawḥīd*), all of its manifestations reflect Unity in one way or another; this is especially true of Sufism, in which the principles of the revelation are most directly reflected. The presence of the principle of Unity in Sufism means, among other things, that its methods and practices unify what in other traditions are usually separate and distinct. To use the terminology of Hinduism—which is a miracle on the religious plane because of the different spiritual forms that have existed within it—the way of *karma* Yoga, *bhakti* Yoga and *jñani* Yoga are combined in Sufism into a single way, one might say into an 'integral Yoga'. It is especially important to note that whereas in Hinduism the *jñani* and *bhakti* types are quite distinct,[21] Sufi spirituality is essentially a *jñani* one which, however, is never divorced from the *bhaktic* element. Some Sufis may emphasize one aspect more than another. Some, like Ibn ʿArabī, Ibn ʿAṭā'allāh al-Iskandarī and Shabistarī, may speak more of gnosis (*maʿrifah*) and some like ʿAṭṭār and Ḥāfiẓ more of love. But in no instance does one find in Sufism a path of knowledge completely separated from love or a path of love without the element of gnosis, like the kind of love mysticism found in Christianity and also in mediaeval Hinduism. Moreover, this combination of knowledge and love in Sufism is always based on the support of the *Sharīʿah*, or, in a sense, on a way of work or action.

Also because of the unitary nature of the Islamic revelation, the contemplative and active ways have never been totally separated either outwardly or inwardly in Sufism. There is no outward monasticism in Islam, and the most intense contemplative life in Islam is carried out within the matrix of life within society. The Sufi has died to the world inwardly while outwardly he still participates in the life of society and bears the responsibilities of the station of life in which destiny has placed him. In fact he performs the most perfect action, because his acts emanate from an integrated will and an illuminated intelligence. Rather than being in any way contradictory, the contemplative and active lives complement each other in all Islamic spirituality,[22] as we shall have occasion to discuss more fully in the next chapter, and the methods and techniques of the contemplative life are such that they can be performed in whatever outward circumstances a person may find himself in and in whichever form of active life he may have to participate.

This unitive character of Sufism, both in its own methods and in its relation to man's outward life in society, offers obvious advantages for men living in the modern world, where inner withdrawal is usually more of a possibility than is outward separation from the world. Also the unitive nature of Sufism is a powerful remedy for the disintegrated life from which so many people in the modern world suffer. The total integration of the personality achieved in Sufi training is the goal sought by much of psychotherapy and psychoanalysis, which, however, can never achieve this goal, for their methods as practised today are cut off from the grace of the Spirit which alone can integrate the psyche and, as a result, they usually lead to its disintegration rather than to its integration. God has placed religion in the world to enable man to overcome his complexes, in addition to performing numerous other functions for him. Any caricature and parody of religion and especially of initiatic techniques cannot but result in a caricature and parody of the effect religion has had over the ages in removing man's complexes and integrating his personality.

The pertinent question that will undoubtedly be asked is: granted that Sufism does contain these characteristics, what are the possibilities of practising it? Of course one cannot gauge the mercy of Heaven, for the 'spirit bloweth where it listeth', but as far as the traditional teachings of Sufism are concerned, it is always emphasized that there is no practice of Sufism possible except through a master who is referred to traditionally as *shaykh*, *murshid* or *pīr*. The only exception is that of special individuals (*afrād*) who are disciples of the ever-living but hidden prophet Khaḍir[23] and who are in any case chosen for the Way by Heaven. Therefore this possibility is not an option for man to choose. As far as the aspirant is concerned, the only way open to him is to find an authentic master. The question of the practical possibility of living according to the disciplines of Sufism, therefore, comes down essentially to the possibility of finding an authentic master who can instruct the disciple as to how and what he should practise. As far as the Western world and especially America are concerned, it is necessary to mention the danger of false masters, of those who pretend to be guides without possessing the necessary qualifications, which are given by God alone. Even in classical times, when the danger of 'false prophets' mentioned by Christ was much less than in these late hours of human history, authentic masters took care to warn against the perils of submitting oneself to an unqualified 'master'. In his incomparable *Mathnawī*, Jalāl al-Dīn Rūmī says:

جون بسی ابلیس آدم روی هست — پس بهردستی نشاید داد دست
حرف درویشان بدزدد مرددون — تا بخواند بر سلیمی زان فسون
کار مردان روشنی و گرمی است — کار دونان حیله وبی شرمی است
جامه پشمین از برای کد کنند — بومسیلم را لقب احمد کنند
آن شراب حق ختامش مشك ناب — باده را ختمش بودگند وعذاب

'Since there is many a devil who hath the face of Adam, it is not well to give your hand to every hand[24]

'The vile man will steal the language of dervishes, that he may thereby chant a spell over (fascinate and deceive) one who is simple,

'The work of (holy) men is (as) light and heat, the work of vile men is trickery and shamelessness.

'They make a woollen garb for the purpose of begging. They give the title of Aḥmad (Muḥammad) to Bū Musaylim . . .

'The wine of God, its seal (last result) is pure musk, (but) as for (the other) wine, its seal is stench and torment.[25]

There is a mystery in the way man chooses a master and a spiritual path, which is alluded to by Rūmī himself and which cannot be solved by rational analysis alone. The problem is this: how can a candidate for initiation who does not as yet possess spiritual vision distinguish a true master from a false one when there must already be a true master to actualize the possibilities within the disciple and to enable him to distinguish the wheat from the chaff? Herein lies that mysterious relationship between the Spirit and its earthly embodiments which escapes being understood discursively. Man believes that he chooses the Way but in reality he is chosen by the Way. What man can do is to pray to find a true master and have reliance upon God while searching. He can, moreover, apply the universal criteria of authenticity and orthodoxy at a time when there are many more pretenders than when Rūmī wrote about them, at a time to which Christ referred in his initiatic saying, 'Many are called but few are chosen.'

The Truth has a way of protecting itself from profanation, but the soul of man *can* be destroyed if moulded in the hands of someone who does not possess the right qualifications and who is no more than a pretender. Better to remain an agnostic or a materialist than to become a follower of some pseudo-spiritual movement which cannot but do harm to what is most precious within man. The Sufis compare man to an egg that must be placed under a hen for a specific period in order to hatch. If, however, it is placed underneath a hen which leaves the egg early or does not take the necessary care of it, then the egg will never hatch and cannot even be eaten.[26] It will become useless and can only be thrown away. This parable depicts the danger of placing oneself in the hands of a pretender, in the care of those who brush aside centuries of tradition for a supposedly higher and more 'evolved' form of spirituality, or who want to crash the gates of Heaven by means of Sufism without the grace and aid of the Prophet of Islam, whose spiritual presence (*barakah*) alone can enable the initiate to rise upon the ladder of perfection extending to Heaven. We live in dangerous times when the possibilities of error are many, but also by compensation the paths towards God are opened before men in ways never dreamt of before. It remains for each individual to practise discernment and to distinguish between the true and the false, between the way of God and the way of Satan, who is traditionally known as the 'ape of God'.

Despite all the false masters and forms of pseudo-spirituality, there are still authentic Sufi masters, and the possibility of practising Sufism in the West is certainly present. But we believe that such a possibility will concern only a few of the vast number of people interested in Sufism today. Most likely in the near future Sufism will exercise its influence in the West not on one but on three different levels. First of all, there is the possibility of practising Sufism in an active way. Such a path is naturally meant for the few. It demands of man complete surrender to the discipline of the Way. To practise it one must follow the famous saying of the Prophet, 'Die before you die.' One must die to oneself and be reborn spiritually here and now. One must devote oneself to meditation and invocation, to inner purification, to the examining of one's conscience and many other practices prevalent among those who actually walk upon the Path (*sālikūn*). There are already some who practise Sufism seriously in the West, and, besides the pseudo-Sufi movements of little import, certain branches of Sufism have already sunk their roots in the West and have established authentic branches there. This group is surely bound to grow, although it cannot embrace all of those who are attracted to Sufism in the West today.

The second level on which Sufism is likely to influence the West is by presenting Islam in a more appealing form to many who would find in Islamic practices what they are seeking today in the name of Sufism. Because of a long historical background of conflict with the West, Islam has, until quite recently, been treated in the Occident in the most adverse manner possible. Many who would find exactly what they are looking for in the daily prayers and the fasting of Islam, in its integration of the secular into the sacred, in its dissemination of the sacerdotal function among all men, in its arts and sciences and many other features, are driven away from it because of the way in which it is usually presented to them. Sufism could help to explain Islam by elucidating its most universal and hence, in a sense, most comprehensible aspect, and therefore making it more approachable to outsiders. Usually when people want to study Hinduism they begin with the *Bhagavad-Gītā* and not the Law of Manu, whereas in the case of Islam, as already stated, the legalistic aspects are usually taught first and the most universal teachings, if touched upon at all, follow afterwards in a disjointed manner. As it becomes more fully realized that Sufism is an integral part of Islam and the flower of this tree of revelation, the possibility of the practice of Islam for many who are now attracted to Sufism but who cannot undertake the difficult disciplines of the Path itself will become more evident.

There is no question here of proselytizing, as far as we are concerned, but the fact remains that many in the West are seeking Oriental religious forms to practise and follow in their everyday lives, but put Islam aside because they do not identify it with its spiritual aspect, of which Sufism is the essence. Once this identification is clearly made, Sufism may play a role in the West similar to the role it played in India, Indonesia and West Africa in spreading Islam itself. Of course in the West its method and the extent of its activity will certainly be different from what we find in the above instances, but its function will be similar. It will open a possibility within Islam for many earnest Western seekers attracted to Sufism today, and it can also make available to them that intermediate region between esotericism and exotericism which is known to those who have studied the structure of Islam carefully.

Finally, there is a third level upon which Sufism can play an important role in the West, that is, as an aid to recollection and reawakening. Because Sufism is a living tradition with a vast treasury of metaphysical and cosmological doctrines, a sacred psychology and psychotherapy hardly ever studied in the West, a doctrine of sacred art and traditional sciences, it can bring back to life many aspects of the Western tradition forgotten today. Until recently, the usual historical works in Western languages on Islam relegated Sufism, along with other aspects of Islamic intellectuality, back to the thirteenth century, and described it as if it had died out long ago. Now, as more people in the West discover that it is a living tradition, contact with its riches can certainly play the role of re-awakening Western man to many of his own forgotten treasures. The trends of the past two decades have not been hopeful, but the possibility is nevertheless present.

Moreover, Sufism possesses teachings concerning the nature of man and the world about him which contain keys to the solutions of the most acute problems of the modern world, such as the ecological crisis.[27] Its teachings, if conveyed in contemporary language, could aid in solving many present-day problems which have come into being in the first place because of the forgetting of first principles. Its very presence could create, through a kind of 'sympathetic vibration', the revival of a more authentic intellectual activity and the revivification of precious aspects of the Western tradition which were covered by the dust created by the storm which shook the West during the period that has paradoxically come to be known as the Renaissance.

If, however, Sufism is to provide for some of the present-day needs of the West, it must be able to preserve its own integrity and purity. It must be able to resist the powerful forces of deviation, distortion and dilution visible everywhere today. It must serve the world about it like a crystal which gathers the light and disseminates it to its surroundings. At the same time it must be able to address the world around it in a language which that world understands. Sufism cannot leave unanswered the appeal of those who call upon it. Nor can it in any way compromise its principles in order to become more fashionable or more widely heard, to become a fad which would disappear from the scene with the same rapidity with which it had become popular.

In order to present Sufism in a serious manner above and beyond transient fads and fancies, it is therefore necessary to remain strictly traditional and orthodox from the point of view of the Sufi tradition and at the same time intelligible to Western man with the particular mental habits he has acquired and the reactions towards things he has developed within himself. Also, in order really to accept and practise the teachings of Sufism, it is necessary for the modern aspirant to realize that, in fact, he is drowning, that sacred tradition is a rope thrown towards him by the Divine Mercy, and that with its aid alone can he save himself. In the present situation, those who are rooted in the Sufi tradition and who can also expound it in a manner that is comprehensible to modern men and that addresses their real needs bear a great responsibility upon their shoulders. It is for them to preserve the purity and integrity of the message, yet to be able to transmit it to men conditioned by the factors that characterize the modern world. But in performing this task, such men fulfil their highest duty and accomplish the most worthy act of charity, for there is no higher form of charity than the expression of the Truth, which alone can provide for man's deepest and most abiding needs.

Notes to Chapter 5

1. We say 'primarily in Sufism' because as far as Islamic esoteric doctrines are concerned Shi'ite gnosis in both its Twelve-Imam and Ismā'īlī forms is also of great importance. Moreover, the theosophy of Suhrawardī and Mullā Ṣadrā, which developed mostly in Persia and within the bosom of Shi'ism, is of particular importance for solving the present *impasse* of Western thought because of its innate metaphysical richness, and because it has a more systematic character than the metaphysical expositions of the school of Ibn 'Arabī, to which it is, in fact, closely related. The comparative method could very profitably be applied to this theosophy to juxtapose its teachings to such subjects as structuralism, evolution, the relation between logic and intuition, etc., with which modern Western thought, in both its religious and its non-religious form, occupies itself. This would be a separate programme to which, without doubt, Muslim intellectuals as well as those in quest of revivifying true intellectual activity in the West will no doubt turn in the future as this theosophy (*al-ḥikmat al-ilāhiyyah*) becomes better known.

2. F. Schuon, *Understanding Islam*, Foreword, p. ii.

3. For the relationship between Sufism and the rest of the Islamic tradition, see F. Schuon, *op. cit.*, Chap. iv; F. Schuon, *The Transcendent Unity of Religions*, trans. by P. Townsend, London, 1953; S. H. Nasr, *Ideals and Realities of Islam*, Chap. v.

4. See S. H. Nasr, *The Encounter of Man and Nature, the Spiritual Crisis of Modern Man*, pp. 124–129; also S. H. Nasr, 'Man in the Universe', in *Eternità e storia. I valori permanenti nel divenire storico*, Florence, 1970, pp. 182–193; also in S. H. Nasr, *Sufi Essays*, London, 1972, Chap. 6.

5. F. Schuon, 'The Contradiction of Relativism', *Studies in Comparative Religion*, Spring, 1973, p. 70.

6. Usually, three stages of certainty are distinguished, based upon the language of the

Quran: 'the science of certainty' (*'ilm al-yaqīn*), 'the eye of certainty' (*'ayn al-yaqīn*) and the 'truth of certainty' (*ḥaqq al-yaqīn*). These stages have been compared to 'hearing a description of fire', 'seeing fire', and 'being burned by fire'. See Abū Bakr Sirāj ed-Dīn, *The Book of Certainty*, London, 1952.

7. See J. Servier, *L'homme et l'invisible*, Paris, 1964.

8. See G. Di Santillana and E. von Dechend, *Hamlet's Mill*, New York, 1967. These examples could be multiplied tenfold in many fields, not the least amazing of which are the remarkable alphabets developed by some of the indigenous nations of Africa.

9. See R. Guénon, *The Reign of Quantity and the Signs of the Times*, trans. by Lord Northbourne, Baltimore, Penguin Metaphysical Series, 1972.

10. We have in mind many spiritual masters and their spiritual organizations who have come to the West in the past few decades and sought to increase their following by disseminating exactly the same techniques and methods to Westerners as they were applying in the East, with the result that many people unqualified for initiation have been allowed to practice methods that have been either fruitless or harmful to them and in certain cases have led to insanity. Many authentic *bhakti* masters from India have spread their message to Western disciples as if they were addressing a traditional Hindu audience. The results of such efforts are clear for all to see. In any case, the tree is judged by the fruit it bears. Such cases must, however, be clearly distinguished from the self-proclaimed masters who do not issue from any orthodox traditional background but have the audacity to place themselves 'above' traditional teachings and the perennial truths expounded by saints and sages throughout the centuries.

11. The whole group of traditional writers in the Western world, consisting of such men as R. Guénon, A. K. Coomaraswamy, M. Pallis, T. Burckhardt and especially F. Schuon, who occupies a special position among them, belong to this category and for this reason play a role of outstanding importance in the spiritual and religious life of the modern world, even if their works have, until recently, been neglected in many circles.

12. Concerning this spiritual station, see S. H. Nasr, *Sufi Essays*, Chap. 5.

13. 'Metaphysical knowledge is one thing; its actualization in the mind quite another. All the knowledge which the brain can hold, even if it is immeasurably rich from a human point of view, is as nothing in the sight of Truth. As for metaphysical knowledge, it is like a divine seed in the heart; thoughts are only very faint glimmers from it.' F. Schuon, *Spiritual Perspectives and Human Facts*, p. 9.

14. For the role of 'faith' in the realization of the highest metaphysical truths, see F. Schuon, 'The Nature and Arguments of Faith', in *Stations of Wisdom*, trans. by G. E. H. Palmer, London, 1961, pp. 52 ff.

15. The great Algerian saint of this century, Shaykh Aḥmad al-'Alawī, often repeated the Sufi saying, 'He whose soul melteth not away like snow in the hand of religion, in his hand religion like snow away doth melt' (trans. by M. Lings in his *A Sufi Saint of the Twentieth Century*, London, 1971). This dictum is a direct allusion to the need for man's separate existence to melt away in the Truth through the attainment of the virtues, which are the only way in which the Truth can become actualized in the being of man. Despite the emphasis upon this basic feature of all authentic spirituality by masters of old as well as by the leading present-day exponents of traditional doctrines

such as F. Schuon and T. Burckhardt, there has now formed a whole group of 'traditionalists' in the West who accept the teachings of tradition mentally but who do not find it necessary to practise the disciplines of an authentic Way and to discipline their souls in order to become themselves embodiments of the Truth. It is in their case that the second part of the saying of Shaykh al-ʿAlawī applies, for religion or Truth simply melts away in their hands instead of becoming actualized in their being.

16. As already mentioned (note 6), the Sufis usually distinguish between three degrees of certainty, which cover the major steps of the initiatic process, from the mental knowledge of the sacred, to its vision and finally to its realization in one's being.

In one of his famous aphorisms, Ibn ʿAṭā'allāh al-Iskandarī, using a somewhat different terminology, refers to these fundamental stages in these words:

شعاع البصيرة يشهدك قربه منك
وعين البصيرة يشهدك عدمك لوجوده
وحق البصيرة يشهدك وجوده لاعدمك ولا وجودك

> The ray of light of spiritual vision (*shuʿā' al-baṣīrah*, corresponding to *ʿilm al-yaqīn*) makes you witness His nearness to you. The eye of spiritual vision (*ʿayn al-baṣīrah*, corresponding to *ʿayn al-yaqīn*) makes you witness your non-being as due to His Being. The truth of spiritual vision (*ḥaqq al-baṣīrah*, corresponding to *ḥaqq al-yaqīn*) makes you witness His Being, not your non-being or your being.

See V. Danner, *Ibn ʿAṭā'illāh's Sufi Aphorisms*, Leiden, 1973, p. 30, no. 36, containing the English translation of the aphorisms which we have here slightly modified. See also P. Nwiya, *Ibn ʿAṭā'illāh et la naissance de la confrérie šāḏilite*, Beirut, 1972, pp. 102–103, no. 33, where both the Arabic original and the French translation are given.

17. 'In knowledge, reasoning can play no part other than that of being the occasional cause of intellection: intellection will come into play suddenly—not continuously or progressively—as soon as the mental operation, which was in its turn conditioned by an intellectual intuition, has the quality which makes of it a pure symbol.' Schuon, *Spiritual Perspectives and Human Facts*, p. 13.

18. Thanks to the efforts of T. Burckhardt, there are excellent summaries with precious notes of both these works in French as *La sagesse des prophètes*, Paris, 1955, and *De l'homme universel*, Lyon, 1953. Burckhardt has also summarized the doctrinal teachings of the school of Ibn ʿArabī in his *Introduction to Sufi Doctrine*, trans. by D. M. Matheson, London, 1959. In English also there are several partial translations of Sufi doctrinal works, including *Studies in Islamic Mysticism*, by R. A. Nicholson, Cambridge, 1919, which contains a translation of parts of al-Jīlī's *al-Insān al-kāmil*, and several translations by A. J. Arberry of al-Kalābādhī, Ibn al-Fāriḍ and others. What are needed, however, are complete translations into English of these and the many other works of those Sufi masters who have given an open exposition of Sufi doctrine.

19. As far as this school of theosophy (*al-ḥikmat al-ilāhiyyah*), to which we have already alluded above, and its importance for an understanding of Islamic metaphysics are concerned, see S. H. Nasr, *Three Muslim Sages*, Chap. 2; Nasr, 'The School of Isfahan' and 'Ṣadr al-Dīn Shīrāzī' in M. M. Sharif (ed.), *A History of Muslim Philosophy*, Vol. II, Wiesbaden, 1966, and the many works of H. Corbin, who has devoted a lifetime to making this as yet little-studied aspect of Islamic intellectual and spiritual life better known in the West. See especially his *En Islam iranien*, particularly

Vols. 2 and 4. He has also translated one of the major treatises of Mullā Ṣadrā, the *Kitāb al-mashā'ir*, into French as *Le livre des pénétrations métaphysiques*.

20. See S. H. Nasr, *Ideals and Realities of Islam*, Chap. iv.

21. Even in Hinduism, however, there is the *parabhakti* form of spirituality which is gnostic but coloured by *bhakti* elements. Therefore, by referring to the clear separation between these two forms of spirituality in Hinduism we did not mean to exclude their synthesis within the Hindu climate.

22. This does not mean to imply that there have never been any hermits or wandering dervishes among Muslims. They can still be found in various parts of the Islamic world today. It means that Islamic spirituality in its main current combines these two modes. Some Sufi orders such as the Shādhiliyyah and the Ni'matullāhiyyah in fact insist on their adepts having a definite profession and practising the contemplative life within active life in society. They prefer the life of the contemplative who lives in society (*mutasabbib*) to the contemplative who is withdrawn from society (*mutajarrid*).

23. Khaḍir, who corresponds to Elias, symbolizes the esoteric function in the story of Khaḍir and Moses in the Quran, and is represented usually as the 'green prophet'. See A. K. Coomaraswamy, 'Khwaja Khadir and the Fountain of Life, in the Tradition of Persian and Mughal Art', *Studies in Comparative Religion*, Vol. 4, Autumn 1970, pp. 221–230. In Shi'ite Islam, the Twelfth Imam fulfils a similar function and in Sufism in general the Uwaysīs are a particular order who are said to receive initiation from the 'invisible master'. See also the numerous studies of L. Massignon on the spiritual significance of Khaḍir, for example, 'Elie et son rôle transhistorique, Khadiriya, en Islam', *Études carmélitaines: Elie le prophète*, Paris, 1956, Vol. 2, pp. 269–290.

24. This is a direct reference to the act of initiation through which a disciple becomes attached to a particular master and order.

25. R. A. Nicholson, *The Mathnawi of Jalālu'ddin Rūmī*, London, 1926, Vol. 2, pp. 20–21, with a small alteration in the verse 'They make a woollen garb', which Nicholson has translated as 'They make a woollen lion', basing himself on another version of the original Persian verse. See also S. H. Nasr, *Sufi Essays*, p. 61 ff.

26. We have dealt more extensively with this theme in *Sufi Essays*, p. 63.

27. See S. H. Nasr, *The Encounter of Man and Nature, the Spiritual Crisis of Modern Man*, Chap. iii.

Chapter 6

The Harmony of Contemplation and Action In Islam

تفكر ساعة خير من عبادة ستين سنة

An hour of meditation is better than sixty years of acts of worship.

Prophetic *ḥadīth*

العلم بلا عمل كشجر بلا ثمر

Knowledge without action is like a tree without fruit.

Arabic proverb

Having dealt with the role that Sufism can play in fulfilling the spiritual needs of modern man in general, we now turn to a particular aspect of the Islamic tradition, namely the relation between contemplation and action, which concerns so directly the present-day plight of Western man and to which brief reference has already been made in the previous chapter (pp. 58–9). One of the basic problems of modern man is the divorce between contemplation and action, and in fact the almost complete destruction of the former by the latter, even in religious circles which were always devoted to the contemplative life. This loss of balance between these two primordial modes of human existence is itself another consequence of the loss of the Centre and the attempt made by modern man to remain content with the periphery, with dispersive action independent of the vision and message from the Centre which alone can prevent human action from becoming meaningless dissipation. It is, therefore, of particular importance, as an instance of bringing the doctrinal and practical teachings of the Islamic tradition to bear upon the existing problems of Western man, to turn to the message of Islam concerning the contemplative and active lives as possibilities for man to follow in his terrestrial journey.

The two quotations at the beginning of this chapter, if interpreted in the light of the question of the relation between contemplation and action, express their just relationship in Islam, a religion which, as already stated, has never allowed the contemplative and active lives to become totally divorced from each other or to be separately institutionalized.[1] For the modern world, which is immersed so completely in a way of acting and doing bound to purely terrestrial ends that it has lost sight of the meaning of contemplation, let alone its primacy over action, it is hardly conceivable that in a civilization such as that of Islam action and contemplation should exist side by side harmoniously and, in fact, complement each other. Today it is difficult to imagine a universe of thought, action and being in which contemplation leads to action, and action on the spiritual plane becomes the way of access to the inner garden of contemplation.

Contemplation in Islamic spirituality, as in other integral traditions, is essentially a knowledge that relates the knower to higher modes of being. It is identified with *shuhūd* (vision) and *ta'ammul* (literally 'to regard attentively') and is related to *tafakkur* (meditation) in traditional Islamic sources. It is referred to constantly in the Quran, which commands man to contemplate the beauties of the Universe and their divine prototypes. The essentially gnostic character of Islamic spirituality lends a contemplative air to all the authentic manifestations of Islam, including, of course, its sacred art,[2] and causes the soul of the Muslim to tend towards contemplation as that of a Christian tends toward sacrifice.[3] There lies deep within the texture of the soul moulded by the message of the Quran a tendency to uproot itself from the world of multiplicity and to establish itself at the centre of that 'void' which symbolizes Divine Unity and whose reflection is to be found in both virgin nature and in Islamic sacred art. There is the tendency within the soul of the Muslim to be satisfied with the contemplation of a single flower, a blade of wheat, a solitary bush or tree, which, being epiphanies of the Divine, all provide even more than the contemplative eye needs to behold, and all serve as the gateway to the Infinite. For as the Persian poem states,

دل هرذره را که بشکافی   آفتابیش درمیان بینی

If thou dissectest the heart of any atom thou shalt behold a sun within it.
Hātif of Ispahan

Moreover, in the Islamic context, this contemplation has always been wedded to action understood in its traditional sense. The contemplative form of Islamic spirituality has never been opposed to correct action and has in fact often been combined with an irresistible inner urge to action. It is this inner unity that made Islamic civilization at the height of its power one of the most virile and active in human history at the same time that it harboured within itself a most intense contemplative life.

Here again the message of the Quran expresses the rapport between contemplation or knowledge and action, between *al-ʿilm* and *al-ʿamal*, which was divinely ordained for the Islamic community. Throughout the Quran the injunction to contemplate God's wisdom in creation as well as in its metacosmic reality is followed by injunctions to act correctly and according to principles derived from that wisdom. The call to daily prayer in its Shiʿite form, based on formulae drawn from the Quran, serves as a good example of this principle, for it summarizes the hierarchic relationship between God's wisdom, man's knowledge of it and the action which issues from this knowledge. The second part of the call to prayer (*adhān*) consists of three phrases: *ḥayy ʿala'l-ṣalāt*, hurry to prayer, *ḥayy ʿala'l-falāḥ*, hurry to salvation, *ḥayy ʿalā khayr al-ʿamal*, hurry to the best act, good works or correct action. Prayer, which in its highest form is contemplative and unitive, leads to salvation or deliverance of the soul from all bondage and imperfection and this in turn leads to correct action. Without prayer or contemplation one cannot *be* in a state of grace or goodness and without *being* good one cannot *do* good. Correct action depends on the correct mode of being, which in turn issues from the correct relation with the source of all existence through prayer, which in its most exalted mode is pure contemplation. How often is this simple truth forgotten in the modern world where men want to do good without *being* good, to reform the world without reforming themselves, to exalt action and belittle contemplation, unaware that without observance of the above hierarchy no action can ever yield completely fruitful results, especially so far as human welfare in its broadest sense is concerned.

In the light of the innate relationship between contemplation and action contained in the formulae of the *adhān* it can be said that although contemplation and action are complementary, they are not on an equal footing. Contemplation and meditation, which is closely related to it, stand above action, as the *ḥadīth* about an hour of meditation being more worthy than sixty years of acts of worship reveals. At the same time, correct action follows from contemplation and is related to the realized aspect of knowledge which contemplation in fact makes possible. The Arabic saying that knowledge without action is like a tree without fruit can be interpreted to mean precisely that theoretical knowledge is incomplete if it is not actualized through contemplation into realization, which in turn leads to a transformation and, in fact, to the 'death and resurrection' of man and thus to the correct mode of action, which issues effortlessly from the newly acquired mode of being. It means that such theoretical knowledge has not fulfilled its proper function. Contemplation alone can turn this theoretical knowledge into concrete realization leading in turn to correct action, which may be inward or outward, depending on the conditions chosen for the man by the hand of destiny. It can turn the theoretical metaphysical doctrine, which is like a purifying snow within the mind, to a fire in the centre of the heart, a fire which not only melts the heart but also enlivens the limbs and provides them with a new vitality.

The relationship between contemplation and action in human life thus described is an echo, in the matrices of time and space, of the principial domain, and an image, although in reverse, of the cosmogonic act itself. In the Quran, the act of creation, the *fiat lux*, is expressed in the majestic verse

إِنَّمَا أَمْرُهُ إِذَا أَرَادَ شَيْئًا أَنْ يَقُولَ لَهُ كُنْ فَيَكُونُ

> But His command, when He intendeth a thing, is only that he saith unto it: 'Be!' and it is.
>
> XXXVI; 82, Pickthall trans.

Creation is related to an act which at the same time bestows existence and knows all things in principle. The act of God is at once the Word or Logos (*al-kalimah*) and the Intellect (*al-ʿaql*). Therefore, not only does God utter the word *kun* (Be!), but also the spiritual root (*malakūt*) of all things resides in His presence, as the Quranic verse immediately following the one above confirms:

فَسُبْحَانَ الَّذِى بِيَدِهِ مَلَكُوتُ كُلِّ شَىْءٍ وَإِلَيْهِ تُرْجَعُونَ

> Therefore glory be unto Him in Whose hand is the dominion (*malakūt* or 'spiritual root') over all things! Unto Him ye will be brought back.
>
> XXXVI; 83

The Divine Act, therefore, is inextricably related to the Divine contemplation of the essences of things, of their *aʿyān*, or to use the terminology of the Quranic verse just cited, their *malakūt*, which means at once 'dominion' and the higher planes of reality or the spiritual world.[4]

Furthermore, in Sufi metaphysics and cosmology, which are based directly on the Quranic revelation, the creation of the Universe is conceived as a 'breathing' by God upon the immutable archetypes (*al-aʿyān al-thābitah*), which are God's knowledge of all things as well as their spiritual essence. The 'breath of the Compassionate' (*nafas al-Raḥmān*) externalizes the Divine possibilities in the form of external objects. The Divine Act creates the cosmos through contemplation, a cosmos which itself *is* the result of God's contemplation of Himself. For it was in order to contemplate His own Beauty that God created the Universe.[5]

Likewise, according to the Islamic philosophers such as Ibn Sīnā, the very substance of the Universe is the result of God's contemplation of Himself. By contemplating Himself, the Necessary Being (*wājib al-wujūd*) causes to exist the First Intellect, and the First Intellect in turn the Second Intellect, down to the world of generation and corruption in which man resides.[6] Contemplation and existence, knowledge and being, are interrelated, and on the highest plane God's act and self-knowledge are ultimately the same.

In the process of spiritual realization, which is in a way the reversal of the cosmogonic act, namely a journey by means of the arc of ascent (*al-qaws al-ṣuʿūdī*) through all the degrees that have been brought into being by the cosmogonic act in the stages of the descending arc (*al-qaws al-nuzūlī*) of cosmic manifestation, contemplation and action are once again interrelated. Contemplation leads to correct action, and action, conceived as inner spiritual travail as well as external acts which put the soul in the right state to undergo the inner alchemy, leads to the doors of contemplation. But because man must know in order to act, contemplation, as already stated, always precedes action in a principial manner. Thus the contemplative man is held in higher esteem in traditional Islamic society than the man of action, as the famous *ḥadīth* testifies:

(يوزن يوم القيامة مداد العلماء ودم الشهداء فيرّجح مداد العلماء على دم الشهداء)

> The ink of the man of knowledge is more worthy than the blood of the martyr.

Yet precisely because there is no monasticism in Islam; because Islam is a society of 'married monks';[7] because the Divine Law of Islam (the *Sharīʿah*) is at once a code of action and a way of preparing the soul for the flights of contemplation in the spiritual world; and because of many other factors, the ink and the blood have never been totally divorced, and the Islamic order has preserved a remarkable balance between the contemplative and the active lives, a balance which cannot be fully understood by a merely theoretical discussion of the subject from the outside. As long as man does not participate in tradition in an operative manner and does not benefit from the grace or *barakah* issuing from its rites and other sacred forms, the complementarity of the contemplative and the active lives is most difficult to conceive. It happens often in the Western world today that both contemplation and action are thought *about* abstractly and categorized logically, but rarely are they lived and practised correctly, with the result that their inner complementarity is rarely appreciated or understood. How often in the modern world does one hear from men who have only a theoretical knowledge of tradition without actual participation in it, that such and such a way of life corresponds to the way of action and such and such another to contemplation; that one must do such a thing according to one particular traditional source and contemplate in such a way according to another, as if one were collecting art pieces from various parts of the world for a museum exhibition. Yet, although all authentic traditional sources speak with authority, they cannot be understood by a simply theoretical grasp of the teachings they contain nor can selections be made from their teachings by men who do not follow one tradition themselves and who ultimately place their own selves as the judge of God-given traditions.

So many modern men, therefore, who rely only on books and simply speak about tradition without practising it, are never able to perform correct action in the spiritual sense, not to speak of reaching states of contemplation which in their pure form, alone possessing spiritual efficacy, belong only to the traditional universe. The man who does not practise a spiritual way cannot experience that inner certitude, that inner attachment of one's being to the Divinity, which makes of action an application of immutable principles[8] and the gateway to the world of contemplation, which brings about a state of unity whereby contemplation and action are wedded in an indissoluble union.[9] In fact, what is invocation (*dhikr*), that central practice of Sufism, but such a wedding between action and contemplation at their highest level? There is an immeasurable difference between the man who does not practise a tradition and does not live 'existentially' attached to a traditional world and one who participates in such a world, especially if he be one whose participation is active, if he be one who lives in the awareness of being motivated and moved at every moment of life by the 'hands' of God according to the Quranic verse

يَدُ اللهِ فَوْقَ أَيْدِيْهِم

The Hand of Allah is above their hands.

XLVIII; 10

As the Alexandrian Sufi Ibn ʿAṭāʾallāh al-Iskandarī states:

> He who is negligent awakens in the morning by considering what he is going to do,
> And he who is wise by considering what God will do with him.[10]

There is an immense difference between the two, even in the context of the traditional world. How much greater is the difference in a world such as the modern one in which many men live in a state of total amnesia or at best a simply theoretical and cerebral understanding of tradition, a state which hides from them the possibilities of practising the traditional life in an active way and of opening inner doors to the world of contemplation amidst external circumstances and situations which, seen only from the outside, appear opposed to such possibilities and incongruent with the spiritual life.[11]

When we turn to the actual possibilities of practising the contemplative life within the Islamic tradition, we are faced at first sight with a situation which seems to leave out the possibility of a contemplative life, if this form of life is identified with one form or another of monasticism, as in Christianity or Buddhism. Monasticism is banned according to the famous dictum,

«لا رهبانيّة في الاسلام»

'There is no monasticism in Islam', but this institutional ban does not by any means imply the closing of the door to the life of contemplation. On the contrary, Islamic spirituality, being gnostic in nature, is based directly upon contemplation and, as stated above, there is in the Muslim soul a tendency toward contemplation which is combined with combativeness (*jihād*), understood in its esoteric sense of removing all the obstacles which veil the Truth and make It inaccessible.[12] As we have seen in the previous chapter, Sufism, the main manifestation of Islamic esotericism, contains within itself the possibility of the most intense contemplative life, not because it is a *monachisme errant* as some orientalists have called it,[13] but because such a perspective lies by nature within the Islamic revelation and constitutes its essence.

The unitary principle of Islam, however, could not permit this contemplative way to become crystallized as a separate social organization outside the matrix moulded by the injunctions of the Divine Law or *Sharīʿah*. It had to remain as an inner dimension of that Law and institutionally as an organization integrated into the Islamic social pattern and inseparable from it.[14] As a result, contemplatives of the highest order have often combined their life of contemplation with the most intense forms of activity, and throughout Islamic history outstanding Sufis have been known to be scholars, artists, teachers and even administrators and rulers. In such cases, the inner contemplative life has intensified and given meaning to their acts rather than in any way diminishing their efficiency or appropriateness.

In the case of women, people with a Christian background familiar with the distinction between Mary and Martha, and aware of the figures of such outstanding Christian women contemplatives and saints as Hildegard of Bingen and Catherine of Sienna, often find it difficult to understand how the possibility of the contemplative life could exist for a woman in Islam. Putting aside certain female ascetics like Rābiʿah, who is one among many female saints and mystics in Islam, most contemplative Muslim women have, like men, found the possibility of the contemplative life within the matrix of the Muslim social order itself. To accept one's destiny as the wife and mother who is of necessity concerned with daily problems, and to submit oneself to one's social position and duties with the awareness that this is in reality submitting oneself to the Divine Will have led many Muslim women to an intensely contemplative inner life amidst, and integrated into, the type of active life imposed upon her by the hands of destiny. The Muslim woman's acceptance of her role and duty as specified by Islamic teachings echoes the state of spiritual poverty or *faqr* and even of *fanā'*, or 'annihilation', in God, and can lead, when combined with true piety and devotion to spiritual practices, to these states. For both men and women in Islam, the contemplative life lies not outside but within the active norms of life specified by the *Sharīʿah*, exceptional cases and circumstances as willed by God being, of course, always possible.

The most essential rapport between contemplation and action in Islam is to be found in prayer, especially in quintessential prayer or invocation (*dhikr*) as practised by the Sufis. Therein contemplation and action become unified. Perfect action, which is the *dhikr*, leads to contemplation (*shuhūd* or *mushāhadah*), while contemplation is itself the *dhikr* inasmuch as the *dhikr* is unified with 'Him who is invoked' (*madhkūr*). In perfect invocation, he who invokes or performs the act of invocation (*dhākir*) becomes united with the *dhikr* and the *madhkūr* in a supreme union which transcends the dichotomy between action and contemplation, knowledge and existence, the knower and the known, and in which all polarities are embraced within the essential and at the same time primordial Unity.[15]

One can, moreover, distinguish in the *dhikr*, or unitive prayer, a contemplative action and an active contemplation. The incantatory methods of Sufism, if practised under the direction of a master and within the protective matrix of traditional orthodoxy, are all forms of contemplative action at the highest level, leading ultimately to union with God. Inasmuch as the process of realization is, as already asserted, in a sense the reversal of the cosmogonic act, the traversing of the ascending arc (*al-qaws al-ṣuʿūdī*) on the path of return to the Source and Origin by means of the contemplative act results in going from a state in which knowledge and existence are separated to a state in which they are united. As a result, in a mysterious fashion the agent who performs the contemplative act is able to transcend his own limited existence as agent through his very action. The secret of this paradox lies in the fact that in the *dhikr* man performs an act, but an act that is preceded by contemplation, an act which is also a state of being, an act which is ultimately not the act of man but the act of God. Hence, in the same way that through the Word God created the world, again through His Word—the *dhikr*, which is mysteriously the act of man participating in the eternal and immutable act of God—creation ascends in the scale of being and finally returns to its Source. Quintessential prayer is a contemplative act which leads to pure contemplation and finally union.

As for active contemplation, it too is nothing but the *dhikr* seen from another point of view. Sufism is not a passive form of mysticism. It is a journey (*sulūk*) in search of Divine Knowledge, the attainment of which leads to union and to the overcoming of the separation between man in his fallen state and man as the Universal and Perfect Man (*al-insān al-kāmil*), who is in eternal union with God because he is the perfect mirror in whom the Divine Names and Qualities are reflected.[16] There is, then, in the very method of Sufism or the *dhikr*, as it is combined with various forms of meditation (*fikr*), an active contemplation of the spiritual realities. For those who actually tread the path, the *sālikūn*, in contrast to the stationary members of Sufi orders who remain satisfied with being simply blessed with the grace of initiation (the *mutabarrikūn*), the whole of the spiritual work is continuously combined with the element of active contemplation in which progress upon the spiritual path is achieved through an active participation of the whole being of the adept.

All this explains why, in Islam, one of the symbols of the Universal Man, who embodies the full realization of the truth and in whom the *dhikr* has become fully operative, is the Seal of Solomon. The triangle with its base toward heaven symbolizes contemplation, and the other, in the reverse position, symbolizes action.[17] It is this perfect harmony and wedding between the two that makes the act of the contemplative at once the sword that discriminates between truth and error and establishes harmony and justice, and the brush that paints upon the canvas of time and space the beauties of the spiritual world and opens thereby the gate for the return to that world through the very contemplation of the forms of beauty thus created.

The relationship between action and contemplation described on its most essential level as quintessential orison is reflected also on the plane of the study of nature and of the creation of art. Islamic science certainly enabled man to gain knowledge of nature and also to act upon nature, as we see in agriculture, medicine and the like. But the final goal of this science was to enable man to contemplate nature and to aid him to act upon himself and to remake himself with the help of the contemplative knowledge thus gained. Islamic science was concerned with a process which also implied the possibility for nature, considered as the theophany (*tajallī*), to act upon the soul of man, as well as the possibility for men to 'act' upon nature through the contemplation of its epiphanies.[18] Islamic science thus began with an objectivization of nature which made it an 'object' of study to achieve a unitive knowledge which finally integrated man with his own prototype as well as with the prototype of nature, so that nature became a 'thou', an intimate witness to the Divine Presence. Moreover, action upon nature has always been regulated and kept within limits in the Islamic perspective because the traditional Muslim knows fully that ultimate happiness comes not from endless action turned outward toward the plundering and devastating of nature but from acting inwardly upon oneself to tame one's own lower nature and to 'Islamize the Satan of one's own being', as the Sufis would say.

In direct contrast to this perspective, modern science, which is marked by the complete lack of a contemplative dimension, has sought since the seventeenth century to drive a wedge between man and nature by extending further and further 'the edge of objectivity',[19] with the result that this 'objectivity' has finally led to the total alienation of man from his natural environment, an alienation which, combined with a theory of action as an aggressive externalization of human energy with the aim of indiscriminately raping and plundering nature, has led the world to its present environmental crisis. The relation between contemplation and action in the Islamic sciences of nature, which is derived from the principial relation already delineated, contains a message of the utmost importance for modern man in search of a means to save himself from the catastrophe brought about by his own folly.

Likewise, in Islamic art there is an intimate relation between action and contemplation which recaptures in the world of forms the complementarity existing between the two in the principial order.[20] The artist obviously makes something: that is, he acts in one way or another upon matter. But because he follows traditional patterns, norms, regulations and procedures which are themselves derived from and are the fruit of contemplative vision, his action is subsequent to contemplation and follows in its wake. In the case of many a traditional artist who is himself engaged in spiritual practice, the phase of making or acting is based upon the direct fruit of his own contemplation as well as the fruit of contemplation of previous masters handed down to him through traditional channels. As a result, the various manifestations of Islamic art themselves serve as an aid to contemplation. Whether it be the courtyard of a mosque, an arabesque design, a verse of Sufi poetry or a traditional musical composition, various forms of Islamic art serve the function of strengthening the wings of the soul for its contemplative flight into the heavenly empyrean. Their beauties are, in fact, so many reminiscences of the beauties of paradise which man can taste even here on earth on the wings of contemplation and spiritual vision. They are beauties which do not externalize the soul but draw it to its own Centre. In Islamic art, as in the Islamic sciences of nature, contemplation and action are intertwined and complementary, while the hierarchic relation according to which contemplation precedes action is always preserved. The relation seen in these domains is, moreover, nothing other than the application to these fields of the principial relation existing between them in the spiritual life, one which is so basic and fundamental that it can be seen in every authentic manifestation of Islam itself and also of its arts and sciences.

As far as the operative and practical aspects of man's spiritual life are concerned, the perfect and exemplary relation between contemplation and action is to be found for every Muslim in the life of the Holy Prophet, who is of necessity the model for every form of spiritual life in Islam. If there are those who, as a result of the influence of modernism, seek to belittle the importance of the contemplative life in Islam, they need only study the life of the Prophet both before the commencement of his prophetic mission and during the twenty-three years when he lived on earth as a prophet. In both periods, he was devoted intensely to contemplation and spent much time in solitude, while at the same time he transformed human history through a series of actions of such far-reaching consequences that they cannot be gauged in ordinary human terms and are beyond the ken of imagination. Likewise if there are those who wish to over-emphasize the importance of external action and to extol action pure and simple as an end in itself, again they need only study the actions of the Prophet, which were always the applications of principles rooted in contemplation and derived from knowledge of the Divine Order.

Of course, no one has the right to claim or to hope to achieve the perfection of a prophet, but the very harmony between contemplation and action, between a heart that was always at peace in the Divine Presence and a mind and body that acted with the utmost determination combined with resignation to the Divine Will—as seen in the exemplary life of the Prophet of Islam—is the perfect embodiment of the ideal relationship and the complementarity between contemplation and action for Muslims. The Prophet thus remains the perfect model (*uswah*) to follow, and in him is to be seen, in a blinding fashion, perfect contemplative action and active contemplation, and the union of action and contemplation in that *coincidentia oppositorum* which transcends all duality and opposition. The end of human life according to Islam is to act according to the Divine Will and finally to reach, through self-purification, such a state of knowledge and vision or contemplation as to see God everywhere. The Prophet was that perfect being who acted according to the Divine Will at every moment of his life, his gaze fixed on the Divine realities, contemplating God both beyond manifestation and in every speck of His creation. In the Prophet is thus to be found the perfect manifestation of the complementarity of contemplation and action which lies at the heart of the Islamic way of life and which characterizes, at its highest level of meaning, the central method of realization in Islamic spirituality. His example not only remains supreme for Muslims but is also of the utmost importance for those in the modern world in search of harmonizing once again the contemplative and the active lives and bringing unity to the life of man, whose total submersion in multiplicity and surrender to dispersive action has already drained his life of spiritual quality and meaning and threatens even to destroy the just equilibrium between the soul and the body upon which all human life depends and without which the essential human nature of man becomes devoured by his accidental animality.

Notes to Chapter 6

1. This does not mean that the contemplative life in its institutionalized form as it exists in other traditions should be disdained, as it is by so many modernized Muslims. The Prophet himself had a special love for Christian monks. In any case, the contemplative life is an absolutely necessary part of any integral tradition, and the form it takes within that tradition depends completely on what God has ordained. Muslims today, who profess to have faith in God and His Providence, should therefore be the last to criticize the presence of contemplative ways of living in other traditions which happen to differ from what is to be found in Islam. It is a total misunderstanding of religion in general and of Islam in particular on the part of modernists to claim superiority for Islam over other religions because Islam does not permit man to pursue the contemplative life in a distinct form. But this is precisely what some Muslim modernists, eager to placate the shallow criticisms of modern Westerners, have claimed, forgetting the numerous *ḥadīth* of the Holy Prophet on the supremacy of contemplation over action.

Concerning the necessity of the contemplative life in traditions where it takes a monastic form, see F. Schuon, 'The Universality of Monasticism and its Relevance in the Modern World', in *Light on the Ancient Worlds*, pp. 119–135.

2. See T. Burckhardt, 'The Foundations of Islamic Art', in his *Sacred Art in East and West*, trans. by Lord Northbourne, London, 1967; and his 'Perennial Values in Islamic Art', in Ch. Malik (ed.), *God and Man in Contemporary Islamic Thought*, Beirut, 1972, pp. 122–131; also in *The Sword of Gnosis*, pp. 304–316.

3. See F. Schuon, *Understanding Islam*, pp. 18–19.

4. In traditional Islamic cosmology, *malakūt* (the domain of royalty) is used to refer to a state of being, or 'Divine Presence' (*haḍrah*) standing below the archangelic world or the *jabarūt* (the domain of power), and above the physical world, or the *mulk*, but in the Quranic verse just cited it refers, according to many of the traditional commentators, to the spiritual root of things which is at once their essence and the highest level of their being residing 'in the hands of God'. See F. Schuon, *Dimensions of Islam*, Chap. 11; and S. H. Nasr, *Science and Civilization in Islam*, pp. 92–97.

5. See Ibn 'Arabī, *Fuṣūṣ al-ḥikam*, ed. by A. Afifi, Cairo, 1946, Chap. 1, where this doctrine is fully expounded. See also Ibn 'Arabī's *La sagesse des prophètes*, trans. by T. Burckhardt, pp. 19–36; T. Burckhardt, *An Introduction to Sufi Doctrine*, pp. 64–72; T. Izutsu, *A Comparative Study of the Key Philosophical Concepts in Sufism and Taoism*, Part One, Chaps. xi, xii and xiii; and S. H. Nasr, *Science and Civilization in Islam*, Chap. xiii.

6. Concerning Ibn Sīnā's ontology and cosmology, see S. H. Nasr, *An Introduction to Islamic Cosmological Doctrines*, Chaps. 12, 13 and 14.

7. This is an expression of F. Schuon. Concerning this aspect of Islamic society and family, see his *The Transcendent Unity of Religions*, Chap. VII.

8. See Marco Pallis, 'The Active Life', in his *The Way and the Mountain*, London, 1960, pp. 36–61.

9. As mentioned in the previous chapter, there are of course rare exceptions, called the *afrād* in Sufism, who are 'given' certain spiritual experiences by Heaven without their systematically practising a regular spiritual way. But this is only the exception which proves the rule and is in any case not a choice open to man. Such exceptions are certainly no excuse for those who refuse seriously to practise a tradition and yet seek enlightenment.

10. الغافل اذا صبح نظر ماذا يفعل
والعاقل ينظر ماذا يفعل الله به

P. Nwiya, *Ibn 'Aṭā'illāh et la naissance de la confrérie šāḍilite*, no. 106. See also V. Danner, *Ibn 'Aṭā'illāh's Sufi Aphorisms*, p. 40, no. 114, where a somewhat different translation is given of the same aphorism.

11. Many people with a contemplative tendency who seek to follow a traditional way in the modern world have refused to accept Islam in general and Sufism in particular because of their external judgment about the incompatibility of the demands that Islam makes on life on the plane of action with conditions imposed by the modern world and also because of what appears as an insurmountable chasm that separates the lives of Sufi saints and contemplatives as recorded in traditional sources from what can be practised and lived in the modern world. Such people neglect certain forms of

cosmic compensation as well as the effect of the *barakah* that issues from traditional forms and practices and the qualitative aspects of action of a traditional nature before the eyes of God. These are all elements which paradoxically make more accessible things which in more normal circumstances were in themselves very difficult to attain. These elements open doors to the world of contemplation through graces which can never be calculated externally by a simply theoretical study of tradition and the relation between action and contemplation as recorded in traditional sources.

12. 'Le genèse d'une religion équivaut à la création d'un type moral et spirituel apparemment nouveau, et même nouveau *de facto* sous certains rapports contingents; ce type, dans l'Islam, consiste en l'équilibre—paradoxal au point de vue chrétien—entre la contemplativité et la combativité, puis entre la sainte pauvreté et la sexualité sacralisée: l'Arabe—et l'homme arabisé par l'Islam—a pour ainsi dire quatre pôles, à savoir le désert, l'épée, la femme, la religion. Chez le contemplatif, les quatre pôles s'intériorisent; le désert, l'épée et la femme deviennent autant d'états ou de fonctions de l'âme.' F. Schuon, 'Images d'Islam', *Etudes Traditionnelles*, no. 432–33, Juillet-Août et Septembre–Octobre, 1972, p. 145.

13. See, for example, R. Brunnel, *Le monachisme errant dans l'Islam*, Paris, 1955.

14. Concerning the relationship of Sufism to the *Sharī'ah*, see F. Schuon, *Understanding Islam*, Chap. iv, pp. 106 ff. Schuon, 'Imam, Islan, Ihsan' in *L'Oeil du coeur*, Paris, 1950, pp. 150–156 (reprinted 1974); and S. H. Nasr, *Ideals and Realities of Islam*, pp. 121–144.

15. Regarding this unity, the Sufi poet Jāmī says:

خوش آنکه دلت زذکر بر نور شده　　در پرتوی آن نفس تومقهور شده

اندیشهٔ کثرت زمیان دور شده　　ذاکر همه ذکر وذکر مذکور شده

How fortunate art thou to have thy heart filled with the light of the invocation,
A light which has conquered thy carnal soul.
The thought of multiplicity has passed away,
The invoker has become the invocation and the invocation the invoked.

See F. Schuon, *Understanding Islam*, pp. 122 ff., where the Sufi doctrine of *dhikr* is expounded majestically.

16. Union (*wiṣāl*) in Sufism does not mean the union of man's imperfect nature with God. This would be sheer blasphemy. As the Sufi poem says:

How can this creature of dust be related to the world of purity?

Union rather means the realization of one's nothingness, the quality of perfect servitude (*'ubūdiyyah*) before the Absolute and becoming a mirror, through this very realization, of God's Names and Qualities. See Ibn 'Arabī, *La sagesse des prophètes*, pp. 19–56; and F. Schuon, 'The Servant and Union', *Dimensions of Islam*, pp. 46–53.

17. The two triangles obviously also symbolize activity and passivity as well as Divine and human nature and their union. For an explanation of this symbol, see Abū Bakr Sirāj ed-Dīn, *The Book of Certainty*, Chap. 1.

18. On this aspect of Islamic science, see S. H. Nasr, *Islamic Studies*, Chap. 13; and Nasr, *Science and Civilization in Islam*, Introduction and Chap. 13.

19. To quote C. Gillespie in his well-known study, *The Edge of Objectivity*, Princeton, 1960.

20. See the numerous works of T. Burckhardt on this question, such as the works already cited in note 2.

Part IV

The Contemporary Muslim between Islam and the Modern World

Chapter 7

Islam in the Islamic World Today

For nearly all of its fourteen centuries of history Islam has filled the whole of the 'living space' of that part of the cosmos called the Islamic world, leaving no vacuum to be filled by elements which could properly be called un-Islamic. The earthly manifestation of Islam was practically synonymous with the Islamic world, and everything in the Islamic world from the method of ploughing fields to composing poetry was inseparable from the spirit and form of Islam. It is only now, when, as a result of the encroachment of modernism, the homogeneity created by the *Sharīʿah* on one level and Islamic art on the other has been partially destroyed, that it is possible to speak of Islam *in* the Islamic world as distinct from other elements of a completely non-Islamic and even anti-Islamic nature which have crept into this world to destroy in part its marvellous unity and homogeneity. It is true that in the traditional world of Islam there were also occasional forms of decadence in both art and thought of the type characteristic of the European Renaissance, but they were so peripheral and so much on the fringe and were, moreover, overwhelmed so rapidly by the spiritual presence of the tradition that they cannot in any way be compared in dimension with the spread of modernism in the Islamic world today.[1] No matter how much effort certain Orientalists spend in seeking to resuscitate the rationalistic tendencies of an Ibn al-Rāwandī or Muḥammad ibn Zakariyyā' al-Rāzī, or to display in art exhibitions certain naturalistic vases, frescoes and paintings of Umayyad, Ottoman, Mogul or Persian origin, they cannot hide the overwhelming evidence of the presence of the spiritual character of the Islamic tradition, a presence which obliterated all such transient phenomena in the Islamic world.

The unity of the Islamic world, however, is now partially broken as never before, not only politically—which had occurred already during the Abbasid period—but even religiously and culturally, by the erosion caused by Westernization, a process which as well as introducing a totally foreign element into the Islamic world also reflects directly an alien world which itself suffers from the most glaring forms of disunity and contradiction. Numerous works have been written in the West with various degrees of success on modern movements in the Islamic world,[2] but few have considered the effect of the inner contradictions and tensions of Western civilization itself upon the confusion caused in the Islamic world by present-day modernizing elements. It is enough to see the difference of perspective and approach existing today among philosophers, sociologists and educators of Muslim universities, reflecting the centres of learning in which they were trained in continental Europe or England or America, to realize how complicated the pattern of Westernization—which of course has been synonymous with modernization until now—actually is.[3]

In addition to the historical accidents of colonization and Westernization, there is also another factor to consider which reflects the multifarious tendencies within Western civilization itself. Because the Islamic world has always been a unity, it has until now functioned as an organism in which each part has played a particular role. During the classical period of Islamic civilization, each part of the Islamic world was especially known for its mastery of a particular art or science, from sword-making to navigation, from astronomy to *Kalām*. On a more inward level, each of the Islamic peoples, such as the Arabs, Persians, Turks, Berbers and Black Africans, emphasized a particular devotional aspect of Islam and even a particular interpretation of the *Sharīʿah*, while the Shariʿite rites as well as the pure metaphysics of *Taṣawwuf* and the techniques for its realization provided the thread of unity through this diversity.

The spread of modernism has had the effect not only of sowing the seed of confusion in the minds of those who are affected by it and therefore loosening the hold of Islam upon them, but also of separating different parts of the Islamic world from each other more than ever before. There is much talk of easy communication today, but as a matter of fact, intellectually and culturally, there is less communication between various parts of the Islamic world today not only than during the period of the classical caliphate but even than after the Mongol invasion, when Moroccans worked along with Syrian astronomers in Maraghah under the leadership of Naṣīr al-Dīn al-Ṭūsī.[4] The various parts of the Islamic world, which for centuries complemented each other and functioned organically and harmoniously, are now left to themselves to recreate a totality from something which was always part of a greater whole and was continuously enriched by other parts of the whole.[5]

As a result, when one studies the situation of Islam and Islamic culture in the Islamic world today, one sees a certain element of this totality better preserved in one land and another element in another land. In one part of *dār al-islām*, certain parts of the *Sharīʿah* are performed impeccably and certain other parts relatively neglected.[6] In one place the juridical sciences are still studied and taught in their fullness, and in another the theological ones or certain other traditional sciences. Some of the Muslim peoples have preserved the formal aspects of the *Sharīʿah* more strictly, and others place more emphasis upon their inner content and are less observant concerning the exactness of the outward forms. Likewise, in the domain of the sacred art of Islam, some have preserved the most beautiful Quranic psalmody, others calligraphy and yet others architecture.[7] Some continue to preserve the traditional dress but are more modernized in their minds and attitudes than others who have been forced to abandon their traditional dress but whose psyche and mind remain less affected by modernism.

Many historical factors, ethnic characteristics, internal social and political elements and the like have created a pattern in which, overlying the deeper layer which unifies the Islamic peoples and displays the unity and totality of Islam, one can observe a differentiated patchwork of modern ways of thinking and acting throughout various Islamic countries, reflecting both the confusion of the Western world and the complicated processes through which this confusion reached the Islamic world. In the periods when Islamic civilization was at its height, when its homogeneity reflected the verities of Islam on all levels of human life, a perceptive Muslim could gain a vision of the totality of the Islamic order through contact with any of its great centres; but today, such an experience of Islam in its totality is not easy to come by, even for a Muslim acquainted with only a part of *dār al-islām*, not to speak of an outsider. For example, in the intellectual field, a person possessing the necessary intellectual and spiritual capabilities and living in Cairo or Damascus or Isfahan of the fourth/eleventh century, or even of the eleventh/seventeenth century, would have been able to gain knowledge through traditional education of the hierarchy of the Islamic sciences extending from the supreme *scientia sacra* contained in Sufism to various traditional schools of philosophy and the natural sciences to theology and the various juridical sciences. Although not impossible today, the task of attaining such a knowledge is certainly much more difficult than before for a Muslim brought up in a traditional *madrasah*, not to speak of one whose Westernized education has cut him off from many of the essentials of his own intellectual heritage. In fact, the spread of modernism in the Islamic world was facilitated precisely by this diminution in the knowledge of Islam's totality on the part of many Muslims. Yet it is precisely this total knowledge, not limited to a single level but embracing the whole, that is necessary if an intelligentsia capable of answering all the challenges that the Western world poses for Islam is to be formed.

Strangely enough, one of the results of the shock received by certain Muslims in their encounter with the Western world has been a re-awakening of interest in the totality of Islam. In these cases, a 'rediscovery' of Islam, and even a kind of renewal of some people's vision of their own faith, has taken place, in such a way that such persons could, in a sense, be called *jadīd al-islām*, (having just become Muslim) with all the positive qualities connected traditionally with this term. The impact of modernism upon the Islamic world, combined with a certain amount of decadence which set in in some domains of life and thought beginning in the twelfth/eighteenth century, destroyed the homogeneity of that world and veiled the totality of the tradition even from Muslims. To understand the nature of the impact of modernism upon the Islamic world, and to prepare to combat its evils, requires on the part of the Muslim intelligentsia a rediscovery of the vision of the whole of their tradition and a stepping outside the boundary of their national and local experience to view the encounter of Islam and modernism in other parts of the Islamic world. For them as well as for the student studying Islam from the outside,[8] the study of the parts cannot but help them to gain a knowledge of the whole.

It must be added, however, that the emphasis laid upon the necessity of studying Islam in each part of the Islamic world today in its confrontation with various forms of modernism must not lead to negligence of the traditional and unchanging aspects of Islamic life so often forgotten in the studies made by Western students as well as by modernistic Muslims. We have had occasion to mention in our previous writings on Islam[9] the danger of the type of method used by most modern students of Islam grounded in such pseudo-sciences as modern sociology and the like or paralyzed by the historicism which grew out of nineteenth-century European philosophy. But it is necessary to repeat here that for a mentality trained to measure and to consider as significant only that which changes, the only noteworthy phenomenon in any part of the Islamic world becomes that which is related to some kind of rebellion against the existing traditional order. If there are a dozen traditional commentaries written upon the Quran they are considered as mere repetitions, but if there is one which breaks with the traditional canons, it is immediately hailed as a significant departure and made known through articles in various European languages. One can hardly emphasize enough how diabolical this propaganda on behalf of perverted tendencies or trivial mental exercises has been and how on the one hand it has led the Western reader to the wrong conclusion about the contemporary state of Islam, and on the other hand it has misled the Muslim in whom the power of faith (*īmān*) has become weakened by the illusion that traditional Islam is something that belongs only to the past and that by identifying himself with modernistic theories and interpretations he is allying himself with forces that must of necessity prevail in the future.

In reality nothing could be further from the truth. Despite serious encroachments upon the body of Islam by modernism and by the confusion caused within the mind and soul of certain Muslims caught between the pull of their tradition and Western ideologies and values, Islam remains very much a living tradition on both the exoteric and the esoteric levels. Were this not so it would hardly be possible to speak of applying the teachings of Islam to the problems faced by modern man. If nothing had been left of Islam save some kind of sentimental or apologetic modern interpretation, one could hardly expect it to provide an antidote for the maladies caused by modernism itself.

But authentic and traditional Islam continues to live. It is there to be studied and rediscovered in its totality by turning both to the oral and written sources of the tradition as it has been lived and transmitted since its revelation, and to its present-day manifestations in the souls and lives of the Muslim peoples in various parts of the Islamic world under the different historical, political and social conditions imposed upon the once unified *dār al-islām* during the most recent period of Islamic history. Being more acquainted with the Arab and the Persian worlds, it is to these parts of the Islamic world that we turn in seeking to understand something of the state of Islam in the Islamic world today and in its confrontation with modernism. These countries form only a part of the Islamic world, but they continue to be of great importance and centrality because of the fundamental role they have played as the heart of *dār al-islām* since the foundation of Islamic civilization.

Notes to Chapter 7

1. It is worthy of note that the emphasis of European Orientalism on certain fringe phenomena in traditional Islamic society has played no small role in the spread of modernism in the Islamic world itself since the late nineteenth century.

2. Of these the most noteworthy are still those of H. A. R. Gibb and W. C. Smith already cited. For a bibliography on the subject, see C. Adams, *A Reader's Guide to the Great Religions*, New York and London, 1965.

3. See S. H. Nasr, *Islamic Studies*, Chap. 8, where this question is discussed for the field of philosophy.

4. It is typical of this lack of communication between various parts of the Islamic world that it is easier to speak by telephone from almost any Muslim capital to London or Paris than to another Muslim capital. In fact in some cases one cannot speak with the capital of a neighbouring country save through some European capital such as Paris or London. Those who have tried to telephone from, let us say, Beirut to Tehran must have been struck by this fact.

5. We remember once having read in one of the treatises of Jābir ibn Ḥayyān that there are certain doors for which God has made one lock with two keys, giving one key to the Arabs and the other to the Persians, the two main ethnic groups who created classical Islamic civilization. Jābir adds that a day will come when the two races will separate and neither will be able to open those doors alone. One wonders how many doors remain closed today not only because of the 'separation' of the Arabs and the Persians but also of the Arabs and the Turks, the Turks and the Persians, the Persians and the Muslims of the sub-continent, etcetera.

6. This does not of course apply to the basic 'pillars' of Islam, which are observed by all practising Muslims everywhere, but to such aspects of the *Sunnah* as congregational prayers, sacrifice of animals, pilgrimage to various holy sites, supererogatory prayers, chanting of litanies and the like.

7. It seems that the Divine Mercy (*Raḥmah*) would exclude the possibility that all the traditional channels for the transmission of grace through forms belonging to sacred art could become closed in a particular Islamic *milieu*, even if this *milieu* be modernized.

It is thus that in certain Muslim cities debased by the ugliest modern architecture one suddenly hears the most beautiful chanting of the Holy Quran or sees striking examples of calligraphy or other sacred art forms which continue to be the channel for the emanation of the *barakah* of Islam.

8. In fact, if the various prejudices and misunderstandings of many Western Orientalists be put aside, it becomes obvious that in their insistence upon studying Islamic civilization as a whole and in basing their studies on the Islamic world itself rather than on parochial divisions, they have rendered a service to serious students of Islam. Many young Muslim intellectuals have regained a vision of the totality of Islam and its civilization through contact with Western studies on Islam, which, because they have approached the subject from the outside, have tried to look upon the whole of Islamic civilization rather than its parts. This merit does not, of course, in any way condone the wilful or unintentional misrepresentations of Islam by many Orientalists whose works have played no small role in wreaking intellectual havoc among many modernized Muslims, especially in countries where a European language is prevalent. See M. Jameelah, *Islam and Orientalism*, Lahore, 1971, where the views of several well-known Islamicists are criticized from the orthodox Shariʿite point of view.

9. See, especially, S. H. Nasr, 'The Immutable Principles of Islam and Western Education', *Muslim World*, Jan. 1966, pp. 4–9; and Nasr, *Ideals and Realities of Islam*.

Chapter 8

Islam in the Contemporary Arab World

The Arabs were chosen as the recipients and the first propagators of the Islamic revelation, and since the inception of Islamic civilization their destiny has remained indissolubly bound with the earthly manifestations of Islam wherever these might be. The vast majority of Arabs are Muslims,[1] and even the few among the Muslim Arabs who have recently rebelled against the faith are nevertheless influenced in many ways by Islam's norms and spirit. Their psychic and mental make-up has been moulded and structured for too long by Islam to allow its influence to be eradicated overnight. In the lives of those Arabs who consciously practise Islam and accept its teachings, and even of the few who have wandered away from its sacred mould, Islam remains the overwhelming reality, penetrating even now into practically every aspect of their individual and collective existence.

But despite this indissoluble bond between Islam and the Arabs, events of the past century have caused the penetration of many foreign ideas, ranging from nationalism and secularism to socialism and Marxism, into the traditional universe of the Arabs, and have brought about some modifications in the understanding of the traditional pattern of religion among certain classes. These factors must, of course, be evaluated and considered in any appraisal of the situation of Islam in the contemporary Arab world, for they form the background of the complex and often bewildering scene observable today.

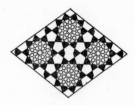

The first element to consider in studying present-day religious life among the Arabs is the shock received by all Muslims, and especially the Arabs, during the nineteenth century, from the domination of the European powers, a domination which for Muslims posed a crisis of cosmic dimensions. For the first time in their history, except for the short episode of the Mongol invasion, Muslims experienced political humiliation at the hands of non-Muslims. The very promise of the Holy Quran to give Muslims victory in the world provided they remained faithful to Islam seemed to have become negated by the experience of history itself. This shock, at once political, social and religious, was the source of a series of reactions of differing natures, ranging from the 'reform' movements, which sought to purify Islam, to various forms of Mahdiism, which saw in the corruption of the times a confirmation of the teachings of the Quran about the latter days, and to out-and-out secularism, which, however, did not gain any notable followers until the present century.

The unitary nature of Islam, combined with the nature of the political shock received from Western domination, has made political considerations a major aspect of the religious thought and writing of many contemporary Arabs. Strangely enough, this emphasis has been fortified in the twentieth century by the final political humiliation of the Arabs in Palestine at the hands of a movement which is itself inseparable from religion, despite its fiercely nationalistic and often secular character. The tragedy of Palestine, which for the Arabs was the final confirmation of the immorality of Western politics, emphasized at the same time for many of them the religious aspect of political activity and the pertinence of the political expression of religious sentiments even in the modern world. Palestine has become for the Arabs at once the supreme political issue and the tracing upon the canvas of history of the image of traditional accounts of eschatological events of the greatest religious importance relating to the city of Jerusalem.

The political preoccupations of the Arabs in the nineteenth century, combined with the development of a sense of frustration and also a sense of cultural weakness *vis-à-vis* the West, resulted finally in the attempt to adopt Western patterns of nationalism. The fire of Arab nationalism, first lit by a group of Western-educated Arabs mostly from Syria and also mostly Christian, soon transformed the political life of the Arab World. First of all it helped to break up the Ottoman Empire, then to bring independence to various Arab states, and finally to bring about the movement to seek to unify them, this last phase remaining still in the stage of trial and experiment. But even this force, which was originally of a purely Western and secularist origin, became gradually Muslimized as it penetrated the masses, to the extent that today Arabism, or *'urūbah*, is identified closely by the majority of the common people almost automatically with Islam.[2] For a simple Arab in the street, any Muslim who knows a few verses of the Quran and can perform his prayers is considered somehow to be 'an Arab', for in his mind to be Arab and to be Muslim are the same. Even in educated circles in such countries as Egypt and Algeria, many people closely identify national and Islamic bonds and affiliations. Politics remains inseparable from religion and a great deal of the religious thinking of the Arabs has been devoted during the past century to political facets of Islam and the Arab World.

The attack of the West upon the Arab World, aside from its political effects, was also a direct attack against Islam as a religion. The Arab has remained conscious of the fact that ever since his political subjugation his religion and his culture have been the target of innumerable assaults, ranging from out-and-out slander by older missionaries and orientalists to much more subtle techniques of 'de-Islamicizing' the minds of Muslim youth in Western-owned and directed educational institutions in the Arab World. Much of Muslim religious thought, therefore, took an apologetic turn from late in the nineteenth century, and gradually there came into being a certain type of Muslim religious thinker who had already unconsciously lost the intellectual battle to modernism and the West, and was now seeking only to defend his faith by showing that somehow every fashionable thought of the time had been Islamic before being adopted by the West. Even discoveries of modern science, which, of course, soon become stale and outmoded, were traced back to the Quran as if to show that the grandeur of the Quran resides in anticipating this or that discovery of physics or biology.[3] The apologetic attitude became, because of the incessant attacks of the West, an almost ubiquitous aspect of the religious thought and writings of modernized Arabs, and to this day it remains, along with the political preoccupation mentioned above, of importance in a certain type of religious writing that is read widely by the modernized classes of society.

The attack made upon Islam hastened another tendency which had been inaugurated in the twelfth/eighteenth century in the heartland of the Arab World by Muḥammad ibn ʿAbd al-Wahhāb and others to 'purify' Islam by returning to the sources of the religion and doing away with the later developments of the Islamic tradition, both intellectual and artistic. Had there not been the shock of Western domination, this movement would have probably developed along lines very different from those which it actually took.[4] As it was, frustration in the face of complete domination by the West forced this movement to become more and more the rallying point for the well-known 'reformist' movement associated with the names of such men as ʿAbd al-Raḥmān al-Kawākibī, Jamāl al-Dīn al-Afghānī (or Astarābādī) and Muḥammad ʿAbduh and Rashīd Riḍā, to the extent that, with Rashīd Riḍā, the intellectual background of the reform of the *Salafiyyah*—as his school was called—was nearly the same as that of the Wahhābīs.[5] In both cases there was, along with a positive emphasis upon the *Sharīʿah*, an opposition to Sufism and the mystical life, to Islamic philosophy and to nearly the whole Islamic intellectual tradition. A 'rationalism' was developed which was combined with 'puritanism' and based upon a juridical and theological attitude which drew much from the writings of Ibn Taymiyyah and his students and which limited the vast horizons of Islamic intellectual life to a small portion of its traditional expanse. The effect of this type of religious thinking among the educated classes in the Arab World is still considerable, especially in the Arab Near East. The Maghrib of the Arab World, however, has been to some extent spared from this wave which swept over Egypt and Syria, not to speak of Wahhābī Saudi Arabia, during the past century.

In opposition to this fundamentalist and puritanical tendency, there developed gradually among the Arabs from the beginning of this century another mode of thought, which preached various degrees of secularism and ranged from mild defences of Western civilization to the writings of Salāmah Mūsā and the early Ṭaha Ḥusayn, who preached the complete adoption of Western culture and a total break with the sacred ambience of traditional Islam. Of course at the very moment when such men began to defend Western culture and secularism, others like Muṣṭafā Ṣādiq al-Rāfiʿī, Muṣṭafa Luṭfī al-Manfalūṭī and Shakīb Arsalān rose and violently attacked their writings. Nevertheless, views similar to those of the secularists have continued to be held by a certain number of influential men, and the present situation of Islam among certain classes of Arab society today cannot be understood without this background, although the present supporters of such a position are of a type somewhat different from the earlier secularists.

In addition to the tendencies and movements already mentioned, another reaction began among the Arabs, mostly after the Second World War, which has modified greatly the effect of these earlier movements. This new reaction was the disenchantment with the West and the realization of its moral bankruptcy, made so evident by the atrocities of the World War and later in the Palestine war and its aftermath.[6] The blind admiration of the West espoused by so many of the 'leaders' of the previous generation gave way to doubt about the value of the civilization for whose sake the Arabs were asked to forsake their own religion and way of life. Some men, like Ṭaha Ḥusayn, even recanted openly in their later writings and expressed serious misgivings about Western civilization and its fruits. This awareness, which is still in the process of transforming the Arab image of the West, has a profound effect upon the role and function of religion among the Arabs, for it must be remembered that since the nineteenth century it has always been on the strength of arguments drawn from Western sources, and by appealing to the success of the West, that Arabs have been asked, and in fact are still being asked by certain purblind leaders of the blind, to abandon their own tradition.

In the Arab World today, besides the purely intellectual and mental factors expressed in currents of thought and affecting religion on its articulate plane, there are factors of a social and economic nature and elements dealing with everyday life that have as much—if not more—effect upon religious life as philosophical and theological ideas. In fact, today in the Islamic world in general and the Arab World in particular, Islam is being corroded more by the penetration of foreign modes of everyday living than by the scientific or agnostic philosophical ideas which have affected Christianity so greatly since the Renaissance. One of the best means of gauging the intensity of Islamic religious life is to study the degree to which the *Sharīʿah*, in its full meaning and embracing all of life, is applied in a particular ambience. In its formal and legalistic aspect, the *Sharīʿah* is applied in varying degrees, from countries like Saudi Arabia and Kuwait, which use only Shariʿite law, to lands like Tunisia, where much of the law is derived from European codes. On the juridical level there is discernible a complex pattern which, for the most part, shows the attempt of most Arab governments to modify the teachings of the *Sharīʿah* but to remain as much as possible within its injunctions and principles.[7]

But the more difficult and profound problem is to study to what degree the mode of life, which was once dictated totally by the *Sharīʿah*, has become secularized. Here one will discover that, surprisingly enough, even in countries where non-Shariʿite laws have been introduced, the concept of secular law or the secularization of life remains singularly alien to the mind of the vast majority of Arabs, save for a few who are thoroughly Westernized. But the encroachment of the kind of mundane and frivolous life which is characteristic of modern industrial societies is to be seen in larger Arab cities. The breaking of the injunctions of the *Sharīʿah* concerning such questions as adultery or the use of alcoholic drinks is an ever more frequent phenomenon in big cities, even by people who consider themselves definitely Muslim and who would protest violently if classified otherwise, but who are generally unaware of the contradictions involved in their manner of living. The modernized Arab, like his Persian or Turkish counterpart, is drawn away from religion more through the temptation to create a sensuous and false 'paradise' around himself than by the attempt to play the role of the divinity like an agnostic Western philosopher. For Islam, the danger comes more from men so engulfed by the life of the senses and mundanity as to forget completely the sacred aspect of life taught by religion than from the type of rationalistic philosopher who in the Renaissance destroyed the unity of Christendom and weakened the hold of faith upon men. The *Sharīʿah* continues to be respected as the concrete expression of God's Will, but more and more men in the big cities allow its hold upon their lives to be compromised by the penetration of completely un-Islamic modes of acting and living.[8]

One of the important aspects of Islam in contemporary life among the Arabs has been the appearance of movements which stand for the re-establishment of the full and complete reign of the *Sharīʿah* over the every-day life of Muslims. These movements range from the Istiqlāl party in Morocco, which has also definite political and social programmes, to the Ikhwān al-Muslimīn, the most important movement of this kind to appear during the past decade in the Arab World. The writings of the intellectual élite of this movement, such as Sayyid Quṭb, are based most of all upon a renewed and vigorous application of the *Sharīʿah* to the whole of human life. The persistence of the influence of this movement, even among the young, reveals a strong desire on the part of a significant portion of even the modernized classes for a moral revivification and renewal. The continuing appeal of men like Ḥasan al-Bannā' and Sayyid Quṭb is due not so much to their intellectual analyses of various contemporary problems, analyses which are often oblivious of the true nature of some of the questions involved, as to their firm belief in the *Sharīʿah* and to their own personal example of adherence to the *Sharīʿah*. The existence of movements such as that of the Ikhwān, despite its naivety *vis-à-vis* the problems posed by the modern world, reveals the continuing hold of religion upon public life in its economic, social and political aspects, not to speak of the inner life of men.

As far as political life in the contemporary Arab World is concerned, its ever greater Islamicization, in spite of existing revolutionary tendencies which bring into power alien forms of government often with anti-Islamic ideologies, is truly amazing. The nationalist leaders are usually forced to come to terms more and more with the Islamic views of the masses, who keep a constant pressure upon them.[9] And many of the leaders themselves combine leftist political tendencies with very strong Islamic convictions. One observes in the Arab World today not only traditional rulers who are devout Muslims or at least espouse the cause of Islam publicly, but also the most revolutionary governments which combine an extreme 'leftist' policy with a degree of adherence to the *Sharīʿah* and the Islamic tradition which seems outwardly incongruent and amazes many a Western observer who has prepared *a priori* criteria, drawn from his own experience in the West, to study the Arab World.[10] The European type of nationalism, therefore, which is by nature against the universalism of Islam, which did much to weaken Islam in the early phases of Arab nationalism, and which has produced anti-Islamic tendencies in many non-Arab Muslim countries, seems after several decades to converge paradoxically enough toward the Islamic ethos within many parts of the Arab World today, although it has done much to alienate Muslim peoples from each other and to dissect and divide the heritage of Islam, which belongs to all Muslim peoples by right.

Parallel with secularizing forces of every kind, one observes forces at play which seek to re-assert Islam in the social and political field. Furthermore, in recent years there have also become discernible tendencies which seek to achieve the same on the intellectual plane. The past few decades have witnessed the turning of the interest of many men of letters to religion and religious subjects, to the extent that some of the best known among them, such as ʿAbbās Maḥmūd al-ʿAqqād and Ṭaha Ḥusayn, not known in their earlier writings for their interest in religion, have written later in life several biographical studies of the Prophet and the Companions, or works on other specifically religious themes. This tendency complements the continuing flow of religious literature from the religious centres, especially al-Azhar, and by graduates of such centres.[11] It also complements a small but growing number of writings by men in other walks of life who are deeply concerned with religion. One of the best known religious works to have appeared in the Arab World during the past decades, the *City of Wrong*, was written by Kāmil Ḥusayn,[12] an Egyptian surgeon.

This revival of intellectual interest in Islam, which of course does not by any means please the modernized and secularized so-called 'intellectuals', usually of ultra-nationalistic or Marxist tendencies, is complemented by a renewal of interest in the whole tradition of Islamic thought, especially philosophy and Sufism. Traditional Islamic philosophy was revived in Egypt by Jamāl al-Dīn al-Afghānī[13] after centuries during which it had ceased to be taught in most Arab *madrasahs* and remained a living intellectual tradition only in Persia and adjacent areas. During this century, an avid study of Islamic philosophy has been carried out in the Arab World, and especially

Egypt, by such men as Muṣṭafā ʿAbd al-Rāziq, Ibrāhīm Madkour, ʿAbd al-Raḥmān Badawī, Fu'ād al-Ahwānī, Muḥammad Abū Rīdah, ʿUthmān Amīn and others. The efforts of such men must be seen not only as simple academic scholarship but also as an attempt to revive the intellectual heritage of Islam. Their work certainly possesses a religious significance and is related in this sense to the writings of men of letters and other classes of educated Arabs on religious subjects. The ever-growing interest in Islamic philosophy in the Arab World is related to the general desire for a new self-discovery on the part of the modern educated classes after the disillusionment with the West, which indeed becomes ever more intense with the rapid decline and, in fact, disintegration of modern Western society and culture as it has been known during the past few centuries.

It must be remembered that the intensity of religious life among the Arabs cannot be gauged at all by studying simply the various reactions of the Arabs to the modern world. One must also study the unchanged but ever-living traditional modes of religious life. Most Western scholars, who as already mentioned are trained by profession to study only change and who have made an *a priori* judgment that only that which changes is significant, have tended to neglect the permanent elements in the traditional religious life of Muslims in general and of the Arabs in particular, and have exaggerated the importance of the so-called 'reform' movement. In reality, today, the influence of the 'reformists' in the Arab World is far less than that of the traditional Muslim authorities both past and present. One would like to know, for example, which work of the modernist 'reformers' compares in popularity with those of an al-Ghazzālī. The heart of the religious life resides and will continue to reside in traditional forms and practices, in the inner being of individuals for whom Islam means an approach to the Divine and a sanctification of human life, and not a mere asset with which to further particular worldly causes, whether they be political, social or economic.

To understand religion in the contemporary Arab World one must also understand the meaning of the still-continuing congregational prayers held in every city, of the countless pilgrims who continue to be attracted to the spiritual pole of Mecca, and of the millions who visit sanctuaries, from Mulay Idris in Morocco to Ra's al-Ḥusayn in Cairo and the Shiʿite sanctuaries of Najaf and Karbala. One must realize the vitality and the continuous subsistence of traditional religious teaching among both Sunnis and Shiʿites. One must be aware of the continuity of the intellectual traditions of Islam among the *ʿulamā'* (religious scholars) and the traditional learned classes, and of the life of faith (*īmān*) among the vast majority of the community, for whom prayer and devotion still constitute the celestial pattern into which human life is integrated. Any changes or reactions caused by the domination of the West and the political and cultural tragedies that have followed can only be understood in the light of the dominant presence of the still-living tradition of Islam. For every Arab, young or old, who speaks of secularism or socialism or Marxism there are many for whom no 'ism' can ever replace the all-embracing reality of Islam. To grasp the religious life of the Arabs in its fullness one must be aware not only of the 'renovators', 'reformers' and rebels whose harm to the traditional order can hardly be over-emphasized, but also of the innumerable elements of permanence and continuity implied by the very notion of a living tradition and displayed fully by Islam in its manifestation among both Arabs and non-Arabs.

Also, in speaking of the religious life of contemporary Arabs it is not possible to overlook Sufism, which lies at the heart of the Islamic tradition and which has acted throughout Islamic history as the source for spiritual and religious regeneration, being the invisible origin of even external and social movements of a religious nature.[14] Strangely enough, however, the majority of modern accounts of religion in the Arab World fail to take account of this basic element, and neglect the Sufi orders and their rejuvenation during the past century, with the sole exception of the Sanūsiyyah Order, which has been studied more often precisely because of its puritanical and 'Wahhābī' tendencies.[15]

The fact is that during the nineteenth century, along with the gradual penetration of modernism and secularism into the Arab World and the rise of the modernist 'reformers' about whom so many studies exist in European languages, there occurred also a genuine renewal of life within several of the Sufi orders by great saints who were in fact 'renewers' (*mujaddid*) in the traditional meaning of the word, which is very different from 'reformer' (*muṣliḥ*) in its modern sense.[16] The renewal of life of the Shādhiliyyah Order and the founding of certain new branches and orders such as the Yashrūṭiyyah, the Badawiyyah and the Madaniyyah, mostly in the Arab Middle East, and the Darqāwiyyah[17] in the Maghrib, marked a revival of an intense spiritual life that has affected the whole religious life of the community to this day.

During this century the same forces of inner renewal can be observed. The influence of the remarkable Algerian Darqāwī master, Shaykh Aḥmad al-ʿAlawī, who founded a new branch of the Shādhiliyyah Order, spread beyond the confines of the Maghrib and even the Arab World[18] and is felt far and wide to this day. Anyone who has frequented a gathering of the Shādhiliyyah-ʿAlawiyyah Order in Damascus or Aleppo has become aware of the degree of influence of this master and the extent of his living grace (*barakah*) within branches of the order founded by his disciples in many Arab lands as far away from each other as Syria, the Yemen and Morocco.

In Egypt also, almost contemporary with Shaykh al-ʿAlawī, another Shādhili master, Salāmah Ḥasan al-Raḍī, founded the Ḥāmidiyyah branch of the order, which soon began to attract many into its fold.[19] Its emphasis upon both the practice of the *Sharīʿah* and spiritual discipline has made it one of the main spiritual forces in contemporary Egypt, attracting adepts from many walks of life, including the young in universities.[20] Its current role in Egypt exemplifies the basic importance of Sufism in the contemporary religious life of many parts of the Arab World.

The events of the past two or three decades have caused major social and political strains in the Arab World and have accentuated many of the tendencies alluded to above as well as causing new ones to come into being. A sense of bewilderment combined with emotional irrationality has captivated the minds of certain men as a result of the extreme despair and unbelievable stress caused by the injustice brought upon the Arabs by the Palestine tragedy and its aftermath, including all the extremist forms of government that this event helped to bring into being. Also, an ever greater degree of destruction of the religious quality of life is to be observed in the bigger cities, especially among notable segments of the youth drawn to the frivolities and trivialities of modern life. Furthermore, out-and-out secularist and anti-Islamic political ideologies have gained power in certain regions of the Arab World.

But along with the growth of all these anti-traditional forces and tendencies one can notice a marked renewal of interest in religion, especially among the youth. It is enough to compare the number of young people who used to visit a place such as the tomb of Ibn ʿArabī in Damascus or Ra's al-Ḥusayn in Cairo two decades ago with the number who are seen there now. Both Sufism and the Shariʿite practices of Islam have been attracting numerous people of late, not only from the traditional classes in the countryside but also from urban classes that only a generation ago showed little interest in religion.[21] Along with the young Arabs studying in the West or in Western-oriented universities in the East who are becoming infatuated with various fashions of Western thought ranging from positivism to Marxism, there are those who are searching again for their own roots and looking within their own tradition for an answer to the dilemma of human existence in an inhuman world whose overt contradictions become more apparent every day. The rise of religious interest in the Arab World during the past decade or two is a phenomenon of central importance which can hardly be brushed aside as a momentary emotional reaction before the inevitable onslaught of complete secularism, as secularist historians would wish to do.

In reality, what has happened during this period is that on the one hand the blinding glitter of Western civilization has begun to fade and its innate faults and present difficulties have become more evident, and, on the other hand, the false gods for whose sake the modernized Arabs sought to brush Islam aside have failed them in the worst way imaginable. The defeat in the 1967 war and the humiliations before and after cannot possibly be blamed in any way upon traditional Islamic institutions. It is the failure of the modern ideologies whose adoption dates back to the nineteenth century that has now come into the open. For many an Arab, recent events have only strengthened their serious disillusionment with the programme of simply aping the West. Rather, they see recent tragedies as a divine punishment for their having forsaken Islam. They have come to view all these difficulties as trials which, according to the teachings of the Quran, the individual Muslim as well as Muslim society as a whole must pass through in this world. They have also come to realize that in order to return to Islam they must re-discover Islam in all its fullness, not in its atrophied and apologetic form as presented by so many of the modernist 'reformers' during the last centuries.

On the scholarly level also, a new class, small but of considerable significance, has come into being which is traditional and at the same time well acquainted with the West without being its slavish imitator. Both on the popular and the intellectual level the awareness of the necessity of taking religion seriously is to be discerned in many circles, whose members thus return to the living stream of the authentic Islamic tradition in both its Shariʿite and its Sufi aspects.

Today the Arab World stands at a most crucial stage of its history. There are still those who would like to secularize the Arab world and separate it from Islam as much as possible. But because Arabic was chosen as the vehicle of the Quranic revelation and the Arabs as the first propagators of Islam, the destiny of the Arabs remains inseparable from that of the whole Islamic world and in fact from the earthly manifestation of Islam itself. Moreover, the future well-being of the Arabs depends upon the degree to which they are able to remember their true identity and to remain faithful to the task which their identification with Islam upon the historical scene has placed upon their shoulders. Inasmuch as it is impossible for men to remove the imprint of the Divine upon the human order, Islam continues today as the most powerful and enduring motivating force within the Arab soul and mind, and an ever-present factor in Arab life in all its aspects. It is the source to which all things must of necessity return, even if they wander away momentarily, and it continues as an objective norm which moulds the lives of, and at the same time serves as the ideal for, the vast majority of Arabs, both individually and collectively. Islam remains a living reality without which it is impossible to understand the Arabs today. To speak of the Arabs is to speak of a people whose language is that of the Quran, and the fabric of whose soul has been woven over the ages from elements of the Quranic revelation in a manner that makes their contemporary history inseparable from Islam and the Islamic universe into which most Arabs still are born and in which they live and die.

Notes to Chapter 8

1. There is also, of course, a sizeable Arab Christian population whose religious life deserves to be studied seriously and in itself. But in this essay we shall confine ourselves to Islam, which, besides being the religion of the vast majority of Arabs, has provided the cultural matrix over the ages for the other religious minorities among them, such as the Christians and the Jews.

2. 'Even today it is still true to say that, to an Arab, Muslim means totally Arab . . .' L. Gardet, *Mohammedanism*, trans. by W. Burridge, New York, 1961, p. 147.

'The synthesis is close: an identification, at times unconscious, of Islam and Arabism.' W. C. Smith, *Islam in Modern History*, p. 99.

3. The writings of such men as, for example, Farīd Wajdī, found mostly in the *al-Azhar Journal*, were once very popular in the Arab World and in fact throughout the

Muslim world. We have dealt with this attitude in many of our writings. See, for example, S. H. Nasr, *Islamic Studies.*

4. This point has been emphasized by H. A. R. Gibb. See especially his well-known *Modern Trends in Islam.*

5. On the 'reformists' there are numerous writings by Western scholars, including the well-known works of Gibb and Smith cited above; also A. Hourani, *Arabic Thought in the Liberal Ages*, London, 1962; and K. Cragg, *Counsels in Contemporary Islam*, Edinburgh, 1965.

Arab authors have also devoted a number of studies to the reformers. See Aḥmad Amīn, *Zuʿamāʾ al-iṣlāḥ fi'l-ʿaṣr al-ḥadīth*, Cairo, 1948; and Tawfīq al-Ṭawīl, 'al-Fikr al-dīnī al-islāmī fi'l-ʿālam al-ʿarabī' in *al-Fikr al-ʿarabī fi miʾah sanah*, Beirut, 1967.

On the 'reformers', Tawfīq al-Ṭawīl writes, 'It is possible to say that in the Wahhābī movement there appeared the emphasis upon the doctrine of Unity (*tawḥīd*), in the Sanūsī movement the connection of the religious call to effort and action with results sought in the life of this world, in Kawākibī the battle against political oppression and the call to Arab nationalism on the one hand and to socialism on the other, in Jamāl al-Dīn al-Afghānī the sacred battle against European colonialism, in Muḥammad ʿAbduh the placing of reason as the criterion for religious thought, and in Rashīd Riḍā zeal in spreading the call of Islam.' *op. cit.*, p. 326. This 'positive' evaluation is characteristic of a certain type of modernized Arab who sees the role of the 'reformers' completely in a positive light and views them as the saviours of Islam during their own days, forgetting the innate weakness of the position of this group *vis-à-vis* Western fads and trends, and their disregard for some aspect or other of the sacred tradition of Islam.

6. See H. A. R. Gibb, 'The Reaction of the Middle East against Western Culture', in his *Studies on the Civilization of Islam*, ed. by S. J. Shaw and W. R. Polk, London, 1962, Chap. 14. J. Bercque has also analyzed this tendency in many of his writings.

7. See N. J. Coulson, *A History of Islamic Law*, Edinburgh, 1964, Part Three.

8. On the central importance of the *Sharīʿah*, see S. H. Nasr, *Ideals and Realities of Islam*, Chap. IV.

9. 'As soon as the nationalists come to power, there opens a hidden inner conflict between the handful of leaders and the relentless omnipresent pressure of those surrounding them, a pressure which has become all the more insistent since the moral bankruptcy of the West and of the Westernized classes has become apparent.' H. A. R. Gibb, *Studies on the Civilization of Islam*, p. 330.

10. A country like Syria is amazing in its combining of 'leftist' political programmes with a remarkable degree of adherence to the *Sharīʿah.*

11. Even as far as Azharite writings are concerned, there are without doubt a greater amount of activity and a wider dissemination among various classes of society of writings by such men as Muḥammad al-Bahiy, Shaikh Shaltūt and others than there were before.

12. *Qariyah Ẓālimah*, trans. by K. Cragg as *The City of Wrong*, London, 1959.

13. See M. Mahdi, 'Islamic Philosophy in Contemporary Islamic Thought', in *God and Man in Contemporary Islamic Thought*, pp. 99 ff.

14. For example, it should be recalled that Ḥasan al-Bannā', the founder of the Ikhwān al-Muslimīn, was a member of a branch of the Shādhiliyyah Order in his youth.

15. See, for example, N. Z. Ziadeh, *Sanusiyah*, Leiden, 1958. As an exception, one can cite the scholarly study of J. Spencer Trimingham, *The Sufi Orders in Islam*, Oxford, 1971, pp. 110 ff., where the traditional revivals within the Sufi orders have been at least listed.

16. Most religious 'reforms' of the kind studied and debated so often by modern scholars are deformations rather than reformations, by men who want to reform religion rather than to reform themselves. 'The only means of "reforming" religion is to reform oneself.' F. Schuon, 'No Activity Without Truth', *Studies in Comparative Religion*, Autumn, 1969, p. 199; also *The Sword of Gnosis*, p. 34.

17. See T. Burckhardt (trans.) *Letters of a Sufi Master*, London, 1969.

18. Thanks to the beautiful exposition of M. Lings, *A Sufi Saint of The Twentieth Century*.

19. See M. al-Kāhin al-Fāsī, *al-Ṭabaqāt al-kubra'l-shādhiliyyah*, Cairo, 1929; and ʿAbd al-ʿAlīm Maḥmūd, *al-Madrasat al-shādhiliyyat al-ḥadīthah*, Cairo, 1969.

20. 'La modération qui caractérise la Hāmidiyya, laquelle reste attachée à la tradition de la Shādhiliyya, tout en l'adoptant à la vie de l'Egypte moderne, explique pourquoi tant de jeunes gens, parmi lesquels on compte des universitaires, se sentent attirés par cette *ṭariqa*, qui est une des expressions les plus remarquables du soufisme.' E. Bannerth, 'Aspects de la Shādhiliyya', *Mélanges de i'Institut Dominicain des Etudes Orientales*, (Cairo), Vol. 11, 1972, pp. 248–49.

21. 'Finally, many educated men have recently become greatly interested in several aspects of religion. Professors, judges, higher civil servants and army officers have been meeting spontaneously and unobtrusively in mosques and private homes to read the Koran together, discuss mysticism and even to perform the famous *dhikr* . . . such groups seem to have increased considerably in the last decade or so.' M. Berger, *Islam in Egypt Today*, Cambridge, 1970, p. 74. The same holds true for most countries of the Arab Near East.

Chapter 9

Islam in Persia, Yesterday and Today

The situation of Islam in the Arab World differs from its situation in the rest of the Islamic world in that the Arab Muslim, even if modernized, does not see in his pre-Islamic past anything but the 'age of ignorance' (*al-jāhiliyyah*), which he can hardly extol even in a modernistic and nationalistic *milieu*, and also in that the contemporary Arab Muslim cannot separate himself from his ethnic and linguistic attachment to the earthly vessel of the Quranic revelation.[1] In contrast to this situation, the non-Arab Muslims have a distinct pre-Islamic past completely different from the background within which Islam was revealed, and do not share the ethnic and linguistic bonds with the earthly embodiment of the Quranic revelation, at least not to the same extent as the Arabs.

This distinction is particularly true of the Persians, who had a brilliant pre-Islamic civilization of great spiritual and artistic beauty, and played a major role in the very foundation of Islamic civilization. They and the Arabs (*al-ʿarab wa'l-ʿajam* in traditional Islamic sources) together founded Islamic civilization and have influenced nearly every phase of its subsequent history. In fact, although Islamic thought and culture succeeded in freeing itself from becoming only 'Arabic' or 'Persian' during the Umayyad and Abbasid periods, both of these peoples left their indelible mark upon its historical deployment and development. The Persians, on the one hand, played a central role in building Islamic civilization[2] and, on the other, were able to integrate within the universal perspective of Islam many elements of their pre-Islamic past, which thus became completely Islamicized. They therefore not only became thoroughly Islamic and have remained one of the most productive of Islamic peoples intellectually and artistically, but they were also able to preserve their own identity and remain distinctly Persian, creating a second cultural focus within the unity of Islamic civilization, which in its classical phase and almost up to modern times could be divided culturally into the Arabic and the Iranian zones. The situation of Islam in present-day Persia, and modernism's threat to the remarkable unity created between Persia's ancient past and Islam, cannot therefore be understood without reference to the historical background and an analysis of the forces and elements that were integrated to create the classical Islamic culture of Persia.[3]

When we look at Persia today we see that it is one of the most overwhelmingly Muslim countries in the world.[4] The life of the vast majority of Persians today is dominated and moulded completely by Islam, while, at the same time, the religious and cultural life of the country naturally reflects the long history of the Persian people. Because the Persians became thoroughly Islamicized and yet created a distinctly Persian Islamic culture related on a certain plane with their pre-Islamic past,[5] to understand their present-day religious life—particularly in the form of Ithnā ʿAsharī or Twelve-Imam Shiʿism, which is dominant in Persia today—it is necessary to cast a brief glance at the religious history of the people who have lived on the Iranian plateau during the past three thousand years.

Persia has been both a centre from which major religious influences have radiated and a cross-roads at which the religious traditions of the Mediterranean world and Asia have met, resulting often in new currents of religious life. Having originally belonged to the same ethnic and linguistic stock as the Aryan conquerors of India, the early Iranians who settled on the plateau possessed a religion akin to that of the Vedas. From this early background there arose the reform of Zoroaster and the establishment of the specifically Iranian religion of Zoroastrianism. Although the dates of Zoroaster are still much debated, there is no doubt that in the fifth century BC his teachings became the official religion of the Persian empire. The sacred book of Zoroastrianism, the *Avesta*, is the most precious religious document of the early history of Persia as well as a basic source for the study of the Iranian languages. Zoroastrianism, with its firm belief in the angelic world, its accent upon the moral dimension of human existence, its emphasis upon the reality of the after-life and Last Judgment, and its stress upon the purity of the elements and the sacred character of human life, left an imprint both on the later religious life of Western Asia and on the general outlook of the Persians.[6]

The positive qualities which this religion implanted in the souls of the Persians survived and became transmuted into the Islamic mould after Zoroastrianism itself had decayed and lost the spiritual struggle against the new forces of Islam. For example, the care that many devout Persians take in keeping their clothing, food and habitat clean in a ritual sense, sometimes even over-emphasizing this element of religion, is founded upon an old Zoroastrian teaching reinforced by the emphasis of Islam upon cleanliness. Whatever survived of Zoroastrianism in the Persian soul was, however, thoroughly Islamized and interpreted in the light of the unitary point of view of Islam.

From the matrix of Zoroastrianism, which is the stable and orthodox background of Iranian religions, there grew several religious movements which had world-wide repercussions and also shook the foundations of Zoroastrianism itself. With the fall of the Achaemenian Empire, Hellenistic influences spread throughout the domain of the Persian people. This cultural movement was combined with a religious one known as Mithraism (considered as a distinct religious movement and not general devotion to Mithra, which ante-dated Zoroastrianism itself) which itself contained important Hellenistic elements. The mystery cult of Mithra, which spread as far West as Germany and Scandinavia, was a synthesis of Zoroastrian, Hellenistic, Babylonian and Anatolian elements, as well as pre-Zoroastrian Persian religious practices. If, for the world at large, this religious movement meant the spread of Iranian religious elements, for Persia itself it implied perhaps more than anything else the establishment of a religious sanction for the syncretic cultural life through which the Persians were now passing as a result of the conquests of Alexander and the establishment of Seleucid rule.

During the Parthian period, Zoroastrianism and the proper Persian cultural tradition began to reassert themselves until, with the advent of the Sassanids, the religion of Zoroaster became once again the official state religion, remaining in this position until the fall of the Sassanid empire. Nevertheless, its authority did not go unchallenged even on the religious plane. In the third century AD, a second world-sweeping Iranian mystery religion, Manichaeism, came into being. Its founder, Mani, first found favour with the Sassanid ruler but was finally put to death through the opposition of the Zoroastrian priesthood. His cult nevertheless spread from China to France and in Persia itself gained many adherents. At once a socially revolutionary and a religiously mystical movement, it marked a major protest against established religious institutions. Although some of its cosmogonic and cosmological teachings found a place in certain forms of Islamic philosophy, for Persians of the later period Manichaeism has appeared as a rebellion against religious authority. It has never enjoyed the same status as Zoroastrianism, from which it came into being and against which it revolted.

The Sassanid period was also witness to other religious movements such as Mazdakism, a 'religious communism' known today mostly through what its enemies, both Zoroastrian and Christian, wrote against it. This movement, which was soon crushed, was again a protest against the Zoroastrian social order and foretold the collapse of this order which occurred with the coming of Islam. Also at this time there developed within Zoroastrianism the philosophico-religious school known as Zurvanism, which indicates a blend of Iranian religious thought with certain Greek philosophical ideas. Finally, it must be remembered that through rivalry with the Byzantines the Sassanids encouraged Oriental Christian sects, especially the Nestorians. These sects were given a free hand to establish schools and missions throughout the Sassanid empire, with the result that notable Christian communities came into existence in Persia and became an important minority religious community in the Islamic period. The Jews also had had several centres in Persia from Achaemenian times, and continued to thrive under both Zoroastrian and Muslim rule. The tolerance toward minority religions shown by Cyrus the Great has been with few exceptions the rule in the religious history of Persia.

The major spiritual transformation in Persia came, strangely enough, not from one of the new members of the family of Iranian religions but from a religion of Abrahamic and Semitic background, namely Islam. Although the military defeat of the Sassanids before the Arab armies was a sudden and rapid process, the spiritual struggle between Islam and Zoroastrianism was a gradual one and did not really terminate until the fourth/tenth century. This fact itself indicates that the Persians accepted Islam, not through force, as is claimed by some modern historians, but because of an inner spiritual need. When the Persians regained their political independence from the caliphate there were still very sizeable Zoroastrian communities in Persia. But instead of showing any inclination to return to this tradition, the newly independent Persian rulers became themselves the champions of the spread of Islam, while insisting on the independence of the literary and cultural life of Persia. Most of the Muslim lands of Asia have, in fact, been Islamicized through the intermediary of the Persian form of Islam. And to this day, when a Persian thinks of the domain of 'Persian culture' he sees before him nearly the whole of the Eastern lands of Islam, from the Western borders of the Iranian plateau to Western China, with Iraq as an intermediary realm where the Persian, Arabic and, later, Turkish elements met.

During early Islamic history Persia was dominated by the Sunni form of Islam. In fact it was from Khurasan that the theological defence of Sunnism was made during the tenth and eleventh centuries, by such masters of theology as al-Juwaynī and al-Ghazzālī, when many other lands of Islam were dominated by Shiʿism. Yet, certain centres in Persia such as Qum were from the beginning Shiʿite and the Persians in general had a particular reverence for the household of the Prophet of Islam from the earliest centuries of Islamic history. The figure of Salmān al-Fārisī, the Persian who in search of the ideal prophet journeyed all the way to Arabia to meet the Prophet and became so close to him as to be called 'one of the members of the household' (*ahl-i bayt*) of the Prophet, has the deepest significance for the religious consciousness of Islamic Persia.[7] During the early centuries, therefore, Persia was at once a major centre of Sunni Islam, producing such scholars and theologians as al-Bukhārī, al-Ghazzālī and Fakhr al-Dīn al-Rāzī, and a land within which important centres of Shiʿism existed, where many of the greatest early Shiʿite theologians such as Ibn Bābūyah and Kulaynī were born and nurtured.

Before the Mongol invasion, a devastating material and social calamity for Persia, the forces of Ismaʿilism were also strong in this land. Although the centre of their power was in the Yemen and later in Egypt, from the third/ninth century onward, there were outstanding philosophers and theologians of this school in Persia, men like Abū Ḥātim al-Rāzī, Ḥamīd al-Dīn al-Kirmānī and Nāṣir-i Khusraw, who have left us so many doctrinal works on Ismaʿilism. Moreover, with the 'resurrection of Alamut', Ismaʿilism gained major political power in Persia and continued to exert political pressure until the destruction of Alamut by Hulagu.

Between the Mongol invasion and the establishment of the Safavids, Persia moved gradually toward Shiʿism through both social, political and purely religious factors marked by the activity of certain Sufi orders and several outstanding Shiʿite theologians.[8] Yet, at the time of the establishment of the Safavids and the recognition of Shiʿism as the official state religion, most of Persia was still Sunni. The change, however, was made relatively rapidly and soon the country became predominantly Shiʿite, although noticeable Sunni elements have survived to this day in such areas as Khurasan and Kurdistan.

Persia was also from the beginning of Islamic history one of the lands in which Sufism, the esoteric and mystical dimension of Islam, spread rapidly and expressed itself in the most striking literary and artistic forms. Some of the greatest early Sufis, like al-Basṭāmī and al-Ḥallāj were Persian, and later the direct influence of Sufism transformed Persian poetry into one of the most universal forms of literature. Both through the direct presence of Sufi orders and through the effect of Sufism upon Persian literature, music, architecture and other forms of art as well as certain social organizations, the spirit of Sufism has left an indelible mark upon many facets of the life of the Persians.[9] It must be remembered, however, that being esoteric in character, Sufism has always preserved its inner teachings for those who have been qualified to follow the Sufi path. It is only the external manifestations of Sufism that have a general cultural and social bearing and are so noticeable a strand in the fabric of Persian life and culture.

It is in the light of this background that we must study the role of Islam in present-day Persia. Because of this long period during which the Persians have become Islamicized in the deepest sense possible, the world view of the Persian today is determined more than anything else by the teachings of Islam. Like other Muslims, the Persian is born, lives and dies with the verses of the Holy Quran echoing in his ears. He sees the world about him in the light of the conception of the Divine and His creation as delineated in the Holy Quran. There is, in fact, in spite of the secularist tendencies of the past fifty years, still no conception of a way of life in which religion is only one element among many or of a world view in which the religious factor is only one dimension. The total world view is religious, and even the apparent negation of religion by certain people has itself a religious significance.

The universe in which the Persian lives, like that of all Muslims, is one created and sustained by Allah, the Omnipotent and Omniscient Creator, Who is at once the Origin and End of all things, the First and the Last. His will reigns supreme over both the world of nature and the lives of men and their societies. He has knowledge of all things and His majesty causes all that is beside Him to melt into nothingness. Yet he has given man free will to pursue his own life and to choose the 'right path' (*al-ṣirāt al-mustaqīm*) of his own accord, without compulsion. The secret of man's life lies between these two logically contradictory assertions, of the absolute Omnipotence of Allah and of man's free will and responsibility before Him as the Supreme Judge.[10]

Every Muslim is aware throughout his life of the ultimate significance of his actions beyond this world of change and corruption. The Persian Muslim, like his other brethren in faith, may, because of his own weakness, sometimes live a life that is mundane and even directly against various Divine injunctions, but he never doubts for one moment the presence of the Divine Command (*al-amr*) and his responsibility to follow it. As already stated for Muslims in general, so also for Persians it can be said that there are some who do not heed the voice of the Divine, but there is practically no one who doubts the presence of 'His voice'. That is why after a life of debauchery a man may become suddenly devout, and even in the midst of the most profane life remains aware of the presence of the transcendent dimension of life.

Inasmuch as the will of God is manifested in Islam in the form of a concrete and all-embracing law, the *Sharīʿah*, the Persian is always aware of the religious character of all facets of life. Since the *Sharīʿah* covers all aspects of human life, to the vast majority of Persians all laws which they encounter and all acts which they perform during their daily lives possess a sacred character even if non-Shariʿite laws have been promulgated in certain domains. Most Persians feel that they are performing a religious duty when they work to make a living, even if the particular work they perform is not itself of a traditional religious nature. By contrast, the small Western-educated classes that have been affected by the Western distinction between the religious and the secular often do not attach this religious significance to their daily work. For them the *Sharīʿah* is identified with specific acts of worship which in fact they rarely perform. But they are a small minority. For most Persians, both the uneducated and the educated, the all-embracing nature of the Divine will which governs all facets of man's life through a sacred law is very much a reality and a permanent factor in their general world view.

The Divine will is also seen by Persian Muslims, as by other Muslims in general, in the world of nature, of which the phenomena, in conformity with the teachings of the Holy Quran, are considered as the 'signs of God'. There is no ultimate distinction between the Divine Law governing men and the laws governing nature, between religious and natural law as understood in the West.[11] Nature is a complementary aspect of the religious reality that is revealed directly through revelation. It can therefore incite the deepest intellectual and contemplative response in the traditional Persian, who turns to it both as a source of enjoyment and as the background for the spiritual life. The very austerity of nature in Persia, the high mountains, the vast deserts, the green valleys hidden high in mountain ranges, evoke an awareness of the transcendent. The visible itself is but a veil for the invisible and the laws of the world of nature but a part of the universal law which of necessity governs all things.

The Persian is also keenly aware of the transient nature of things, a point so often emphasized in Islam. He lives with the reality of death and a realization of the instability of all that surrounds him. For him the angelic world, the hierarchy of spiritual beings that stands above the world of material forms, is a constant reality, one that is emphasized in both the ancient religions of Iran and in Islam. If this world is impermanent and transient, there stands beyond it the permanent and luminous world of angelic substances.[12]

The awareness of the transient nature of this world is combined with a great joy in life and its beauties which reflect the beauty of the higher orders of existence. Few people are given as much to the enjoyment of life's pleasures and beauties as the Persians, but this attitude is always compensated for by the realization that a moment once gone never returns and all that is physical and sensual has an ephemeral character about it. These two attitudes are often reflected even in the distinctly religious activity of chanting the Holy Quran, during which people weep and are carried beyond worldly cares, but which is frequently held in the most beautiful gardens where the best refreshments are served and the voice of the reciter possesses the finest musical quality. At their most spiritual level, these two attitudes are to be found in all Persian Sufi poetry: here one is constantly reminded that the Infinite reflects an aspect of Its beauty at each moment, but because of Its Infinity Its theophanies (*tajalliyāt*) never repeat themselves.[13]

There is also an element of tragedy which characterizes the Persian and which is seen fully in the ethos of Shiʿism. This is not the humanistic tragedy of the later Greeks, a rebellion of man against the gods, associated with the Promethean mentality so characteristic of the decadent period of Greek culture and post-mediaeval Europe, but is a spiritual quality based on man's submission to God and yet his separation from Him.[14] The tragic and sad element (*ḥuzn*), which does not at all negate the aspect of joy (*faraḥ*) in life, is always of a religious character and a basis for contemplation. It is most directly reflected in classical Persian music, where the apparently sad quality is in reality a nostalgia for the Divine. It is a tragedy based on the realization that the human condition contains an apparent contradiction. Man is in desperate need to realize the Divine and to become aware of his own spiritual nature. Yet this realization is made well-nigh impossible by the distance that separates him from the Divine and by his need to await Divine assistance to accomplish this end.[15]

Closely connected with this point of view is the concept of the intermediary and intercessor before God, and the expectation of a future saviour, both so important to Shiʿism; man is in need of an intermediary between himself and God. Even after the descent of a revelation, the role of the intermediary must continue. Therefore, after the Prophet of Islam there must be Imams who act as intermediaries between men of later generations and God. There must also be a future saviour, the *Mahdī*, who will redeem the world from its state of corruption. From the Shiʿite point of view, he too is an Imam, in fact the twelfth Imam of Shiʿism, but an Imam who, although living and present, is in occultation (*ghaybah*) and will not reveal himself until a future moment known only to God. The very expectation of his appearance (*intiẓār*) is a religious virtue. The ideals of appealing to saints and Imams and of patiently awaiting one who will in the future eradicate injustice and corruption and therefore end the hardships of present-day life are constant elements of the Persian religious outlook.

As far as religious institutions and organizations are concerned, the most important centre in the life of the Persians, as in that of other Muslims, is the mosque, whose size varies from the colossal Friday mosques of major cities to single rooms in small towns and villages. Its architecture also varies from ornate tiled mosques to mud structures whose walls are covered by whitewash. In all its forms, the mosque is the centre of both religious and social activity in the community. Its door being always open, it remains a calm sanctuary amid the turmoil of daily life, a place where people wander in to say their prayers as well as to consider a transaction or simply to relax with friends in the contemplative and peaceful atmosphere which the mosque creates. In the cities, in fact, the bigger mosques are nearly always situated in the bazaars and are an inseparable part of daily life.[16]

The mosque is also used for congregational prayers, particularly those of Friday, as well as for special occasions of religious mourning or feasting or funerals. The Friday prayers, however, are less emphasized in Persia than in those Muslim lands where Sunni Islam predominates. This is because in the absence of the *Mahdī* the Friday prayers do not carry any political significance as they do in Sunni Islam, and their importance is not greatly emphasized by the *'ulamā'*. Rather, the religious climate is such that the canonical prayers performed individually and often at home are considered as important as prayers at mosques, so that many who do not go regularly to mosques nevertheless do perform their prayers and other religious rites privately at home.

The role of the mosque differs both between the life of the country dweller and the city dweller, and between that of the traditional and the modern Persian. In the countryside, the *imām* of the mosque often acts as the teacher for elementary education, especially early religious education, and he is the arbitrator in most disputes. After daily prayers, people usually gather about him to pose questions about problems which would otherwise have to be taken to court. In the smaller cities, these customs are retained to a certain degree, but in larger cities both functions, elementary education and judging cases, are performed outside the mosque, although in the second case the arbitrator is himself usually a religious authority. The larger mosques in big cities also perform an educational service on a higher level, in that they are usually affiliated with a religious school or *madrasah* in which more advanced religious education is carried out.

As for the modern educated classes, particularly those who have been educated in the West, as a rule they do not go to mosques except on special occasions. Many of them do make pilgrimages or participate in the mourning of Muḥarram or funeral rites, all of which are usually connected with mosques, but they rarely attend their local mosques for daily prayers. Although there are notable exceptions, one can say that in this aspect of religious life they are sharply distinguished from the rest of Persian society.

The *madrasah* system, which has its roots in the early centuries of Islamic history, is the means whereby the intellectual aspect of the religious tradition is kept alive. In these schools, which are endowed and usually connected with a major mosque, students who have undergone an early religious education continue their studies. They are fully supported by the *madrasah*, receiving accommodation on the premises as well as board and other expenses. There is no pressure on them to finish their studies in a certain period as in modern universities, nor are any specific degrees conferred upon them. Some stay in a *madrasah* for their whole life and, if competent, become teachers in their turn. The students mostly choose the field of the transmitted (*naqlī*) sciences, studying law, the principles of jurisprudence, Quranic exegesis, *ḥadīth*, etc. Some, however, choose the intellectual (*ʿaqlī*) sciences, and pursue logic, Islamic philosophy, theology, etc.

The largest *madrasah* system today, which is in Qum, has over six thousand students, and there are other major centres in Mashhad, Tehran, Isfahan and several other cities. Moreover, besides the official lessons taught in the *madrasah*, classes are often held in the homes of individual professors and masters, often in more advanced phases of study. These classes are particularly important in the field of traditional Islamic philosophy or theosophy (*ḥikmah*) as well as in gnosis (*ʿirfān*). In these private circles, many who do not belong to the *madrasahs* also participate, including often some who have had a modern, rather than a purely traditional, education. One could even say that most of the teaching of the Islamic intellectual sciences in Persia today is performed outside formal institutions and in private circles.

Shrines, or tombs of the Shiʿite Imams, their descendants and Sufi saints, play a major role in the life of all classes of Persians. They consist usually of a mausoleum and a mosque, often with a *madrasah* and a library attached, and are supported by endowments and donations. Of those within Persia itself, the most important is that of the eighth Imam, ʿAlī al-Riḍā, in Mashhad, which is visited by hundreds of thousands of people every month. It has a vast complex of mosques and courtyards around the central mausoleum, as well as dispensaries, hospitals, a major library, a museum, a *madrasah*, etc. Over a thousand people are fed at each meal free of charge and there is no time of the year when the shrine is not completely filled with throngs of the faithful from not only all corners of Persia itself but also the Arab World and the Indo-Pakistani sub-continent. Next to Mashhad, the holy city of Qum is the most important, inasmuch as it is the site of the tomb of Imām Riḍā's sister, Haḍrat-i Maʿṣūmah, and the seat of the most influential Shiʿite *mujtahids*.[17] It, too, is frequented by many pilgrims throughout the year. The tombs of Haḍrat-i ʿAbd al-ʿAẓīm near Tehran in Rayy, Shāh Chirāgh in Shiraz and Shāh Niʿmatallāh Walī, the famous Sufi, near Kirman, are all shrine institutions of first importance. Other shrines are located on tops of mountains in difficult locations, in awesome sites of nature connected with the traditional science of sacred geography. There is no city or town without a site of pilgrimage and a saint to whom the people turn in their moments of trial as well as in moments of thankfulness. All of these shrines play a fundamental role in daily religious life, inasmuch as people turn to these saints as intermediaries between them and God and ask through them what they wish to ask of God. There is hardly anyone in Persia, even the most modern, for whom the power of the grace or *barakah* of these shrines has ceased to exist.

The Sufi centres, called *khānaqāh* in Persian, are also major focuses of religious life, although Sufism itself transcends the exoteric dimension of religion and is concerned with the esoteric teachings of Islam. The *khānaqāh* is usually either the home of a living Sufi master or the tomb of a dead one which has become the centre of the order. In either case, it is a complex of buildings in which the *fuqarā'*, or dervishes, meet for their sessions of spiritual practice and where there are rooms for travelling dervishes as well as cells for those who make spiritual retreats (*khalwah*). On special religious holidays such as the birthdays of the Prophet and ʿAlī as well as during days of mourning, the *khānaqāhs* open their doors to all who come to participate in the ceremonies held there. Even at other times the *khānaqāh* acts as a pole of spiritual attraction for the community itself, even if those outside its organization are not completely aware of all that is taught within its walls to members of the order.

The major Sufi orders in Persia today are the Niʿmatallāhī, with many branches throughout the country; the Gunābādī (itself a branch of the Niʿmatallāhī) centred in Khurasan; the Dhahabī with its major centre in Shiraz; the Qādirī, powerful mostly in Kurdistan and the Persian Gulf region; the Khāksār, popular especially among craftsmen; and the Naqshbandī, having its centre in Kurdistan. These orders, many of which have close contacts with branches in other Muslim lands, continue to influence the general structure of society and cultural life, in particular literature, music and calligraphy. The very presence of a living gnostic path of spirituality also has its effect on intellectual pursuits, especially traditional Islamic philosophy, which for this very reason is not just a rational form of knowledge but a theosophy or *ḥikmah*, ultimately an aid to spiritual realization. But, of course, because of the nature of Sufism, the profoundest influence of its teachings remains confined within the circle of the spiritual élite.

The institution of religious endowment (*waqf*), which is one of the important Islamic institutions, is the means whereby the above-mentioned religious organizations as well as many others are in most cases supported. Usually cultivated lands, but also pastures, wells, trees, etc., are given as endowment for a particular religious institution. A person is chosen to act as keeper and executor of the endowment, and under his direction the income is to be spent in accordance with the will of the founder. Today, a certain amount of organization has been given to this matter through the establishment of a department of *waqf* by the government.[18] But the institution is far from being government-controlled, and in most cases it is still the person in charge of the endowment or his family who hold power in their hands.

In traditional Persian society, as in other traditional societies, every social institution possessed religious and spiritual significance. In modern times, although, as a result of the encroachment of secularism, some of these institutions no longer have a direct religious colouring, others have a religious connection even if they are not, strictly speaking, religious organizations. Of these the guilds (*aṣnāf*) are of great importance. Existing in all the bigger cities, the guilds draw members of a particular occupation such as bakers, bricklayers or carpet-weavers into an organization which still preserves in many fields its original connection with Sufi orders and the chivalrous brotherhoods or *futuwwāt*. Most of the guilds have a particular reverence for ʿAlī, the traditional patron saint of all Islamic guilds, and possess a strong feeling of fraternity. Even labour organizations which resemble unions in the Western sense possess some of the characteristics of the guilds, and it is difficult in most cases to draw a line between the guild and the union.

In certain quarters, some social significance still pertains to the remnants of orders of chivalry centred around gymnasia called *zūr-khānah*. Again closely connected with the name of ʿAlī, these orders served traditionally to enhance the spirit of chivalry (*jawān-mardī*) and to build up moral and spiritual character. In their centres, bodily exercises are performed to the beating of a drum and the chanting of religious and epic verses. Traditional Persian cities, like other Muslim cities, have had local strong men who have kept the peace and protected the morals (*nāmūs*) of their quarters of the city. Such types have usually been connected in Persia with the *zūr-khānah* and still perform this function in many cities, although they stand in rather stark contrast to some of the Westernized youth in the modernized parts of Tehran who are devoid of the traditional virtues of chivalry inculcated by these orders.

Finally, mention must be made of certain recently founded organizations usually connected with bureaucratic professions and some which are affiliated to Sufi orders. There are also lodges of Freemasons which, in the Persian climate, have in a few cases gained a Muslim colouring, while some attempt has even been made to connect them to certain of the *khānaqāhs*.[19] In a few cases, there has come into being a Persian version of an organization resembling these lodges but of a more directly religious character and attracting many from the modern educated classes. In all these cases, a religious element is present, though it varies from one organization, and even from one individual, to another.[20]

Because of the all-embracing nature of the Sacred Law or *Sharīʿah*, there is in reality no aspect of social life in Persia, as in the rest of the Muslim world, which is completely divorced from religious principles, even if modernism and older historical forces resuscitated as a result of the influence of modernism have removed certain aspects of social life from the direct jurisdiction of the *Sharīʿah*. Those domains of social life in which the *Sharīʿah* is still directly applied in Persia are personal law such as marriage, divorce, etc., as well as much of civil law. In this domain, even what was taken from European codes was taken with the approval of the *ʿulamāʾ* and was integrated into the matrix of the *Sharīʿah* through the practice of 'independent juridical opinion' or *ijtihād*. Moreover, those who practice law and administer it are nearly all either products of the *madrasahs* or the law schools and theological faculties where they have been exposed to Islamic jurisprudence (*fiqh*).

It is rather in the domain of economic life that non-Sharīʿite practices are most often seen. In the field of taxation, non-Islamic systems have been used from Umayyad times in addition to the Islamic religious tax which, in Shiʿism, consists of *zakāt* and *khums*. Many wealthy men, especially merchants in bazaars, do, however, continue to pay the religious taxes in addition to those demanded by the government. The religious tax is, in fact, a major source of support for centres of Shiʿite learning in such cities as Qum.

The religious spirit manifests itself in economic life not so much in specific norms as in attitudes. The Islamic view of the permitted (*ḥalāl*) and forbidden (*ḥarām*), the condemnation of usury, of amassing wealth in gold and silver, of usurping the right of orphans, and many other injunctions, even if not practised by all, penetrate subtly into economic life. Also, the more philosophical attitude of uncertainty about what tomorrow will bring, distrust of purely human causation, the feeling of the impermanence of things, all play their role in fields of economic life where specific religious norms may seem to be absent.

As for political life, since Shiʿism in contrast to Sunnism does not accept the religious legitimacy of the institution of the caliphate and believes monarchy to be the best form of government in the absence of the *Mahdī*, the Persian monarchy possesses a positive religious aspect. Ever since the establishment of Shiʿism as the official state religion by the Safavids, the monarch has been considered from the religious point of view as the legitimate ruler who should govern with the consent of the 'religious scholars' or *ʿulamā'*, and whose duty it is to uphold the *Sharīʿah* and to promulgate Islam. This view is explicitly mentioned in the present Persian constitution. The connection of the monarchy with the religious structure of Shiʿism in Persia has been a persistent element of Persian history during the past four centuries, and gives a religious tone to political life even if parliamentary government is not itself an institution of Islamic origin.

The confrontation between religious and modern secular norms is best seen in the present educational system in Persia. There are, in fact, two systems of education, one the *madrasahs* which produce religious scholars, lawyers, *imāms* of mosques, etc., and the other the modern educational system leading to university degrees in various fields. Here religion is taught as a subject among others in the elementary and secondary school curricula, but one does not find the pervasive religious character of all education that has always existed in traditional Islamic society. In the universities also, besides faculties of theology, subjects connected with religious philosophy, law etc., are taught in faculties of letters and law, but here again other subjects are left outside the religious sphere. There is a direct confrontation between religious and 'secular' disciplines of learning, a confrontation which did not exist in the traditional Islamic world view where every science, be it natural, mathematical or philosophical, possessed a traditional and sacred aspect and was never divorced from the total religious and intellectual life of Islam.

As far as philosophy is concerned, it is important to note that traditional Islamic philosophy is still very much alive in Persia.[21] Secular European schools of philosophy are taught in universities but have had comparatively little effect upon the general intellectual life of the country. In fact the very presence of a living Islamic intellectual tradition has prevented facile and shallow modern interpretations of Islam in Persia such as are found in some other Muslim countries. Moreover, as mentioned before, even modern philosophical discussions, once translated into the Persian language, have had to take cognizance of the presence of the Islamic philosophical tradition.

In literature, architecture, the plastic arts, music, theatre, and other forms of artistic and cultural life, traditional forms which have a completely religious and spiritual basis subsist while modern forms have been introduced with varying degrees of 'success' among certain classes. In such cases as the theatre, where the traditional form consisted solely of passion plays, Western forms of theatre depicting problems of Western man have had little appeal to the vast majority of the population, their popularity remaining limited to the few, among Western-educated people located mostly in Tehran. A few attempts have also been made to use Persian and Islamic themes and motifs. In the other arts, the traditional forms have sometimes been used in new contemporary settings, occasionally with success, but often with a result that falls far short of genuine traditional art forms. But by and large, the traditional religious forms of artistic and cultural expression subsist and in certain cases dominate, while the modernized minority in Persian society surrounds itself ever increasingly with various aspects of Western artistic expressions and forms.[22]

The most important religious practices of Persians, like those of all Muslims in general, are the rites of prayers, fasting, pilgrimage and sacrifice, which are all slightly coloured by the secondary aspects that these rites have acquired against the background of Persian culture. Their essential element is that of the universal norms of Islam itself. The daily prayers, which most Shīʿites usually perform three times a day by connecting with a short pause those of noon and afternoon as well as those of evening and night, punctuate the rhythm of daily life. It would not be an exaggeration to say that the conception of time and the flow of life itself are determined by these canonical prayers, which are considered as the pillar of Islam. In addition the very devout perform supererogatory prayers (*nawāfil*) and there are special prayers connected with hope, fear, expectation, etc.

Fasting as a religious rite is connected particularly with the holy month of Ramaḍān, although, again, many devout people fast on different occasions throughout the year, especially the beginning, the middle and the end of the lunar Islamic month. During Ramaḍān the rhythm of life changes and there is a perceptible transformation of the most external aspects of daily life. Many of the modernized Persians do not fast, but on the whole the fast is observed throughout the country. During the holy month, days become calm and sombre and the evenings gay. Many more social calls are made to relatives during the evening, and at this time after the breaking of the fast religious and social life become completely intertwined.

The climax of the holy month comes during the nights of the 19th to the 21st, the period during which the first Imam ʿAlī was struck on the head while praying in the mosque at Kufa and died of the wounds two days later. During these nights, all amusements and parties are halted and mourning is observed in both homes and mosques. The period culminates in the night of the 21st, called the 'night of vigilance' (*iḥyā'*), during which mosques are thronged until the morning hours. People perform a hundred prostrations (*rakʿah*) of prayer and chant litanies and supplications (especially the famous Shiʿite prayer called *Jawshan-i kabīr*) until the rising of the sun.

Pilgrimage, as already pointed out, plays a major role in Persian religious life. The obligatory pilgrimage is, of course, that made to Mecca (*ḥajj*), by virtue of which man crowns the religious performances of his life. Since making this pilgrimage requires financial means and the ability to provide for one's family in advance, those who make the *ḥajj* (who are called *ḥājī* in its Persian pronounciation) are identified with a certain wealth and economic well-being. The *ḥājī* is respected by all devout people, but, in the bazaar particularly, to be a *ḥājī* also confers social and economic advantages. And since all *ḥājīs* in the bazaar are not always beyond reproach in their dealings, some criticism of them can be sensed among the modernized classes. For many years, in fact, making the *ḥajj* had become rarer in the modern educated segment of Persian society. But this has changed completely in the last decade, and now the annual *ḥajj* caravan includes people from every walk of life.

The other places of pilgrimage, especially Najaf, Karbala, Samarra, al-Kazimayn in Iraq, and Mashhad and Qum in Persia, are also of the greatest significance in daily religious life. These centres, as well as the smaller sites connected with different saints, bring the *barakah* of the centre of Islam and of the Prophet to the outer territories. These centres are all echoes of the supreme centre where Heaven and earth meet. There is hardly a Persian who does not make at least a few pilgrimages to a tomb of some saint with the continuous hope of being able to visit the more 'central' ones whenever possible. Although some pilgrimages involve special hardship, the centres being located on mountain-tops or places with a bad climate, most pilgrimages combine religious asceticism with the enjoyment of God's bounties and the beauties of art and nature. For a large segment of the population, such a pilgrimage is the most enjoyable experience of the year, although it is also a time of the most intense purification, a period of prayer and asking for forgiveness that leaves its mark upon the person long after the pilgrimage has come to an end.

The *ḥajj* terminates with the feast of sacrifice (*ʿīd-i aḍḥā* or *ʿīd-i qurbān*) commemorating the sacrifice of Abraham. During this day, not only in Mecca but throughout the Muslim world, sheep are sacrificed. Herds are marked with special colours and brought into the city before the occasion, and on the morning of the *ʿīd* the sacrifice is made, the meat being given to the poor and to neighbours. But besides this, sacrifice is made throughout the year. Firstly, all meat that is used for daily food is slaughtered ritually and sacrificed, and secondly, on almost any joyous occasion, such as the arrival of a traveller from a long journey, the birth of a child (particularly a son), the arrival of an honoured guest, and the building of a new house, sacrifices are made, usually of sheep but sometimes of other lawful animals, including, occasionally, camels.

A religious practice that is particular to the Shiʿite world, especially Persia, is the *rawḍah*, which was developed in its present form during the Safavid period. The *rawḍah* (a word derived from the title of the work *Rawḍat al-shuhadā'*, meaning the 'Garden of Martyrs') consists of sessions during which sermons are delivered combined with the chanting of verses of the Quran and religious poems, with special emphasis on the tragedy of Karbala. These sessions are held most of all during the two-month period of Muḥarram and Ṣafar, revolving around the death of Ḥusayn and its aftermath. Much religious and moral preaching to the public takes place on these occasions. The *rawḍah* is held in mosques as well as in private homes. On the crucial dates of the ninth and tenth of Muḥarram on which the tragedy of Karbala itself occurred, there are even government-sponsored *rawḍah* throughout the country. The sessions are marked by sobbing and wailing, particularly on the part of women, as all discourse is brought back periodically to the theme of the death of the members of the household of the Prophet.

Religious practice also enters into daily life at the critical moments of birth, marriage and death as in other parts of the Islamic world and, in fact, in other religions. At the moment of birth there is the simple recitation of the 'testimony of Islam' or the *Shahādah* in the ear of the new-born child. In the case of boys, the rite of circumcision is perhaps even more directly connected with religious practices than birth itself. As for marriage, although it is a contract and not a sacramental act, nevertheless, since it is made valid by virtue of the *Sharīʿah*, it is definitely a religious act. The verses binding the contract are usually read by one of the *ʿulamā'* although any male Muslim can perform this and other functions of a priestly nature.

It is naturally at the moment of death that religious rites become most vividly remembered and seriously practised. The acts of washing the body and burial are all performed in accordance with Islamic law. Afterwards, a funeral service is held which men attend in a mosque, and another where women gather in the home of the deceased or of one of his or her relatives. Since to attend those services is a social duty and most men have many friends and relatives, attendance at funeral services in mosques is a regular event throughout one's life. The sermon delivered after the chanting of the Holy Quran is the best means available to religious authorities to reach the higher strata of society, especially those who hold political power in their hands. That is why a funeral service held for a member of the government or for a person of high reputation holds a special significance in the religio-political life of Persia. In fact, several political assassinations and attempts toward this end have been made on such occasions during the modern history of Persia.

There is also a practice called preparing *sufrah*, popular among women, at which a table is laid full of all kinds of food, to which friends and neighbours are invited. During the 'feast', a person specializing in performing the *rawḍah*, called *rawḍah-khwān*, chants the Quran and religious poems and preaches on religious themes. The rest of the food is then given to the poor and some taken to each participant's home and given to friends and relatives, especially those who are ill, as an object possessing *barakah* (*tabarruk*). The *sufrah*, being especially for women, is usually connected with important events in the lives of women in the household of the Prophet such as Fāṭimah and Zaynab. The whole process of preparing the table, which is done with the greatest care and the best taste, is considered as a religious labour, one in which, once again, denial of the world is combined with the enjoyment of God's bounty.

The *sufrah*, as well as pilgrimage and many other religious acts, is often performed as a result of a vow and solemn promise to God (*nadhr*) in return for which the person asks something of God. The practice of *nadhr* is very popular in all segments of Persian society, especially among women. Women make a vow to pay so much money to the poor or set a *sufrah* if they bear a child or if their daughter finds a suitable mate. Students often vow to fast or perform a certain pilgrimage if they pass their examinations. Merchants in the bazaar make the *nadhr* to sacrifice so many sheep if their business transactions succeed. There is continuous 'religious barter', in which Persians, like other traditional people, ask of God something in exchange for which they perform acts pleasing to Him. One can hardly understand the psychology of the Persian and the tensions of hope and fear within him without understanding his attitude toward *nadhr* and the 'barter' he makes continuously with the Creator. Only the saintly man lives fully according to the will of God without asking anything in return. But this highest spiritual attitude does not in any way invalidate the general exoteric religious form of it.

Besides religious practices that have been sanctioned and protected by the *ʿulamāʾ*, and represent the conscious, intellectual aspects of Islamic tradition, there are many popular practices which are often combined with the most intense religious fervour and enthusiasm. During the month of Muḥarram, long processions are organized by men who, dressed in black, celebrate the passion of Karbala by chanting religious poems and often beating themselves until they fall into a state of frenzy. Occasionally these practices are carried to extremes, some beating themselves with chains and even swords until they faint from loss of blood. Most processions, however, march through the streets of cities to the solemn rhythm of drum beats and the harmony of human voices choking with grief. In larger cities, the sight of thousands of men and boys marching behind religious emblems and symbols of the family of the Prophet is a most moving religious experience.

There is also the passion play (*taʿziyah*), which, although developed into an aristocratic art in Safavid and Qajar times, is essentially a popular religious manifestation. It is not usually encouraged by the *ʿulamāʾ*, although they do not oppose it since it is a medium for profound religious expression. Varying from simple versions in the villages to elaborate ones in big cities, the *taʿziyah* depicts the events that led to the martyrdom of Ḥusayn at Karbala. The climax is usually performed at high noon on the day of *ʿĀshūrā*, the tenth of Muḥarram, when the third Shiʿite Imam, Ḥusayn, died and was beheaded. In a city like Qum, where several thousand people participate in the performance of the drama and thousands more flock from the countryside to join the population of the city in observing the *taʿziyah*, one sees one of the most overwhelming manifestations of religious life in Persia.

Finally, among popular religious phenomena one cannot overlook the interest in omens, magic and other occult arts. Islam, on the Shariʿite level, opposes the practice of magic, but that has not prevented people, especially women, from utilizing it often in combination with specifically Muslim practices. Furthermore, there is a complete traditional science of the 'magic-like' use of Quranic phrases, that is, the recitation of formulae for appropriate occasions. Although this science is itself far from being 'popular' in the usual sense, it has a widely extended field of application in daily life. There are also prayers (*duʿā'*) connected with the names of Imams and Sufi saints which people carry about with them or recite on various occasions. Besides their purely religious aspect, practices of this kind have also acquired a kind of magical quality. The 'prayer writer' (*duʿā'-niwīs*), like the practitioner of geomancy (*rammāl*), is a permanent fixture in the life of Persian women in both the city and the countryside. He combines strictly religious elements with all forms of fortune-telling and both occult and pseudo-occult sciences.

The rhythm of life in Persia is determined by a number of holidays, many Islamic, some derived from ancient Persia and a few celebrating modern national events. Both the Islamic and the ancient Persian dates have a wholly religious aspect. Even the ancient Zoroastrian *naw-rūz* or 'New Year', which marks the Persian new year to this day, has acquired a completely Islamic colour. At the moment of the vernal equinox, people place the Quran on their tables along with the seven objects beginning with the letter 's' (the *haft sīn* or seven s's) that have survived from Zoroastrian days. Prayers are also said and benedictions invoked upon the Prophet and his family.

As for the Islamic religious dates, the festivities of *aḍḥā* at the end of the *ḥajj*, *ʿīd-i fiṭr* at the end of Ramaḍān, the date of the birth of the Prophet, the birthday of ʿAlī and *ʿīd-i ghadīr*, when according to Shiʿite belief ʿAlī was chosen by the Prophet as his successor, are widely celebrated as joyous occasions. Also of great importance is the date of birth of the Mahdī, when all cities are illuminated with countless lights.

The calendar is also dotted with tragic events, the most important being the 10th of Muḥarram, the death of Ḥusayn, the 21st of Ramaḍān, the death of ʿAlī, the 28th of Ṣafar, the death of the Prophet and the second Imam Ḥasan, as well as the dates of the deaths of other Imams and of Fāṭimah. All these dates mark an intensification of religious life and a transformation of many aspects of daily life. The tragic element in the Persian soul expresses itself at the highest levels during these occasions, which have the effect of cleansing the individual and society from the dross of neglecting their religious vocation.

There exist in Persia today a number of sects which are marked by their emphasis upon a certain aspect of Shiʿite teachings at the expense of other elements, and by their ensuing separation from the main community. Of these the Ismaʿilis are perhaps the oldest, being the remnant of the much larger Ismaʿili community of early mediaeval times. In religious beliefs they are close to the Twelve-Imam Shiʿites except on the question of the Hidden Imam or Mahdī. Theologically, of particular interest are the Shaykhīs, centred mostly in Kirman, and founded by Shaykh Aḥmad Aḥsā'ī two centuries ago. They emphasize the role of *ta'wīl*, or spiritual hermeneutics, and have a special reverence for the Imams. The ʿAlī-Allāhī and Ahl-i Ḥaqq have followers in Kurdistan, Mazandaran and some of the southern provinces. Some members of these sects even go to the extreme of believing in the divinity of ʿAlī and also in re-incarnation.

The significance of these sects from the point of view of the general religious life of Persia is that most of them belittle the practice of the *Sharīʿah*, and some do not even perform the daily prayers in the usual manner. In most cases they represent Sufi orders that have become politicized or have taken on an external social character resulting in the destruction of the equilibrium which characterizes the orthodox Muslim community, Sunnite and Shiʿite alike. They are nevertheless Islamic sects in that they are still within the total matrix of the Islamic tradition. Such is not, however, the case with Babism and Bahā'ism, particularly the latter, which broke completely away from the structure of Islam and cannot in any way be considered as an Islamic movement or sect. The presence of Bahā'ism in Persia today, therefore, even if limited in its membership, has a role to play in the process of secularization and in the destruction of the religious unity of the country.

In conclusion it must be noted that the Persian psyche possesses an elasticity that makes the study of religion in Persia based on external forms alone difficult. From outward signs, one sees the superimposition of a modern, Westernized class, more or less torn away from religious practices, upon the traditional Persian society, nearly all aspects of whose life are dominated by the religious spirit. Even pre-Islamic norms have become, for those living in the matrix of the traditional Persian world, totally Muslimized. But even among the modernized who outwardly seem completely secularized there exist many traditional religious tendencies which in a people of less elastic mentality would not be conceivable. One often sees women who dress in the latest European fashions and try to act like Western women but who, at the same time, display a completely traditional religious attitude at moments of stress or sorrow or on religious occasions. Likewise, many men who present a rationalistic front indifferent to religion become totally transformed in holy places of pilgrimage or at moments of participation in religious ceremonies.

It can therefore be said that most of contemporary Persian life is still dominated in its universal principles as well as in its daily acts by the spirit and form of the Islamic revelation, which also integrated into its world view elements of older religions which were in conformity with its own principles.[23] Moreover, whereas certain domains of life have drawn away from the orbit of traditional religious life as a result of the advent of modernism, even in these domains religious elements and attitudes persist. Of course in Persia, as in the Arab World, there are the few who have become torn away completely from Islam, at least outwardly, and who possess a world-view based upon imitation of various Western ideologies and who experience constantly that tension between East and West alluded to in earlier chapters concerning Muslims in general. But for the vast majority of Persians, the religious truths by which they have lived and died for centuries continue to dominate the horizon of their lives today, even if occasional clouds momentarily obscure the horizon from some eyes. The clouds, however, can never be permanent, and there is hardly anyone who during his lifetime does not gain some kind of vision of that horizon which has co-ordinated and oriented the lives of Persians, as of other Muslims, throughout the ages and continues as the most abiding reality today.

Notes to Chapter 9

1. In fact, the error of modernized Arab Muslims, especially those affected by intense forms of nationalism, is in the other direction. It is in 'nationalizing' Islam by seeing the Holy Prophet solely as an Arab hero and Islam as a kind of product of the Arabic genius, forgetting the role of the Archangel Gabriel and the Origin of the Quranic revelation. This view of the Holy Prophet as simply a 'racial hero' of the Arabs is reflected in many modern biographical studies written not only by Arab Muslims but even by Arab Christians.

2. For the contribution of the Persians only to the purely religious sciences of Islam, see S. H. Nasr and M. Muṭahharī, 'The Religious Sciences', *Cambridge History of Iran*, Vol. IV, Cambridge, 1975, pp. 464–480; as for Persian contributions to Islamic philosophy and the sciences see S. H. Nasr, 'Philosophy and Cosmology', *ibid.*, pp. 419–441 and 'Life Sciences, Alchemy and Medicine', *ibid.*, pp. 396–418; see also H. Corbin, *Terre céleste et corps de résurrection.* The most thorough discussion of the mutual influence and interplay of Islam, its civilization, and the Persians is to be found in the Persian work of M. Muṭahharī, *Khadamāt-i mutaqābil-i Islām wa Irān*, Tehran, 1349 AH solar.

3. We have chosen to discuss Islam in Persia in greater detail than in the last chapter concerning the Arab World because there are so few studies of a serious nature concerning Islam in Persia in European languages. Nearly every Western study of Islam today, such as the well-known works of H. A. R. Gibb, W. S. Smith and K. Cragg, fails to include a chapter on Persia.

4. Of the nearly thirty-three million inhabitants of present-day Persia, about 98 per cent are Muslim, the rest belonging to the Zoroastrian, Christian and Jewish religious communities as well as to various branches of Babism and Bahā'ism. Of the Islamic population, about nine-tenths are Shi'ite and one-tenth Sunni.

5. On the question of the 'continuity' of Persian culture, see S. H. Nasr, 'Cosmographie

en l'Iran pré-islamique et islamique, le problème de la continuité dans la civilisation iranienne', *Arabic and Islamic Studies in Honor of H. A. R. Gibb*, Leiden, 1965, pp. 507–524. Also S. H. Nasr, 'The Life of Mysticism and Philosophy in Iran: Pre-Islamic and Islamic', as well as Corbin, *op. cit.*

6. On the Iranian religions, see G. Widengren, *Die Religionen Irans*, Stuttgart, 1965, where a bibliography of major works on the subject can be found.

7. On the significance of Salmān for Persian Muslims, see the still valuable study of L. Massignon, *Salmān Pāk et les prémises spirituelles de l'Islam iranien*, Paris, Société des études iraniennes, 1934; English translation by J. M. Unvala, *Salmān Pāk and the Spiritual Beginnings of Iranian Islam*, Bombay, 1955. On the significance of the *Ahl-i bayt* in Shi'ism see 'A. Ṭabāṭabā'ī, *Shi'ite Islam*, ed. and trans. by S. H. Nasr, Albany (N.Y.), 1975.

8. On the rapport between Shi'ism and Sufism and the role played by Sufism during the post-Mongol period in the spread of Shi'ism, see M. Molé, 'Les Kubrâwiya entre Sunnisme et Shi'isme aux huitième et neuvième siècles de l'Hégire', *Revue des Études Islamiques*, XXIX, 1961, pp. 61–142. Also S. H. Nasr, *Sufi Essays*, Chap. VIII, and M. Mazzaoui, *The Origin of the Safavids*, Wiesbaden, 1972.

9. As an example of the influence of Sufism on various facets of Persian culture, see N. Ardalan and L. Bakhtiyar, *The Sense of Unity, The Sufi Tradition in Persian Architecture*, and S. H. Nasr, 'The Influence of Sufism on Traditional Persian Music', trans. by W. Chittick, in *The Sword of Gnosis*, pp. 330–342.

10. For a discussion of Divine Omnipotence as related to the possibility of freedom of human action and evil in the world, see F. Schuon, *Islam: the Perennial Philosophy*, London, 1976, especially the chapter on theodicy.

11. We have dealt extensively with this doctrine in many of our writings, especially *Science and Civilization in Islam.*

12. Of course these elements, being aspects of the Islamic world view in general, are also to be found in various forms and with different degrees of emphasis among other Muslim peoples. What perhaps characterizes Persian culture in particular is its special concern with refinement and the expression of beauty in nearly every facet of life as the reflection of Divine Beauty, and its combining a special sense of the ephemeral character of the world with an intense sense of joy in life.

13. According to the well-known Arabic saying *lā takrār fi'l-tajallī*, 'there is no repetition in theophanies.'

14. This tragic ethos is therefore closely associated with the sense of nostalgia for man's celestial origin. Both spiritual attitudes, *ḥuzn* and *faraḥ*, are to be found in perfect complementarity and harmony in the Sufi poetry of such masters as Ḥāfiẓ and Rūmī.

15. 'Sanctity is a tree which grows between impossibility and miracle.' F. Schuon, *Spiritual Perspectives and Human Facts*, p. 209. Yet the tree does grow and there are saints through the grace of Heaven. Their presence is, in fact, precisely a miracle which reveals the special, central position man possesses in the order of universal existence, at once the farthest removed from the Origin and the only creature in the terrestrial environment who can achieve union with God and gain the state of sanctity.

16. For the relation of the mosque to the bazaar in traditional Persian cities see Ardalan and Bakhtiyar, *op. cit.* (note 9).

17. A *mujtahid* in Shīʿism is one who can practice *ijtihād*, that is, give independent views on matters pertaining to Islamic law.

18. The attempt to organize the *waqf* by establishing a governmental institution, even a ministry, to supervise it is, of course, not confined to Persia. The governments of most Islamic countries today have some kind of a department concerned with the organization and administration of *awqāf*.

19. We have in mind the particular development that has taken place within the Ṣafī ʿAlī Shāhī Order during the past half century. It must be added, however, that most of the other orders have kept strictly away from any connection with Masonic lodges.

20. In such cases there is also always the danger of perversion and deviation from the authentic traditional perspective, in view of the kind of influence that can be found within Freemasonry in the West from the time of the so-called reforms which took place during the French revolution and which made Freemasonry speculative, cutting it away from the operative practice of actual masonry and its basis in the crafts.

21. Concerning Islamic philosophy in present-day Persia, see S. H. Nasr, 'The Tradition of Islamic Philosophy in Persia and its Significance for the Modern World', trans. by W. Chittick, *Iqbal Review*, Vol. 12, no. 3, Oct., 1971, pp. 28–49; and H. Corbin, 'The Force of Traditional Philosophy in Iran Today', *Studies in Comparative Religion*, Winter, 1968, pp. 12–26.

22. There is also an opposite tendency among modernized Persians, to return to an appreciation of traditional art which, however, remains often superficial because of the lack of appreciation of the spiritual forces responsible for the production of such an art.

23. One of the main differences between the modernized Persian and the modernized Arab lies precisely in this domain, in that the force of modernism combined with extreme nationalism makes those Arabs affected by it look with a sense of pride towards all that is Arabic, including Islam, which is seen in this case as a purely Arabic 'phenomenon', and with disdain towards the non-Arab Muslims, especially the Persians and the Turks. The same forces make the Persian affected by them feel an intense tension within himself between his Islamic and pre-Islamic past, and, when the forces of Islam weaken within him, a disdain for the Arabs, even to the extent of wanting to 'purify' the Persian language of the Arabic influences which enriched it so much and enabled it to become the universal language of Islamic culture throughout Asia for a millennium.

Chapter 10

Decadence, Deviation and Renaissance: Their Meaning in the Context of Contemporary Islam

Having dealt with the present state of Islam in the Islamic world, it is now necessary to turn to more specific problems caused by the advent of modernism within the mind of those Muslims of various Islamic lands who, while modernized, still concern themselves with Islam and its history. In contrast to traditional Islamic scholarship, where in all branches of the sciences terms are clearly defined and always used with a specific meaning in mind, there has appeared during the past century among a large number of modernized Muslims dealing with their own tradition a tendency toward ambiguity and the careless use of many important terms, a tendency which reflects a confused state of mind to say the least. Words and expressions have been used by many of them in such a way as to betray the state of cultural shock and often the sense of inferiority *vis-à-vis* the West from which they suffer. Their writings reveal most of all a slavery of the mind to the norms and judgments of Western civilization. Moreover, these norms are usually hidden under the veil of an 'Islam' of which there often remains little more than a name and certain emotional attachments, an Islam which has become devoid of the intellectual and spiritual truth which stands at the heart of the Islamic revelation. In the present analysis, it is our aim to discuss three widely used expressions, namely 'decadence', 'deviation' and 'renaissance', which are employed often in reference to Islamic history and to the present-day Islamic world, and which reflect in a profound fashion the attitude of a certain type of modernized Muslim toward the whole of Islam as a religion and as an historical reality.

Let us begin with the term 'decadence', which appears very often in the writings of modern Muslim scholars, who continually refer to the condition of the Islamic world before the advent of modernism as one that could aptly be described as 'decadent'. This value judgment immediately raises the following question: 'decadence with respect to what, or in respect to which norm?' There must be a norm by which something is measured and in relation to which it is judged to have decayed. Here, while some take the early centuries of Islam as a norm, most often it is the value-system adopted consciously or unconsciously from the modern West that provides, in a hidden and subtle manner, the norm and criterion for determining the state of decadence. This can be best illustrated by the question of science understood in its current Western sense. Many modernized Muslims, like so many other Orientals, equate science with civilization and judge the value of any human society and its culture by whether or not it has produced science, disregarding completely the lessons of the history of science itself.[1] Islamic civilization is then considered to have begun to decay when it ceased to produce outstanding scientists as the West understands the function of the scientist today. And even the date of this cessation of activity is taken by most Muslim writers from Western sources, where, until very recently, interest in all aspects of Islamic intellectual life has for the most part been limited to the period when Islam influenced the West. As a result, everything in Islam from philosophy to mathematics suddenly 'decays' mysteriously somewhere around the seventh/thirteenth century, exactly when the intellectual contact between Islam and the West came, for all practical purposes, to an end.[2] Modern Muslim authors who hold this opinion do not even bother to do any research of their own or even to delve into the more recent and less-known research of those Western scholars who have shown how important Islamic astronomy was in the ninth/fifteenth century or how actively Islamic medicine was pursued in Persia and India until the twelfth/eighteenth century.[3]

The result of this concept of decadence, which is based upon the modern Western criteria for 'civilization' in its worldly aspect[4] rather than on the traditional Islamic perspective which looks upon the Medina community as the most perfect Islamic society—a society according to which all other Islamic 'societies' are judged—has been to atrophy the minds of young Muslims and make them lose confidence in themselves and in their own culture. Rather than depicting the decadence which did take place in the Islamic world as a gradual and normal process of 'aging' and of becoming ever farther removed in time from the celestial origin of the revelation, and without, moreover, emphasizing the very recent nature of this decadence, such authors posit the fantastic and abhorrent theory that the Islamic world began to decay in the seventh/thirteenth century. They remain completely oblivious of the fact that if this had been the case it would have been impossible for Islam to continue to nurture a vast civilization and remain a living force to this day. They brush aside such masterpieces of art as the Shah Mosque of Isfahan, the Blue Mosque of Istanbul, or the Taj Mahal, or the literary masterpieces of a Jāmī or a Ṣā'ib Tabrīzī, or the metaphysical and theological syntheses of a Mullā Ṣadrā or a Shaykh Aḥmad Sirhindī, not to speak of the ever-living spiritual tradition of Islam contained within Sufism, which has continued to produce great saints to this day. Surely, had decadence, as envisaged by those modernized Muslim writers who have adopted completely Western norms of judgment, taken hold of the Islamic world at the early date so often posited by this group, there would have been no Islamic civilization left for such a group to 'revive' during the present century. Islamic civilization would have died out long ago and become only a subject of archaeological interest, as in fact so many orientalists would like to consider it.

As for the term 'deviation', it is in fact rarely used by modernists, and is seen only in the writings of the more orthodox Muslim writers who are still aware of the presence of a spiritual and religious norm by which to judge any human society including their own, for to speak of 'tradition' in the widest sense of the word *al-dīn* is also to speak of the possibility of deviation. In fact, in the place where this term should be used, namely in reference to modern Western civilization, which is itself a major deviation and anomaly, not to say 'monstrosity' to use the words of R. Guénon,[5] the group of modern writers with whom we are concerned shy away from utilizing it, again precisely because they lack an objective norm with which to judge the temporal flux determining the specific conditions of time and space of any particular 'world', a norm which must of necessity transcend this flux. This is all the more startling since traditional Islamic sources provide all the material that is necessary to discover such a norm and to formulate such a critique in a language comprehensible to contemporary man.

When we come to the word 'renaissance', we find a profusion of the wildest uses of this term in nearly every context, ranging from art and literature to politics. The modernists never tire of speaking of nearly every form of activity in the Islamic world as a renaissance, whose Arabic translation, *al-nahḍah*, has become such a prevalent word in contemporary Arabic literature. There is something insidious about the carefree use of this word, for it recalls the Renaissance in the West when the re-birth of certain elements of Graeco-Roman paganism, deadly from the spiritual point of view—not the positive elements of this ancient tradition which had already been integrated into Christianity by the Church Fathers, especially St Augustine—dealt a staggering blow to Christian civilization and prevented it from reaching its natural period of flowering as a *Christian* civilization. One cannot but recall in connection with the Renaissance the coming to life once again in the West of the Promethean and Titanesque spirit which stands at the very antipode of Islam.[6] What many Muslims today often take as renaissance is usually precisely the re-birth in one form or another of the very forces that Islam came to supplant, forces which are identified in the traditional Muslim imagery with the age of ignorance or *jāhiliyyah*. That is not to say that a form of 'renaissance' in a particular domain is impossible, for the appearance of a great saint can cause a 'renaissance' of spirituality in a particular region of the Islamic world.[7] A great master of Islamic art can revive a particular artistic form, or a powerful intellectual figure can cause the revival of some aspects of Islamic intellectual life, provided he is himself genuinely rooted in the Islamic intellectual tradition.[8] But most of what is paraded as 'renaissance' today is nothing of the kind. How often has a directly anti-Islamic form of thought been hailed as the 'renaissance' of Islamic thought, or an activity directly opposed to the teachings of the *Sharī'ah* as an Islamic social renaissance! Intellectual honesty would require us at least to avoid using the epithet 'Islamic', even if the term 'renaissance' must, for some reason, be employed. Here again, it is the lack of vision of the objective Islamic norms which causes many people entranced by the errors of the modern world to identify simply any change and activity in the Islamic world with an Islamic renaissance, in the same way that in the secular world of the West and its dependencies in other continents any change is equated with 'progress' and 'development', even if this change is in every way a debasement and diminution of the quality of human life.

In all these cases, the common error results from the loss of vision of the objective, transcendent and immutable Islamic principles which alone can enable one to judge from an Islamic point of view whether a particular form or activity or period of human society is decadent, deviated or resurgent with the characteristics of a true renaissance. Without the Absolute the relative can never be fully understood, and without the Immutable one cannot gauge the direction of flow of that which changes. But because of a 'metaphysical myopia' combined with a blind submission to the follies of the modern West, which has lost its vision of the Immutable, the group of modernized Muslims under discussion possess neither the intellectual vision to perceive the immutable essences of things, their *malakūt* in Quranic terminology, nor the binding faith to remain steadfast to the norm established by the prophetic tradition (*Sunnah* and *Ḥadīth*). Since the first of these ways of reaching the immutable principles of things is of an intellectual and spiritual order, it is brushed aside by the modernists of the type in question without too much popular opposition, and their energy is then concentrated on the subversion of normal faith in the immutable structure of traditional Islam, an undertaking which, because of its clearly religious colour, is bound to arouse greater opposition among believing Muslims. But in both cases the ultimate motive is the same. It is to remove the only objective Islamic criteria according to which one could judge present day Islamic society and in fact the modern world in general.

The desire to remove these objective and God-given criteria becomes, therefore, concentrated in the attempt to weaken, in the eyes of faithful Muslims, the trans-historical significance of the prophetic *Sunnah* and *Ḥadīth* by subjecting them to the so-called method of 'historical criticism', according to which the absence of the record of something is usually equated with the non-existence of the thing itself. The Holy Prophet provides for Muslims, both individually and collectively, the perfect norm for their private and collective lives, the *uswatun ḥasanah* of the Holy Quran. As long as his *Sunnah* is respected and kept intact, there remains within the Islamic community a divinely appointed norm by which to judge human behaviour and, along with the Holy Book itself, the means to provide the basis for the collective life of human society as well as for the inner religious life of its members.[9] The attack against the integrity of the *Ḥadīth* literature has as one of its major objectives, whether realized consciously or not, to remove the divinely ordained criterion for judging Muslims and therefore to leave the door open for men to follow the line of least resistance before modernism and to surrender to their passions or to the transient fashions of the day, however demonic they may be. All of this is done, moreover, in the name of an 'Islamic renaissance' and by criticizing as reactionary or decadent any group which refuses to imitate blindly the cheapest products of Western civilization. The ambiguous and often wishy-washy judgments of many of the modernists with respect to Islam, past and present, is inseparable from the attempt to blur the clear example and norm for human life provided by the Quran and the *Sunnah*. And, conversely, many orthodox Muslims who have sought to defend the integrity of Islam have found it necessary to emphasize over and over again the significance of the prophetic norm as contained in the *Ḥadīth* and *Sunnah*, without which even the message of the Holy Quran would become, in many parts, incomprehensible to men.

It may now be asked, 'Once this criticism has been made of the prevalent use of such terms as renaissance, decadence and deviation, what can these terms really signify if we accept the full authority of the Quran and the *Sunnah*, as well as the gradual unfolding of the tradition in stages to our own day?' To this question one can give a precise answer, which, however, because of the difference in premisses and point of departure, will be very different from that given by the modernist group in question.

Renaissance in the Islamic sense can only mean a rebirth, or literally renaissance, of Islamic principles and norms, and not just a rebirth of no matter what. Every sign of life is not a sign of spiritual life, and every activity that occurs among Muslim peoples is not necessarily an Islamic activity, especially during this age of the eclipse of so many aspects of the Truth. A renaissance in its Islamic sense would correspond to *tajdīd*, or renewal, which in its traditional context is identified with the function of a renewer or *mujaddid*. Islamic history has been witness to many renaissances in the true sense of the word in the form of the activity of a *mujaddid* in one part or another of the Islamic world. But always such a *mujaddid* has been the embodiment *par excellence* of the principles of Islam, which he has sought to re-instate and apply to a particular situation. He thus differs profoundly from the 'reformer' in the modern sense,[10] who is usually a 'deformer' because he is willing to sacrifice an aspect of the Islamic tradition for this or that contingent factor, most often made to appear irresistible by being called 'an inescapable and unavoidable condition of the times'. One wonders what would have happened to Islam during and after the Mongol invasion if such 'reformers' had appeared and had tried to make Islam conform to what were then surely the most irresistible 'conditions of the time', those connected with the victorious Mongols and their ways of life. A true Islamic renaissance is, then, not just the birth or re-birth of anything that happens to be fashionable at a particular moment of human history but the re-application of principles of a truly Islamic nature.

And here the primary condition for a genuine Islamic renaissance becomes clear. This condition in our day resides in independence from the influence of the West and from all that characterizes the modern West. A Muslim far away from the influences of modernism can possibly experience spiritual renewal while remaining oblivious to what is going on in the modern world. But a Muslim intellectual or religious leader who wishes to renew the intellectual and religious life of the Islamic world, now under such heavy pressure from the West and from modernism in general, cannot hope to bring about an Islamic renaissance on either the intellectual or the social level except through a profound criticism of modernism and of the modern world itself. To speak of an Islamic renaissance and at the same time to accept without any discrimination all that the modern world stands for is a pure chimera and the wildest of dreams, a dream which in the end cannot but turn into a nightmare. Today, truly Islamic activity, especially on the intellectual plane, cannot take place without a profoundly critical attitude towards the modern world, combined with a deep understanding of this world. Nor is the practice of giving opinion, or *ijtihād*, possible in the field of Islamic law for a mind that has been transformed by the tenets of modernism. If, despite all the talk about an Islamic renaissance among Muslim modernists during the past century, no such thing has taken place—certainly not issuing from their quarter—it is precisely because they lack this absolutely necessary critical view and at the same time a profound knowledge of the modern world and the means to assess its transient values in the light of the eternal principles of Islam. It is certainly time for those who want to speak in the name of the Muslim intelligentsia and who wish to bring about a renaissance of Islam to stop speaking from a position of inferiority *vis-à-vis* the West and begin to apply the sword of metaphysical discrimination, contained in its purest form in the *shahādah*, to the modern world itself.

Within such a perspective, the meaning of decadence and deviation also becomes clear. Decadence is always a falling off from a perfect norm, but following a course that is still related to that norm, while deviation is a complete departure from that norm itself. Moreover, there are two forms of decadence, one passive and the other active: one which the civilizations of the East have undergone during the past few centuries, and the other which has been followed by the modern West during the same period[11] and which, because of the active and dynamic quality of the West, became properly speaking a deviation. Many Orientals—Muslims as well as others—have mistaken this activity for true life precisely because they have seen it in contrast to the relative lack of dynamism and activity within the traditional Oriental world. Today, strangely enough, before the startled eyes of many modernized Easterners, this deviation of the West is turning into decadence of a form that is easily recognizable, even for them. It can, in fact, be said that the curve of life of modern Western civilization, beginning with the termination of its spiritual normalcy during the Middle Ages, has gone from 'renaissance' to deviation to decadence, this last phase becoming ever more evident during the last two decades. As for that interpretation of Islam of the group of modernists just mentioned, the curve can be described as going from decay to 'renaissance' to deviation—a deviation which will surely be followed by another phase of decadence, but of a type different from that which the modernists sought to remedy to begin with. Fortunately, however, the totality of the Islamic tradition remains above this process.

There is only one way to escape the insidious chain of deviation leading to decadence. It is to remain faithful to the eternal and immutable principles of Islam, which stand above all becoming, and then to apply these principles to whatever situation Muslims are faced with, to whichever 'world' presents itself to them. To take any transient spatio-temporal set of conditions or 'world' as the criterion of the validity of Islamic principles and teachings is to reverse the natural order of things. It is to put the cart before the horse; it is to make the contingent the criterion of judgment for the eternal. Its result can only be an unfolding similar to the fatal course pursued by the West, the end of which is the *impasse* which modern civilization now faces and which threatens the very existence of man on earth.

The Muslim 'intelligentsia' cannot do anything better than to benefit from the lessons that can be drawn from a deeper study of the stages in the history of the modern West which have brought it to its present crisis. If they wish to speak for Islam and to renew its life they must remember the extremely heavy responsibility they bear. It must be recalled that a true death is better than a false life, and that if one wishes to renew the life of the Islamic community it must be the renewal of a life whose roots are sunk deeply in the Divine. There is no way to avoid both decadence and deviation and to achieve a true renaissance but to re-apply the principles and truths contained in the Islamic revelation, which have always been valid and will always continue to be so. And in order to be able to apply these principles to the outside world it is first of all necessary to apply them to oneself. Man must become spiritually revivified before being able to revive the world about him. The greatest lesson that all true reformers today can learn from the numerous failures of even well-intentioned reformers in the modern world is that the real reform of the world begins with the reform of oneself. He who conquers himself conquers the world, and he in whom a renewal of the principles of Islam in their full amplitude has taken place has already taken the most fundamental step toward the 'renaissance' of Islam itself, for only he who has become resurrected in the Truth can resurrect and revive the world about him, whatever the extent of that 'world' might be according to the will of Heaven.

Notes to Chapter 10

1. See S. H. Nasr, *Science and Civilization in Islam*, where we have dealt extensively with this question, especially in the Introduction, pp. 21 ff.

2. There were, of course, occasional contacts between the Ottomans and Europe, but they were of a completely different nature from the intellectual exchange which transformed the history of mediaeval Europe.

3. The situation for Islamic philosophy is even more startling, since Islamic philosophy and metaphysics have never really decayed at all. See S. H. Nasr, *Islamic Studies*, Chaps. 8 and 9; Nasr, 'The Tradition of Islamic Philosophy in Persia and its Significance for the Modern World'; also Nasr, 'Persia and the Destiny of Islamic Philosophy', *Studies in Comparative Religion*, Winter, 1972, pp. 31–42.

4. For Western man, especially after the seventeenth century, 'civilization' became wholly identified with the purely human and in fact with the self-aggrandisement of terrestrial man which reaches its peak with Louis XIV. See F. Schuon, 'Remarks on Some Kings of France', *Studies in Comparative Religion*, Winter, 1972, pp. 2 ff.

5. See the two fundamental works of Guénon on the modern world, *Crisis of the Modern World* and *The Reign of Quantity and the Signs of the Times*. See also the masterly analysis of F. Schuon, *Light on the Ancient Worlds*.

6. Any Muslim whose taste in art has not been completely destroyed abhors the worldly nature of Renaissance and Baroque art and architecture, even of a religious kind. Now, this art which appears so worldly and unspiritual to the Muslim onlooker is only the reflection of the revolt against Heaven embedded in Renaissance humanism, which succeeded in destroying in the West the traditional concept of man as the *imago Dei*.

7. As an example of this kind of 'renaissance' may be mentioned the appearance of the great Algerian Sufi Master, the Shaykh al-ʿAlawī, in North Africa at the beginning of this century. See M. Lings, *A Sufi Saint of the Twentieth Century*.

8. See H. Corbin, 'The Force of Traditional Philosophy in Iran Today'.

9. On the significance of the prophetic *Hadīth* and for a reply to its modern critics, see S. H. Nasr, *Ideals and Realities of Islam*, pp. 79 ff.; and F. Schuon, *Understanding Islam*, Chap. 3. See also S. M. Yusuf, *An Essay on the Sunnah*, Lahore, 1966.

10. Usually called *muṣliḥ*, he who reforms (*iṣlāḥ*), in contrast to him who renews (*tajdīd*) the tradition from within. See p. 96 above.

11. 'All civilizations have decayed; only they have decayed in different ways; the decay of the East is passive and that of the West is active.

'The fault of the East in decay is that it no longer thinks; the West in decay thinks too much and thinks wrongly.

'The East is sleeping over truths; the West lives in errors.' F. Schuon, *Spiritual Perspectives and Human Facts*, p. 22.

Chapter 11

The Western World and its Challenges to Islam

Finally, it is necessary to turn to the specific challenges of an intellectual and spiritual order which the modern West has placed before the contemporary Muslim and to the role that the Islamic tradition can play in providing the means to answer these challenges. As already mentioned, it is in the nature of things in the present-day situation that if one wishes to discuss the challenges to Islam of the West and in fact of modern civilization in general, one must begin by using the sword of discrimination and by embarking on a kind of 'intellectual iconoclasm' to clear the ground of all the 'idols' which clutter the contemporary scene. Modern civilization, whether in the West or in its overflow in the East, takes pride in having developed the critical mind and the power of objective criticism, whereas in reality it is, in a fundamental sense, the least critical of all known civilizations and the one farthest removed from a true sense of discernment, for it does not possess the objective criteria to judge and criticize its own activities. It is a civilization which fails in every kind of basic reform because it cannot begin with the reform of itself.

There is a traditional Islamic saying according to which Satan hates sharp points and edges. This old adage contains a most profound truth, which applies directly to the present-day situation. The Devil, being everywhere, manifests his influence by dulling all sharp points and edges which are accessible to him, so that sharp distinctions disappear in the milieu dominated by his influence. The edges of doctrines become corroded and their sharp form gradually fades away. Truth and error become ever more confused, and even sacred rites and doctrinal formulations, which are the most precious gifts of God to man, become hazy and indefinite as a result of this corroding influence which makes everything appear indistinct and ambiguous. To discuss the challenge of the modern world to Islam requires, therefore, that this haze be dispelled through a rigorous application of intellectual discernment based ultimately upon the *shahādah*, whose first stroke when written in Arabic is, in fact, in the form of a sword. This sword must be used to break the false idols of the new age of ignorance (*jāhiliyyah*), idols which so many Muslims accept without even bothering to question their nature. It must be used to cut away and remove all the false ideas and 'isms' that clutter the mind of modernized Muslims. It must help to chisel the soul of the contemporary Muslim from an amorphous mass into a sharp crystal which glows in the Divine Light, for a crystal glows precisely because of its sharply defined edges.

It should never be forgotten that in the present situation any form of criticism of the modern world based upon metaphysical and religious principles is an act of charity in its profoundest sense and in accordance with the most central virtues of Islam. Also one should never forget—considering a certain attitude prevailing among some Muslims who are afraid of being critical for fear of seeming discourteous, or lacking in *adab* (which in the traditional Islamic languages means at once courtesy, correctness of manners, culture and literature)—that the Prophet of Islam (upon whom be peace) not only possessed *adab* in its most perfect form but also asserted the Truth in the most straightforward and naked manner. There were moments of his life when he was extremely categorical, and he never sacrificed the Truth for the sake of *adab*. Islam has never taught that one should accept that two and two make five in order to display *adab*. In fact, *adab* has always been the complement to the perception and assertion of the Truth in every situation and circumstance. Once, an eminent spiritual authority from North Africa said, 'Do you know what *adab* is? It is to sharpen your sword so that when you have to cut a limb it does not hurt.' It is this type of attitude that is needed by Muslims in their discussion of the West and its challenges to Islam. The Truth not only has a right to our lives and our beings but also has the prerogative to ask us to make sense to others and to express and expound it whenever and wherever possible. Today we need to be critical, even to the degree of stringency, precisely because such an attitude is so rare and so much in demand.

What is lacking in the Islamic world today is a thorough examination and careful criticism of all that is happening in the modern world. Without such a criticism nothing serious can ever be done in confronting the West. All the statements of modernized Muslims which begin with the assertion, 'The way to harmonize Islam and . . .'—whatever may follow the 'and'—are bound to end in failure unless what follows is another divinely revealed and inspired world-view. Otherwise, attempts to harmonize Islam and Western socialism or Marxism or existentialism or evolution or anything else of the kind are doomed at the start by the very fact that they begin without exposing the system or 'ism' under question to a thorough criticism in the light of Islamic criteria, and also because they consider Islam as a partial view of things to be complemented by some modern ideology rather than as a complete system and perspective in itself, whose very totality excludes the possibility of its becoming a mere adjective to modify some other noun which is taken almost unconsciously as central in place of Islam. The rapid change in fashions of the day which makes Islamic socialism popular one day and liberalism or some other Western 'ism' the next is itself proof of the absurdity and shallowness of such an approach. He who understands the structure of Islam in its totality knows that it can never allow itself to become reduced to a mere modifier or contingency *vis-à-vis* a system of thought which remains independent of it or even hostile to it.

The defensive and apologetic attitude adopted by so many modernized Muslims towards various fashionable modes of thought that issue from the West almost with the rapidity of seasonal changes is closely allied to their lack of a critical sense and of a discerning spirit. Usually, obvious shortcomings and that which is easy to criticize *are* criticized, but few have the courage to stand up and criticize the basic fallacies of our times. It is easy to point out that the life of students in traditional *madrasahs* is not hygienic, but it is much more difficult to take a firm stand and assert that much of what is taught in modern educational institutions is far more deadly—for the soul of the students—than the physically unhealthy surroundings of some of the old *madrasah* buildings. There are too few people in the Islamic world who can confront the West and criticize and answer with the sword of the Intellect and the Spirit the very basis of the challenge with which the West confronts Islam. Such is the case today—but it does not have to be so. There is no logical reason why a new intellectual élite could not develop in the Islamic world, an élite which would be able to provide an objective criticism of the modern world from the point of view of the eternal verities contained within the message of the Islamic revelation, applying the God-given treasures of Islam to the wretched situation of modern man and the ever more serious plight he faces.

As already mentioned in previous chapters, there are today essentially two main classes of people in the Islamic world concerned with religious, intellectual and philosophical questions: the '*ulamā*' and other religious and traditional authorities in general (including the Sufis), and the modernists still interested in religion. Only now is a third group gradually coming into being which is traditional like the '*ulamā*' but also knows the modern world. As far as the '*ulamā*' and other traditional spiritual authorities are concerned, it has already been shown that they usually do not possess a profound knowledge of the modern world and its problems and complexities. But they are the custodians of the Islamic tradition and its protectors, without whom the very continuity of the tradition would be endangered. They are usually criticized by the modernists for not knowing European philosophy and science or the intricacies of modern economics and the like. But this criticism, which is again of the facile kind, is for the most part ill-directed. Those who possessed the financial and political power in the Islamic world during the past century rarely allowed the *madrasahs* to develop in the direction of making it possible for the '*ulamā*' to gain a better knowledge of the modern world without becoming corrupted by it. In the few places where attempts were made to modify the *madrasah* curriculum, the hidden intention was more often to do away with the traditional educational system by deforming it beyond hope, rather than to really extend its programme to embrace courses which would acquaint the students with the modern world as seen in the light of Islamic teachings. Furthermore, few attempts have been made to create institutions which would provide a bridge between the traditional *madrasahs* and modern educational institutions. In any case, the modernists have no right to criticize the '*ulamā*' for a lack of knowledge of things which they never received the opportunity to master.

As for the second class, whose attitudes have been analyzed in previous chapters, they are the product of either Western universities or universities in the Islamic world which more or less ape the West. Now, universities in the Islamic world are themselves in a state of crisis which stems from the question of identity, for an educational system is organically related to the culture within whose matrix it functions. A jet plane can be made to land in the airport of no matter which country in Asia or Africa and be identified as part of that country. But an educational system cannot be simply imported; the fact that modern universities are facing a crisis in the Islamic world of a different nature from that which is found in the West is itself proof of this assertion. The crisis could not but exist because the indigenous Islamic culture is still alive. Moreover, this crisis affects deeply those who are educated in these universities and who are usually called the 'intelligentsia'. This term, like that of 'intellectual', is a most unfortunate one, in that often those so characterized are the farthest removed from the domain of the intellect in its true sense. But, by whatever name they are called, most of those who are products of Western-oriented universities have one feature in common: a predilection for all things Western and a sense of inferiority relative to things Islamic. This sense of inferiority *vis-à-vis* the West among so many modernized Muslims, which is, moreover, shared by modernized Hindus, Buddhists and other Orientals in general who are affected by the psychosis of modern forms of idolatry, is the greatest malady facing the Islamic world, and afflicts most deeply the very group which one would expect to face the challenge of the West. The encounter of Islam with the West cannot therefore be discussed without taking into consideration that mentality which is in most cases the product of a modern university education,[1] a mentality which, during the past century, has been responsible for most of the apologetic Islamic works concerned with the encounter of Islam and the West.[2]

This apologetic, modernized approach to the crisis of the encounter of Islam and the West has tried to answer the challenge of the West by bending over backwards to show in one way or another that this or that element of Islam corresponds to just what is fashionable in the West today, while other elements, for which there could not be found a Western equivalent by even the greatest stretch of the imagination, have been simply brushed aside as unimportant or even extraneous later 'accretions'.[3] Endless arguments have been presented for the hygienic nature of the Islamic rites or the 'egalitarian' character of the message of Islam, not because such things are true if seen in the larger context of the total Islamic message, but because hygiene and egalitarianism are currently accepted ideas and norms in the West—or at least they were before the Hippie movement. By affirming such obvious and too-easily defensible characteristics, the apologists have evaded the whole challenge of the West, which threatens the heart of Islam and which no attempts to placate the enemy can avert. When surgery is needed there must be a knife with which to remove the infected part. Also, when error threatens religious truth nothing can replace the sword of criticism and discernment. One cannot remove the negative effect of error by making peace with it and pretending to be its friend.

The apologetic attitude is even more pathetic when it concerns itself with philosophical and intellectual questions. When one reads some of this apologetic literature, which issued mostly from Egypt and the Indian sub-continent at the beginning of this century and which tried to emulate already very stale and dead debates between theology and science in Victorian England or in France of the same period, the weakness of such works, which were supposed to answer the challenge of the West, becomes completely evident, even more so against the background of the decades that have since gone by. Of course at that time one could also hear the strong voice of the traditional authorities, who, basing themselves on the immutable principles of the Islamic revelation, tried to answer these challenges on a religious level, even if they were not aware of the more abstruse and hidden philosophical and scientific ideas involved. But this voice gradually diminished, without of course ceasing to exist altogether, while the other, that of the modernists, became ever more audible and invasive.

This phenomenon has led to the rather odd situation today in which, among the educated classes, practically the most ardent defenders of modern Western civilization in the world are Westernized Orientals. The most intelligent students at Oxford or Harvard are far less confident in the West and its future than those modernized Orientals who for some time have sacrificed everything at the altar of modernism and are now suddenly faced with the possibility of the total decomposition of their idol. Therefore, they try ever more desperately to cling to it. For the modernized Muslims, especially the more extreme among them, the 'true meaning' of Islam has been for some time now what the West has dictated. If evolution is in vogue, 'true Islam' is evolutionary. If it is socialism that is the fashion of the day, the 'real teachings' of Islam are based on socialism. Those acquainted with this mentality and the works it has produced are most aware of its docile, servile and passive nature. Even in the field of law, how often have completely non-Islamic and even anti-Islamic tenets been adopted with a *bismillāh* added at the beginning and a *bihi nastaʿīn* at the end, while the substance of the material contained in between has been derived or even copied from some Western code?

Now suddenly this group, who were willing to sell their soul to emulate the West, see before their eyes the unbelievable sight of the floundering of

Western civilization itself. What a painful sight it must be for such men! Therefore they try, in the face of all evidence, to defend the Western 'value system' and become ferociously angry with those Westerners who have themselves begun to criticize the modern world. Probably, if the obvious decomposition of modern civilization, which became gradually evident after the Second World War, had become manifest after the First World War, when the traditions of Asia were much more intact, a great deal more from these traditional civilizations could have been saved. But the hands of destiny had charted another course for mankind. Nevertheless, even in the present situation, there is a great deal that can be done, for as the Persian proverb says, 'As long as the root of the plant is in water there is still hope.' On the plane of true activity, according to traditional principles, the possibility of doing something positive always exists, including the most obvious and central act of stating the truth, and acting accordingly.[4] Despair has no meaning where there is faith (*īmān*). Even today, if in the Islamic world there comes to be formed a true intelligentsia at once traditional and fully conversant with the modern world, the challenge of the West can be answered and the core of the Islamic tradition preserved from the paralysis which now threatens its limbs and body.

To realize exactly how much can still be saved in the Islamic world, it is sufficient to remember that for the vast majority of Muslims even now, Islamic culture is still a living reality in which they live, breathe and die. From Indonesia to Morocco, for the overwhelming majority, Islamic culture must be referred to in the present tense and not as something of the past. Those who refer to it in the past tense belong to that very small but vocal minority which has ceased to live within the world of tradition and mistakes its own loss of centre for the dislocation of the whole of Islamic society.

The tragedy of the situation resides, however, in the fact that it is precisely such a view of Islam as a thing of the past that is held by most of those who control the mass media in many countries in the Islamic world and who therefore exercise an influence upon the minds and souls of men far beyond what their number would justify. In many lands, those who control such means as radio, television and magazines live in a world in which Islamic culture appears a thing of the past precisely because they are so infatuated with the West that no other way of seeing things than the Western one seems to have any reality for them, even if that other way be a still living reality existing on their very doorsteps.

Strangely enough this Westernized minority in the Islamic world has gained a position of ascendancy at the very moment when the West has lost its own moorings completely and does not know what it is doing or where it is going. If a simple Arab or Persian peasant were to be brought to one of the big Middle Eastern airports and asked to observe the Europeans entering the country, the contrast in nothing more than the dress, which varies from that of a nun to practically nude, would be sufficient to impress upon his simple mind the lack of homogeneity and harmony of the products of Western civilization. But even this elementary observation usually escapes the thoroughly Westernized Muslim, who, though usually well-meaning if nothing else, does not want to face the overt contradictions in the civilization he is trying so avidly to emulate.

Of course, despite the predominance and continuation of this attitude in many circles the situation *has* changed somewhat during the past three decades. Muslims who went to Europe between the two world wars thought of the trees along the Seine or the Thames practically as *Shajarat al-ṭūbā* and these rivers as the streams of Paradise. Whether consciously or unconsciously, most members of this generation of modernized Muslims transferred almost completely their image of Paradise and its perfections to Western civilization. But today this homogeneity of reaction and blind acceptance of the West as an idol is no longer to be observed. The inner contradictions of the West that have become ever more manifest during the past three decades no longer permit such an attitude. The present-day generation of modernized Muslims is much less confident about the absolute value of Western civilization than their fathers and uncles who went to the West before them. This in itself can be a positive tendency if it becomes the prelude to a positive and objective evaluation of modernism. But so far it has only added confusion to the ranks of modernized Muslims, and only here and there has it resulted in the appearance of a handful of Muslim scholars who have awakened to the reality of the situation and have ceased to emulate the West blindly. But alas! The main problem, which is the lack of a profound knowledge of the real nature of the modern world based upon the criteria of Islamic culture, remains. There are still too few 'occidentalists' in the Islamic world who could perform for Islam the positive aspect of the function which 'orientalists' have been performing for the West since the eighteenth century.[5]

Despite the weakening of the confidence in the West on the part of modernized Muslims, the Muslims are still on the receiving end in the realm of both ideas and material objects. Lacking confidence in their own intellectual tradition, most modernized Muslims are like a *tabula rasa* waiting to receive some kind of impression from the West. Moreover, each part of the Islamic world receives a different kind of baggage of ideas, depending on the part of the Western world to which it has become closely attached. For example, in the domain of sociology and also, as mentioned above, in philosophy, the Indian sub-continent has closely followed English schools for the past century, and Persia has followed French schools.[6] But everywhere the modernized circles are sitting and waiting to adopt whatever comes along. One day it is positivism and the next structuralism. Rarely does anyone bother to adopt a truly Islamic intellectual attitude which would act from an immutable centre and in a positive manner with discernment toward all that the wind blows our way. The intellectual situation is as bad as the domain of women's fashion, where in many Islamic lands women remain completely passive as obedient consumers and emulate blindly whatever a few Western fashion-makers decide for them. In dress fashion as in philosophical and artistic fashion, modernized Muslims have no role to play at the source where decisions are made.

It is, of course, true that even Western people themselves are hardly aware of the deeper roots of the movements that sweep the West one after another, and that twenty years ago no one foresaw that such an extensive movement as that of the Hippies would become widely spread in the West. But modernized Muslims are even farther removed from the current in that they are unaware not only of the roots but even of the stages of incubation and growth of such movements and wait until they occupy the centre of the stage, and then react either with surprise or again in a state of blind surrender.

The ecological crisis is a perfect example of this state of affairs. Muslims have waited until the crisis has become the central concern of a vast number of Western people before even becoming aware of the presence of the problem. And even now, how many people in the Islamic World are thinking of this crucial problem in the light of the extremely rich tradition of Islam concerning nature which, in fact, could provide a key for the possible solution of this major crisis, were men to make use of it?[7]

To study in a more concrete fashion the challenges of the West to Islam, it is necessary to take as example some of the 'isms' which are fashionable in the modern world today and which have affected the cultural and even religious life of the Islamic world. Let us start with Marxism, or more generally speaking, socialism.[8] Today in many parts of the Islamic world there is a great deal of talk about Marxism, which, although it does not usually attack Islam directly, has an important indirect effect upon religious life—not to speak of economic and social activity. Many who speak of Marxism or socialism in general in the Islamic world do so with certain existing problems of society in mind for which they are seeking solutions. But very few of them actually know Marxism or theoretical socialism in a serious sense. In spite of all the young Muslim students speaking about Marxism in so many university circles, one wonders how many have actually read *Das Kapital*, or even important secondary sources, or could defend the Marxist position seriously on a purely rational plane. The Marxist fad has become an excuse for many young Muslims to refuse to think seriously about the problems of Islamic society from the Islamic point of view and within the matrix of their own social situation. It is enough to accept the label of this black box with its unknown contents to have one's ego inflated and one's mind fall into the illusion that one has become an 'intellectual' or a member of the liberated 'intelligentsia', but an intelligentsia who, following the already established Marxist solutions to all kinds of problems, thought out in a completely different socio-cultural context in other lands, no longer have any responsibility to think in a fresh manner about the problems of Islamic society *as* an Islamic society. It is precisely this blind following of Marxism as a package whose content is never analyzed, or as an aspirin to soothe every kind of pain, that prepares the ground for the worst kind of demagogy. Instead of discussing problems in a reasonable and meaningful manner, those who have fallen under the influence of what is loosely called Marxism develop a blind and unintelligent obedience which leads to a senseless confrontation and finally a mental sclerosis resulting in untold harm to the youth of Islamic society—not to speak of its obvious harm to the life of faith.

Unfortunately, the response given by Islamic authorities to the challenge of dialectical materialism has for the most part consisted until now of arguments drawn from the transmitted (*naqlī*) or religious sciences rather than from the rich intellectual tradition of Islam contained in the traditional intellectual (*ʿaqlī*) sciences.[9] Now, religious arguments can be presented only to those who already possess faith. Of what use is it to cite a particular chapter of the Quran to refute an idea held by someone who does not accept the authority of the Quran to start with? Many of the works written by the *ʿulamāʾ* in this field can be criticized precisely because they address deaf ears and present arguments which have no efficacy in the context in question. This is especially saddening considering the fact that the Islamic tradition possesses such a richness and depth that it is perfectly capable of answering on the intellectual level any arguments drawn from modern European philosophy. In reality, what is all modern philosophy before traditional wisdom but a noise that would seek in its self-delusion to conquer Heaven? So many of the so-called problems of today are based on ill-posed questions and on ignorance of truths, and are of a nature which traditional wisdom alone can solve, a traditional wisdom found from ancient Babylonia to mediaeval China, and found, in one of its most universal and certainly most diversified forms, in Islam and in the vast intellectual tradition which Islam has brought into being during its fourteen centuries of existence.

The danger of Marxism for Islam has become aggravated recently by the appearance in certain Islamic countries, especially within the Arab world, of a Marxism with an Islamic veneer, creating a most tempting trap for certain simple souls. This insidious use of religion, often with direct political aims in mind, is in fact more dangerous than anti-religious and at least 'honest' Marxism, and corresponds to the thought and attitude of that class of men whom the Quran calls the *munāfiqūn* (hypocrites). In this case also there is no way to give an Islamic response save to answer such pseudo-syntheses intellectually and to demonstrate clearly that Islam is not just anything at all provided a *bismillāh* is added at the beginning, but a total vision of reality which cannot compromise with any half-truths whatsoever.

Another 'ism' of great danger to Islam, one with a longer history of intrusion into the Islamic world than Marxism, is Darwinism or evolutionism in general, whose effect is particularly perceptible among the Muslims of the Indian sub-continent, obviously because of the strong British influence in education in that area. We have already had occasion to speak of the works of outstanding European biologists against evolution[10] and to allude to the proofs brought forth by contemporary anthropologists to show that whatever may have occurred before, man himself has not evolved one iota since he first set foot upon the stage of terrestrial history.[11] But, unfortunately, almost no contemporary Muslim thinker has taken note of these sources and made use of their arguments to support the traditional Islamic view of man. For a notable segment of modernized Muslims, evolution remains practically like a religious article of faith whose overt contradiction with the teachings of the Quran they fail to realize.

In fact, the Darwinian theory of evolution, which is metaphysically impossible and logically absurd, has been subtly woven in certain quarters into some aspects of Islam to produce a most unfortunate and sometimes dangerous blend. We do not mean only the shallow Quranic commentators at the turn of the century, but have in mind even a thinker of the stature of Iqbal, who was influenced by both the Victorian concept of evolution and Nietzsche's idea of the superman. Iqbal is an influential contemporary figure of Islam but, with all due respect to him as a poet, his ideas should be studied in the light of the *ijtihād* which he himself preached so often. He should certainly not be put on a pedestal. If we analyze his thought carefully we see that he had an ambivalent attitude towards many things, including a love-hate relationship with Sufism. He admired Rūmī yet expressed dislike for a figure like Ḥāfiẓ. This is due to the fact that he was drawn, on the one hand, by the Sufi, and more generally speaking Islamic, idea of the Perfect Man (*al-insān al-kāmil*) and on the other by the Nietzschean idea of the superman, two concepts which are, in fact, the very antipodes of each other. Iqbal made the great mistake of seeking to identify the two. He made this fatal error because, despite his deep understanding of certain aspects of Islam, he had come to take the prevalent idea of evolution too seriously. He demonstrates on a more literate and explicit level a tendency to be found among the many modern Muslim writers who, instead of answering the fallacies of the theory of evolution, have tried to bend over backwards in an apologetic manner to accept it and even to interpret Islamic teachings according to it.[12]

The general tendency among Muslims affected by the evolutionist mentality is to forget the whole Islamic conception of the march of time.[13] The later Quranic chapters about eschatological events and the latter days of mankind are forgotten or passed over in silence. All the *ḥadīths* pertaining to the last days and the appearance of the Mahdī are laid aside or malconstrued, either through ignorance or by ill intention. Just the one *ḥadīth* of the Prophet that asserts that the best generation of Muslims are those who are his contemporaries, then the generation after, then the following generation until the end of time, is sufficient to nullify, from the Islamic point of view, the idea of linear evolution and progress in history. Those who think they are rendering a service to Islam by incorporating evolutionary ideas, as currently understood, into Islamic thought are, in fact, tumbling into a most dangerous pitfall and are surrendering Islam to one of modern man's most insidious pseudo-dogmas, one created in the eighteenth and nineteenth centuries to enable men to forget God.

Moreover, accepting the evolutionary thesis brings into being overt paradoxes in daily life which cannot be easily resolved. If things are going to evolve for the better, then why bother to spend one's effort on improvement? Things are going to get better by themselves anyway. The very dynamism preached by modernists stands in opposition to the usually accepted idea of evolution. Or, seen from another point of view, it can be argued that if the effort, work, movement and the like preached in the modern world are effective, then man can influence his future and destiny. And if he can affect his future then he can also affect it for the worse, and there is no guarantee of an automatic progress and evolution to say the least. All of these and many other paradoxes are brushed aside in certain quarters because of an enfeebled intellectual attitude which has as yet to produce a serious and widely known Islamic response of a metaphysical and intellectual nature to the hypothesis of evolution. The challenge of evolutionary thought has been answered in contemporary Islam in nearly the same way as has the challenge of Marxism. There have been some religious replies based upon the Holy Book, but not an intellectual response which could also persuade the young Muslims whose faith in the Quran itself has been in part shaken by the very arguments of the evolutionary school. Meanwhile, works of evolutionary writers, even of the nineteenth century such as Spencer, who are no longer taught as living philosophical influences in their own homeland, continue to be taught in universities far and wide in the Islamic world, especially in the Indian sub-continent, as if they represented the latest proven scientific knowledge or the latest philosophical school of the West. Few bother even to study the recent anti-evolutionary developments in biology itself or the reassertion of the pre-evolutionary conception of man—views which are gaining ever greater adherence in many circles in the West itself today. And what is worse, there are too few efforts on the part of the Muslim intellectual élite to formulate from Islamic sources the genuine doctrine of man and his relation to the Universe which would act as a criterion for the judgment of any would-be theory of man and the cosmos, evolutionary or otherwise, and which would also provide the light necessary to distinguish scientific facts from mere hypotheses and scientific evidence from crass philosophical materialism parading in the dress of scientific fact or even religious belief.[14]

Another important 'philosophical' challenge to the Islamic world concerns the Freudian and Jungian interpretation of the psyche. The modern psychological and psychoanalytical point of view tries to reduce all the higher elements of man's being to the level of the psyche, and moreover to reduce the psyche itself to nothing more than that which can be studied through modern psychological and psychoanalytical methods. Until now, this way of thinking, in its scientific form, has not affected the Islamic world as directly as has evolutionism, and we do not know of any important and influential Muslim writers who are Freudian or Jungian, but its effect is certain to increase soon. It must therefore be remembered that Freudianism, as well as other modern Western schools of psychology and psychotherapy, are the by-products of a particular society very different from the Islamic. It needs to be recalled also that Freud was a Viennese Jew who turned away from Orthodox Judaism. Few people know that he was connected to a messianic movement which was opposed by the Orthodox Jewish community of Central Europe itself, and that therefore he was opposed to the mainstream of Jewish life, not to speak of Christianity. Many study Freudianism but few delve into its deeper origins which reveal its real nature.[15]

Recently one of the outstanding figures of Sufism from the East wrote a series of articles on Sufism and psychoanalysis in French, making a comparison between the two. With all due respect to him it must be said that he has been too polite and lenient towards psychoanalysis, which is truly a parody of the initiatic methods of Sufism. Fortunately for Muslims, until now the influence of psychoanalysis has not penetrated deeply among them, nor have they felt the need for it. This is due most of all to the continuation of the practice of religious rites such as the daily prayers and pilgrimage. The supplications, 'discourses' and forms of pleading that are carried out in religious centres by men, women and children open the soul to the influx of Divine Grace and are a most powerful means of curing the soul's ailments and untying its knots. These forms of prayer achieve a goal which the psychoanalyst seeks to accomplish without success and moreover often with dangerous results, for he lacks the power which comes from the Spirit and which alone can dominate and control the soul.

But psychoanalytical thought, which is agnostic or even in certain cases demonic, is bound to penetrate gradually into the Islamic world, probably mostly though the translation of Western literature into Arabic, Persian, Turkish, Urdu and other Islamic languages. The effect of such translations will be to bring into being, and in fact is already bringing into being, a so-called 'psychological literature' opposed to the very nature and genius of Islam. Islam is a religion which rejects individualistic subjectivism. The most intelligible material symbol of Islam, the mosque, is a building with a space in which all elements of subjectivism have been eliminated. It is an objective determination of the Truth, a crystal through which radiates the light of the Spirit. The spiritual ideal of Islam itself is to transform the soul of the Muslim, like a mosque, into a crystal reflecting the Divine Light.

Truly Islamic literature is very different from the kind of subjective literature we find in the writings of Franz Kafka or at best in Dostoevsky. These and similar writers are, of course, among the most important in modern Western literature, but they, along with most other modern Western literary figures, nevertheless present a point of view which is very different from, and usually totally opposed to, that of Islam. Among older Western literary figures who are close to the Islamic perspective, one might mention first of all Dante and Goethe who, although profoundly Christian, are in many ways like Muslim writers. In modern times, one could mention, on of course another level, T. S. Eliot, who, unlike most modern writers, was a devout Christian and possessed, for this very reason, a vision of the world not completely removed from that of Islam.

In contrast to the works of such men, however, the psychological novel, through its very form and its attempt to penetrate into the psyche of men without possessing any criterion with which to discern Truth as an objective reality, is an element that is foreign to Islam. Marcel Proust was, without doubt, a master of the French language and his *In Search of Time Past* is of much interest for those devoted to modern French literature, but this type of writing cannot under any conditions become the model for a genuinely Muslim literature. Yet it is this very type of psychological literature that is now beginning to serve as a 'source of inspiration' for a number of writers in Arabic and Persian. It is of interest to note that the most famous modern literary figure of Persia, Sadeq Hedayat, who was deeply influenced by Kafka, committed suicide because of psychological despair and that, although certainly a person of great literary talent, he was divorced from the Islamic current of life. Today, in fact, his ideas are opposed by Islamic elements within Persian society. Nevertheless, such writers, who often deal with psychological problems and disturbances found in Western society, problems which the Muslims have not experienced until now, are becoming popular among the Muslim youth who thereby become acquainted, and even inflicted, with these new maladies.

One of the worst tragedies today in the Muslim world is that there has appeared recently a new type of person who tries consciously to imitate the obvious maladies of the West. Such people, for example, are not really in a state of depression but try to put themselves into one in order to look modern. They compose poetry that is supposed to issue from a tormented and depressed soul whereas they are not depressed at all. There is nothing worse than a state of nihilism except its imitation by someone who is not nihilistic but tries to produce nihilistic literature or art only to imitate the decadence of Western art. The influence of psychology and psychoanalysis, combined with an atheistic and nihilistic point of view and disseminated within the Islamic world through literature and art, presents a major challenge to Islam which can be answered only through recourse to traditional Islamic psychology and psychotherapy contained mostly within Sufism, and also through the creation of a genuinely Islamic literary criticism which would be able to provide an objective evaluation of so much that passes for literature today.

The degree of penetration of anti-Islamic psychological as well as philosophical Western ideas through literature into the Islamic World can be best gauged by just walking through the streets near universities in various Middle Eastern cities. Among the books spread on the ground or on stands everywhere one still observes traditional religious books, especially of course the Quran. But one observes also a larger number of works in Islamic languages dealing with subjects ranging all the way from Marxism and existentialism to pornography, presented usually as 'literature'. There are, of course, rebuttals and answers as well, for Islam and its spirituality are still alive. But the very presence of all this writing itself reveals the magnitude of the challenge.

As far as nihilism is concerned, the Islamic answer is particularly strong and, putting pretenders aside, the Muslims, even the modernized ones, have not experienced nihilism in the same way as have Westerners, for whom nihilism has become an experience of almost central importance. The main reason for this is that in Christianity the Spirit has been almost always presented in a positive form, as an affirmation, as the sacred art of Christianity reveals so clearly. The void or the *nihil* has not usually been given a spiritual significance in Christian theology and art, as it has been for example in Islam and also in the Far East.[16] Therefore, as a result of the rebellion against Christianity, modern man has experienced the *nihil* only in its negative and terrifying aspect, while some have been attracted to Oriental doctrines especially because of the latter's emphasis upon the Void.

In contrast to Christianity, where the manifestation of the Spirit is identified always with an affirmation and a positive form, Islamic art makes use of the 'negative' or the 'Void' itself in a spiritual and positive sense in the same way that metaphysically the first part of the *shahādah* begins with a negation to affirm the vacuity of things *vis-à-vis* Allah. The space in Islamic architecture is essentially a 'negative space'. Space in Islamic architecture and city-planning is not the space around an object or determined by that object. Rather, it is the negative space cut out from material forms, as for example in traditional bazaars. When one walks through a bazaar one walks through a continuous space determined by the inner surface of the wall surrounding it, and not by some object in the middle of it. That is why what is happening architecturally in many Middle Eastern cities—such as the building of a large monument in the middle of a square to emulate what one finds in the West—is the negation of the very principles of Islamic art and is based on a lack of understanding of the positive role of negative space and the *nihil* in Islamic architecture.

To return to the question of psychology and psychoanalysis, it must be added that the presence of this perspective in so much art criticism in the West has permitted this kind of thinking to seep into the mind of a small but significant portion of Islamic society through art as well as literature—significant because it wields influence and often forms the taste of the psychologically passive masses of traditional Muslims. Traditional Islamic literary tastes are thereby being influenced by the completely anti-traditional ideas emanating from Jungian and Freudian circles and threatening one of the most central and accessible channels of Islamic norms and values. It might, furthermore, be added that, as already mentioned, Jungian psychology is more dangerous than Freudian in this respect in that it appears to be dealing with the sacred and the noumenal world whereas in reality it is deforming the image of the sacred by confusing the spiritual and the psychological domains and subverting the luminous and transcendent source of archetypes into a collective unconscious which is no more than the dumping ground for the collective psyche of various peoples and their cultures. Islamic metaphysics, like all true metaphysics, stands totally opposed to this blasphemous subversion as well as to the methods of profane psychoanalysis which are, as already stated, no more than a parody of Sufi techniques. But how many contemporary Muslims are willing to stand up and assert their basic differences rather than try to glide over them in order to placate the modern world with all its fundamental errors and subsequent evils?

Another challenge to Islam which has come to the fore only since the Second World War is the whole series of movements of thought and attitudes loosely bound together under the title of existentialism, which is the latest wave of Western thought to reach the Muslims following various forms of positivism. There are of course many branches of existentialism, ranging from the *Existenz Philosophie* of the German philosophers to the theistic philosophy of Gabriel Marcel and finally to the agnostic and atheistic ideas of Sartre and his followers. This type of philosophy, which developed on the European continent early in this century, still holds the centre of the stage in many continental countries. Although it has not, as yet, had a serious effect upon the Muslim world, during the past few years its influence—which can be characterized categorically as negative—is beginning to make itself felt, again through art, and more directly through philosophical works as such, which are beginning to influence some Muslims concerned with philosophy and the intellectual life. Because of the anti-metaphysical attitude of much of what is taught in this school and the fact that it has forgotten the meaning of Being in its traditional sense, which lies at the heart of all Islamic philosophy, the spread of existentialism, especially in its agnostic vein, is a most insidious danger for the future of Islamic intellectual life.

Furthermore, there is the tendency in certain quarters to interpret Islamic philosophy itself in the light of Western modes of thought, the latest being the existential school. Muslim 'intellectuals' are directly to blame for this dangerous innovation (*bidʿah*), which, strangely enough, is also the most blind and unintelligent type of imitation (*taqlīd*).[17] If this type of interpretation continues it will cost the new generation of Muslims very dearly. Today, one sees everywhere in various Muslim countries people learning about their own intellectual and philosophical past from Western sources, many of which may contain useful information and may be of value from the point of view of scholarship, but nearly all of which are of necessity written from a non-Muslim point of view. In the field of thought and philosophy in its vastest sense the countries that have suffered most are those which use English or French as media of instruction in their universities: countries such as Pakistan, the Muslim sectors of India, Malaysia and Nigeria, or the Islamic Maghrib such as Morocco and Tunisia. It is certainly long overdue, with all this talk of anti-colonialism, for Muslims to overcome the worst type of colonialism possible—the colonialism of the mind—and to seek to see and study their own culture, especially its intellectual and spiritual heart, from their own point of view. Even if, God forbid, there are certain Muslims who want to reject some aspect of their intellectual heritage, they would first of all have to know that heritage. Both acceptance and rejection of anything must be based upon knowledge, and there is no excuse for ignorance, no matter what direction one wishes to follow. One cannot reject what one does not know any more than one can accept something in depth without true knowledge. Nor can one throw away what one does not possess. This is a very simple truth, but one that is too often forgotten today.

Some years ago a famous Zen master visited a leading Western university. After his lecture on Zen, a graduate student asked, 'Don't the Zen masters believe that one should burn the Buddhist scrolls and throw away the Buddha images?' The master smiled and answered, 'Yes, but you can only burn a scroll which you possess and throw away an image which you have.' This was a most profound answer. The master meant that you can only transcend the exoteric dimension of religion if you practice that exotericism and subsequently penetrate into its inner meaning and transcend its forms. He who does not practice exotericism cannot ever hope to go beyond it; he merely falls below it and mistakes this fall for a transcending of forms. The same applies on another level to man's traditional intellectual heritage. One cannot go 'beyond' the formulations of the sages of old when one does not even understand them. He who tries to do so mistakes his pitiful ignorance and 'expansion' and apparent 'freedom' from traditional norms of thought—an ignorance which is in reality the worst kind of imprisonment within the limitations of one's own nature—for the true freedom which comes solely from the illimitable horizons of the world of the Spirit and which can be reached only through the vehicle provided by religion and its sapiential doctrines.

Contemporary Muslims should be realist enough to understand that they must begin their journey, in whatever direction they wish to go, from where they are. A well-known Chinese proverb asserts that 'the journey of a thousand miles begins with a single step.' Now this first step must of necessity take place where one is located, and that is as much true culturally and spiritually as it is physically. Wherever the Islamic world is to 'go', it must begin from the reality of the Islamic tradition and from its own real, and not imagined, situation. Those who lose sight of this fact actually do not travel effectively at all. They just imagine that they are journeying. A Pakistani or a Persian or an Arab 'intellectual' who wants to be a leader of thought for the Muslim people must remember who he is, if he wishes to be effective and not be cut off from the rest of Islamic society. No matter how hard he tries to make a corner of Lahore or Tehran or Cairo belong to the setting of Oxford or the Sorbonne, he will not succeed. The so-called Muslim intellectuals of the Westernized kind who complain that they are not understood and appreciated by Islamic society forget that it is they who have refused to appreciate and understand their own culture and society and are therefore rejected by their own community. This rejection is, in fact, a sign of life, an indication that Islamic culture still possesses vitality.

As far as philosophy is concerned, the countries where Muslim languages are used for university instruction are in a somewhat better position, especially Persia, where Islamic philosophy still continues as a living tradition and where it is not easy to say anything at all in the name of philosophy without being seriously challenged by the traditional intellectual élite. But of course even this part of the Muslim world has not been completely spared from condescending and apologetic studies of Islamic thought from the point of view of Western philosophy, though relatively speaking there is less Western philosophic influence there because of the two reasons alluded to above: the language barrier and a still-living tradition of Islamic philosophy. It would be interesting in this connection to compare the effect of the publication in Pakistan of Iqbal's two philosophical works in English, *The Development of Metaphysics in Persia* and *The Reconstruction of Religious Thought in Islam*, with the effect of their publication in Persia in their fairly recent translations into Persian.

Yet even in lands using Islamic languages books do appear in languages such as Persian, and particularly Arabic, on philosophy from a perspective totally alien to that of Islam and bearing such titles as *Falsafatunā*, *Our Philosophy*, as if philosophy as a vision of the Truth or quest after wisdom or *sophia* could ever be 'mine' or 'ours'. No Arab or Persian traditional philosopher ever used such an expression. For Muslims who have cultivated Islamic philosophy, philosophy has always been *al-falsafah* or *al-ḥikmah*, '*the* philosophy', a vision of the truth transcending the individualistic order and derived from the Truth (*al-Ḥaqq*) itself. The very appearance of such concepts and terms as 'our philosophy' or 'my thought' in Islamic languages itself reveals the degree of departure from the Islamic norm. It is against such errors that the weapon of the traditional doctrines contained in the vast treasury of Islamic thought must be used, and answers drawn from these sources be provided, before any further erosion of Islamic intellectual life takes place.

Returning to the question of existentialism and traditional Islamic philosophy in Persia, it must be mentioned that because of the kind of traditional philosophy surviving there, based on the principiality of existence (*aṣālat al-wujūd*), and itself called *falsafat al-wujūd* (which some have mistakenly translated as 'existentialism'), existentialism of the European kind has encountered strong resistance from traditional circles. Actually anyone who has studied traditional Islamic philosophy from Ibn Sīnā and Suhrawardī to the great expositor of the metaphysics of being, Ṣadr al-Dīn Shīrāzī (Mullā Ṣadrā), will readily understand the profound chasm which separates the traditional Islamic 'philosophy of being' from modern existentialism, which, even in its apparently most profound aspects, can only reach, in a fragmentary fashion, some of the rudimentary teachings contained in their fullness in traditional metaphysics. Henry Corbin, the only Western scholar who has expounded to any extent this later phase of Islamic philosophy in the West, has shown the divergence of views between Islamic philosophy and existentialism and the correctives which the former provides for the latter, in the long French introduction to his edition and translation of Ṣadr al-Dīn Shīrāzī's *Kitāb al-mashā'ir* (rendered into French as *Le Livre des pénétrations métaphysiques*).[18] It is incidentally interesting to note that it was through Corbin's translation of Heidegger's *Sein und Zeit* that Sartre was first attracted to existentialism, while Corbin himself turned completely away from this form of thought to the ocean of the 'Orient of Light' of Suhrawardī and the luminous philosophy of being of Ṣadr al-Dīn Shīrāzī.

One last but urgent and basic problem must be mentioned, and that is the ecological crisis, which was brought into being by modern civilization but which is now a challenge to the very life of men everywhere, including, of course, Muslims in the Islamic world. Anyone who is aware of the situation of the modern world knows that the most immediate problem, at least of a material order, which faces the world is the ecological crisis, the destruction of the equilibrium between man and his natural environment. Islam and its sciences have a particularly urgent and timely message which, as mentioned above, can help to solve, to the extent possible, this major challenge to the world as a whole. However, this message unfortunately receives the least attention from modernized Muslims themselves.

We know that Muslims avidly cultivated the sciences of nature, such as astronomy, physics and medicine, and made great contributions to them without losing their equilibrium and their harmony with nature. Their sciences of nature were always cultivated within the matrix of a 'philosophy of nature' which was in harmony with the total structure of the Universe as seen from the Islamic perspective. There lies in the background of Islamic science a true philosophy of nature which, if brought to light and presented in contemporary language, can be substituted for the present false natural philosophy. For it is this latter philosophy which, combined with a lack of true metaphysical understanding of first principles, is largely responsible for the present crisis in man's relation with nature.[19]

Unfortunately, the Islamic scientific heritage has only too rarely been studied by Muslims themselves, and when such a study has been made, it has usually been based again on a sense of inferiority which has impelled the authors to try to prove that Muslims preceded the West in scientific discoveries and therefore are not behind the West in their cultural attainment. Rarely is this precious Muslim scientific heritage seen as an alternative path, a science of the natural order which could and did avoid the catastrophic *impasse* which modern science and its applications through technology have created for men. Muslims with vision should be only too happy that it was not they who brought about the seventeenth-century scientific revolution whose logical outcome we see today. Muslim scholars and thinkers must be trained to revitalize the philosophy of nature contained in the Islamic sciences and to study these sciences themselves.

The end thus proposed is very different from the goal of so many modernized Muslims who pride themselves upon Islam having paved the way for the Renaissance. They reason that since the Renaissance was a great event in history and since Islamic culture helped create the Renaissance, therefore Islamic culture must be of value. This is an absurd way of reasoning, which completely ignores the fact that what the modern world suffers from today is precisely the result of steps taken by the West, mostly during the Renaissance, when Western man rebelled to a large extent against his God-given religion.

Muslims should be grateful that they did not rebel against Heaven and had no share in that anti-spiritual humanism which has now resulted in an infra-human world. What Islam in fact did was to prevent the individualistic rebellion against Heaven, the manifestation of the Promethean and Titanesque spirit which is so clearly shown in much of Renaissance art and which stands diametrically opposed to the spirit of Islam, which is based on submission to God. It is true that Islamic science and culture were a factor in the rise of the Renaissance in the West, but Islamic elements were employed only after they were divorced from their Islamic character and torn away from the total order in which alone they possess their full meaning and significance.

Muslims should revivify the study of the Islamic sciences, first in order to demonstrate to young Muslims, so many of whom have the tendency to stop praying upon learning the first formulae of algebra, the fact that for many centuries Muslims cultivated the sciences, including most of the mathematics taught in secondary schools today, and yet remained devout Muslims; and second, to bring out the underlying harmony of the Islamic sciences with Islamic philosophy, theology and metaphysics, a harmony that is closely related to the philosophy of nature alluded to above. The great masterpieces of Islamic science, such as the works of Ibn Sīnā, al-Bīrūnī, Khayyām and Naṣīr al-Dīn Ṭūsī, can all be employed with both ends in view.

To conclude, it must be asserted categorically once again that to preserve Islam and Islamic civilization, a conscious and intellectual defence must be made of the Islamic tradition. Moreover, a thorough intellectual criticism must be made of the modern world and its shortcomings. Muslims cannot hope to follow the same path as the West without reaching the same *impasse* or an even worse one, because of the rapidity of the tempo of change today. The Muslim intelligentsia must face all the challenges mentioned here, and many others, with confidence in themselves. They must cease to live in the state of a psychological and cultural sense of inferiority. They must close ranks among themselves and also join forces with the other great traditions of Asia, not only to cease to be on the defensive but also to take the offensive and provide from their God-given treasury of wisdom the medicine which alone can cure the modern world of its most dangerous malady and save it from its present-day plight, provided of course that the patient is willing to undergo the necessary cure. But even if we take the most pessimistic point of view concerning the present day situation and believe that nothing can be saved, the assertion of the truth itself is the most valuable of all acts, and its effect goes far beyond what can usually be envisaged. The truth must therefore be asserted and the intellectual defence of Islam made on every front on which it is challenged. The result is in God's Hands. As the Quran asserts, 'Truth hath come and falsehood hath vanished away. Lo! falsehood is ever bound to vanish.' XVII; 81, Pickthall translation.

Wa'llāhu a'lam.

(جَآءَ الْحَقُّ وَزَهَقَ الْبَاطِلُ اِنَّ الْبَاطِلَ كَانَ زَهُوقاً).

Notes on Chapter II

1. It must be said, however, that because of the very rapid decadence of Western society during the past two decades, some of the younger Muslims who have experienced the Western world on an 'intellectual' level are far less infatuated with it than before and have in fact begun to criticize it. But of these the number that think within the Islamic framework are very limited. The various works of Maryam Jameelah contain many thoughtful pages on this theme and the whole problem of the confrontation of Islam and Western civilization. See especially her *Islam versus the West*, Lahore, 1968.

2. A few of the modernized *'ulamā'* must also be placed in this category. See W. C. Smith, *Islam in Modern History*, where the style and approach of such an apologetic attitude, especially as it concerns Egypt, is analyzed.

3. It is here that 'fundamentalist' puritanical movements such as that of the Salafiyyah and the modernist trends meet.

4. See F. Schuon, 'No Activity without Truth', *Studies in Comparative Religion*, Autumn, 1969, pp. 194–203; also *The Sword of Gnosis*, pp. 27 ff.

5. We do not mean that Muslim 'Occidentalists' should emulate the prejudices and limitations of the Orientalists, but that they should know the West as well as possible from the Islamic point of view in the same way that the best among Orientalists have sought to know the East well, albeit within the frame of reference of the West. Of course, because of the anti-traditional nature of the modern West, such a frame of reference has not been adequate when dealing with the religious and metaphysical teachings of Oriental traditions, but that is another question, which does not concern the present comparison.

6. See S. H. Nasr, *Islamic Studies*, Chap. 8.

7. See S. H. Nasr, *The Encounter of Man and Nature*, pp. 93 ff.

8. As far as socialism in its non-Marxist form is concerned, which is now enjoying great popularity in the form of 'Islamic socialism', 'Arab socialism' etc., it is usually a misnomer for social justice and is adopted in many circles, without an analysis of its real meaning, for political expedience or simply to appear modern and progressive. See A. K. Brohi, *Islam in the Modern World*, Karachi, 1968, pp. 91 ff.

9. A major exception to this is the five-volume *Uṣūl-i falsafah* of 'Allāmah Sayyid Muḥammad Ḥusayn Ṭabāṭabā'ī, one of the most venerable masters of traditional Islamic philosophy in Persia today, with the commentary of Murtaḍā Muṭahharī, Qum, 1932 (AH Solar). As far as we know this is the only work of an Islamic character which has tried to answer dialectical materialism from a philosophical point of view, drawing from traditional Islamic philosophy, especially the school of Mullā Ṣadrā.

10. See Chap. 1, note 7.

11. See, for example, A. Leroi-Gourhan, *Le Geste et la parole*, 2 vols., Paris, 1964–1965; J. Servier, *L'homme et l'invisible;* E. Zolla, (ed.), *Eternitá e storia. I valori permanenti nel divenire storico;* and G. Durand 'Défiguration philosophique et figure traditionnelle de l'homme en Occident'. Even an academic authority like Lévi-Strauss, the founder of structuralism, has said, 'les hommes ont toujours pensé aussi bien.'

Servier, while offering a vast amount of scientific evidence against the idea of man's evolution, criticizes modern evolutionists in these terms: 'Il vaudrait mieux admettre que l'évolutionnisme matérialiste est une religion demandant beaucoup à la foi et peu à la raison. Darwin a parlé des 'lunettes obscures du théologien' et le mot a fait fortune. Mais quelles lunettes de ténèbres chaussent le nez des évolutionnistes!' Servier, *op. cit.*, p. 9.

12. It must be said, however, that fortunately in Islam there have not as yet appeared any figures representing 'evolutionary religion' possessing the same degree of influence as can be seen in Hinduism and Christianity, where such men as Sri Aurobindo and Teilhard de Chardin have rallied numerous supporters around themselves. The metaphysical teachings of Islam based upon the immutability of the Divine Principle has until now been too powerful to permit the widespread influence of any such deviation.

13. See Abū Bakr Sirāj ed-Dīn, 'The Islamic and Christian Conceptions of the March of Time', *Islamic Quarterly*, 1954, Vol. I, pp. 229–235.

14. See Lord Northbourne, *Looking Back on Progress*, London, 1971; M. Lings, *Ancient Beliefs and Modern Superstitions*, London, 1965; and F. Schuon, *Light on the Ancient Worlds.*

15. See W. N. Perry, 'The Revolt against Moses', *Studies in Comparative Religion*, Spring, 1966, pp. 103–119; F. Schuon, 'The Psychological Imposture', *ibid.*, pp. 98–102; and R. Guénon, *The Reign of Quantity and the Signs of the Times*, Chaps. XXIV *et seq.* As far as Jung is concerned, his influence can be even more dangerous than that of Freud, precisely because he deals more with traditional symbols but from a psychological rather than spiritual point of view. See T. Burckhardt, 'Cosmology and Modern Science III', *Tomorrow*, Vol. 13, no. 1, Winter, 1965, pp. 19–31; also in the *Sword of Gnosis*, pp. 122 ff.; see also his *Scienza moderna e saggezza tradizionale*, Torino, 1968, Chap. 4.

16. On the significance of the void in Islamic art, see, T. Burckhardt, 'The Void in Islamic Art', *Studies in Comparative Religion*, Spring, 1970, pp. 96–99; and S. H. Nasr, 'The Significance of the Void in the Art and Architecture of Islamic Persia', *Journal of the Regional Cultural Institute*, (Tehran), Vol. V, nos. 2 and 3, 1972, pp. 121–128; also in *Islamic Quarterly*, Vol. XVI, nos. 3 and 4, 1972, pp. 115–120.

17. See S. H. Nasr, *Islamic Studies*, Chaps. 8 and 9.

18. See Mullā Ṣadrā, *Kitāb al-mashāʿir* (*Le livre des pénétrations métaphysiques*), Chap. IV of the Introduction. See also T. Izutsu, *The Concept and Reality of Existence*, Tokyo, 1971, where a profound analysis of Islamic ontology is to be found, even if in Chapter II certain comparisons are made with Western existentialism which appear to us as difficult to accept. We have also dealt with this subject in our forthcoming *The Transcendent Theosophy of Ṣadr al-Dīn Shīrāzī.*

19. See S. H. Nasr, *Science and Civilization in Islam; An Introduction to Islamic Cosmological Doctrines*, and *The Encounter of Man and Nature*, Chap. 2.

Select Bibliography

A. K. Brohi *Islam in the Modern World*, Karachi, 1968.

T. Burckhardt *Alchemy*, trans. by W. Stoddart, London, 1967.

— *Fes, Stadt des Islam*, Lausanne and Freiburg, 1960.

H. Corbin *Le livre des pénétrations métaphysiques*, Tehran–Paris, 1964.

— 'The Force of Traditional Islamic Philosophy in Iran Today', *Studies in Comparative Religion*, Vol. 2, 1968, pp. 12–26.

— *En Islam iranien*, 4 Vols., Paris, 1971–2.

G. Durand 'Défiguration philosophique et figure traditionnelle de l'homme en Occident', *Eranos-Jahrbuch*, Vol. XXXVIII, Zurich, 1971, pp. 45–93.

R. Guénon *The Reign of Quantity and the Signs of the Times*, trans. by Lord Northbourne, Baltimore, 1972.

T. Izutsu *The Concept and Reality of Existence*, Tokyo, 1971.

Maryam Jameelah *Islam versus the West*, Lahore, 1968.

M. Lings *Ancient Beliefs and Modern Superstitions*, London, 1965.

Abul Hasan Ali Nadwi *Saviours of Islamic Spirit*, trans. by M. Ahmad, Lucknow, 1971.

S. H. Nasr *The Encounter of Man and Nature, The Spiritual Crisis of Modern Man*, London, 1968.

— *Islamic Studies*, Beirut, 1967.

— *Science and Civilization in Islam*, Cambridge, 1968; New York, 1970.

— *Ideals and Realities of Islam*, London, 1966; Boston, 1972.

— *Sufi Essays*, London, 1972, trans. J. Peter Hobson, Albany (N.Y.), 1973.

J. Needleman (ed.) *The Sword of Gnosis*, Baltimore, 1974.

Lord Northbourne *Religion in the Modern World*, London, 1963.

— *Looking Back on Progress*, London, 1971.

F. Schuon *Islam: the Perennial Philosophy*, London, 1976.

— *Light on the Ancient Worlds*, trans. by Lord Northbourne, London, 1965.

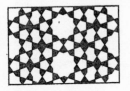

— *Understanding Islam*, trans. by D. M. Matheson, London, 1963; Baltimore, 1972.
— *Logic and Transcendence*, trans. P. Townsend, New York, 1975.
— *Dimensions of Islam*, trans. by P. Townsend, London, 1970.
J. Servier *L'homme et l'invisible*, Paris, 1964.
E. Zolla (ed.) *Eternità e storia. I valori permanenti nel divenire storico*, Florence, 1970.

General Index

Index of Authors mentioned in notes